SHELLEY'S POETRY: THE DIVIDED SELF

Shelley's Poetry

The Divided Self

Simon Haines

Department of English
Australian National University, Canberra

First published in Great Britain 1997 by
MACMILLAN PRESS LTD
Houndmills, Basingstoke, Hampshire RG21 6XS and London
Companies and representatives throughout the world

A catalogue record for this book is available from the British Library.

ISBN 0–333–59707–9

First published in the United States of America 1997 by
ST. MARTIN'S PRESS, INC.,
Scholarly and Reference Division,
175 Fifth Avenue, New York, N.Y. 10010

ISBN 0–312–16551–X

Library of Congress Cataloging-in-Publication Data
Haines, Simon, 1955–
Shelley's Poetry : the divided self / Simon Haines.
p.   cm.
Includes bibliographical references (p.   ) and index.
ISBN 0–312–16551–X (cloth : alk. paper)
1. Shelley, Percy Bysshe, 1792–1822—Criticism and interpretation.
2. Emotions in literature.   3. Reason in literature.   4. Self in
literature.   I. Title.
PR5438.H33   1997
821'.7—dc20   96–27679
                                                       CIP

This book is printed on paper suitable for recycling and made from fully managed and sustained forest sources.

10   9   8   7   6   5   4   3   2
06   05   04   03   02   01   00   99   98

Printed and bound in Great Britain by
Antony Rowe Ltd, Chippenham, Wiltshire

307573

For Jane, Catherine and William
and
for my mother and father

Contents

Preface

How many critical books on Shelley or any poet are read nowadays by people who are neither teachers nor students in a university? Why write yet another such book for a small and sated coterie? Why, even worse, write one questioning the reputation of a poet supposedly still recuperating from a savage critical assault more than fifty years ago?

This book is intended to encourage general readers as well as university teachers and students to think about poetry as itself, and for themselves. Too much contemporary writing about poetry assumes that it has to be explained chiefly in terms of some other thing: in Shelley's case, of the poet's life, of British and European politics from the 1780s to the 1820s, of scepticism or Platonism, of theory of language or mind, and so on. Poetry in this light looks like an oddly shaped container for ideas about these subjects. At best its task may be to find what might be termed "thin" symbols for a finally unrepresentable Truth or Idea. The poet, in this case Shelley, appears as a political radical, a cad, a metaphysician, a mystic, a systematic philosopher, a theorist of something or other: rarely as a poet. Readers are to think of themselves as theorised, contextualised or otherwise dissolved into some greater reality. But poetry may also be represented as a distinctive manner of thinking, a kind of human perception that resists dissolution into philosophical or historical categories. Nor need one necessarily find the poetry in question appealing in order to represent it in this way. Indeed a predominantly (but not entirely) disapprobatory criticism of such an influential and admired poet may be particularly effective in encouraging such a way of seeing poetry, as well as salutary in helping to discover a certain style of mind widespread in the eighteenth and nineteenth centuries, and also in our own times.

When I embarked with great enthusiasm on a study of Shelley's poetry many years ago I soon found the few adverse criticisms of him, especially those by Hazlitt, more telling than the many appreciations; I still do. This book attempts to explain why. I hope Shelley's admirers will not dismiss it out of hand as merely an old-fashioned and long-discredited kind of sniping at a great poet, and that they will find something here worth thinking about. No one can contemplate Shelley's career as a poet without admiration and humility. But responsible reading entails honesty, and honest doubt may promote responsive reading, reawaken poetic faith, better than half the creeds currently promoting themselves as the keys to all reading.

I am most grateful to Jane Adamson, Timothy Clark and Stephen Prickett, who read an earlier draft of this work and made many helpful suggestions; and to Roy Park, who supervised the thesis in which it had its origin. Without the encouragement and conversation of Jane Adamson, Frances Dixon, Fred Langman, Anne Loftus, Sam Goldberg and David Parker this would have been a much worse book, if it had ever been done at all.

Parts of Chapters 1 and 4 appeared in *The Critical Review*, 1990 and 1993. I am grateful to the editors for permission to use these materials in a revised form.

S. H.

Canberra, 1996

1
The Case of Shelley

INTRODUCTION

Shelley's reputation in this century has often been represented by his vindicators as if it were a kind of sandcastle, knocked down with a kick or two in the 1930s by those philistine bullies, T. S. Eliot and F. R. Leavis, and since then painstakingly rebuilt by a faithful band of sensitive but disinterested scholars. Frederick Pottle's 1952 essay, "The Case of Shelley", is still the classic statement of this slightly aggrieved and beleaguered position. Writing in the very shadow of the New Critical volcano, Pottle pointed out a number of fundamental misreadings of the poet in crucial essays by Eliot, Leavis and Allen Tate, and called for less "prescription" and more "calm, patient, neutral description" in modern criticism in general.[1]

In the case of Shelley, at least, Pottle's call seems to have been resoundingly answered; indeed, it was already being answered by the time he made it. Since the 1930s dozens of books and hundreds of articles have been published on the poet, most of them admirably patient and unprescriptive, provided that one grants their frequently unargued premises: that Shelley is a great poet, and that his greatness warrants every kind and any amount of research into all aspects of his life and work. From the main founts of twentieth century Shelley scholarship,[2] and from many important subsidiary sources, there has flowed for sixty years a ceaseless river of textual studies, bibliographical studies, biographies, political studies, studies in the history of ideas; studies of Shelley's political thought, of his religious thought, of his scientific thought, of his critical thought, of his mythopoeic thought; Marxist, Freudian, post-structuralist, feminist, Lacanian and New Historicist studies. The 1980s and 1990s alone have witnessed the publication of a dozen major books on Shelley, to say nothing of all the articles, dissertations, monographs and other book-length works. For those who would prefer not to drown in this flood,

1

but who would like at least to get their feet wet, collections of critical essays have been edited in the last few years by Kelvin Everest, Miriam Allott and G. Kim Blank, and handy survey reviews of recent work have been written by Denis Donoghue, Angela Leighton and Richard Holmes. If studies of Shelley now constitute a small library, the very surveys and bibliographies of those studies fill a large shelf. Stuart Curran's 70-page commentary, published in 1985, is still the best of these, as well as one of the briefest and most recent; but the line of book-length surveys alone stretches back from Karsten Engelberg in 1988 *via* Clement Dunbar and Nancy Fogarty in the 1970s and 1960s to Sylva Norman, Julia Power and Francis Clairborne Mason in the 1950s, 40s and 30s. The formidable *Keats-Shelley Journal*, with its own annual bibliographies, edited since 1981 by Curran, and the even more formidable *Shelley and His Circle, 1773–1822*, a catalogue-edition with commentaries, edited first by Kenneth Neill Cameron and now by Donald H. Reiman, thunder on at the head of a platoon of journals and other publications associated with the poet.[3] As for the essential scholarly business of editing Shelley's own writings, the uninitiated may be surprised to learn that we still have no complete authoritative annotated edition of either the poems or the prose (except for the letters). Still, there are good reasons for this; we very soon will have them; and meanwhile there are some excellent selections.[4] In short, Pottle's prediction that the decline in Shelley's reputation would "one day be reversed"[5] must long ago have come true, at least if academic productivity is any measure of reputation. In a survey of 100 British and North American universities carried out for his book Blank reports that Shelley and Keats were regarded as ranking about third or fourth in "'importance as a Romantic' relative to the other major Romantic poets".[6]

The sandcastle now seems to be made of adamant; surely against this industrious army Eliot and Leavis stand no chance. But is "neutral description", no matter how copious, an adequate response to evaluative detraction, or is its very copiousness a sign of lingering unease? Blank, Everest, Allott and Holmes all still feel obliged to glance irritably, or nervously, over their shoulders at those grim philistine shades. The "critical attack ... still bites very deep after more than fifty years", wrote Holmes, Shelley's outstanding modern biographer, in 1992,[7] surveying some of the bicentenary tributes. "Leavis and the New Critics were not ready for a poetry where the play of language is at least as esteemed as the work of signification", sniffed Blank in his introduction to one of those tributes,[8] a post-structuralist collection already beginning to sound curiously dated. What was it about that "attack" that has bitten so deep, that still seems to force such authoritative but dissimilar readers to acknowledge, rebut, regret or belittle? Why the defensive tone? We shall pursue these questions properly in the rest of this chapter. Briefly, however, what Shelley's defenders have spent most time denying is some variant or other of Leavis's charge of "sensory weakness": of his claim that the poet has a "weak grasp on the actual", that he is "unexacting about sense" and "weak in his hold on objects".[9] The method adopted by Pottle's "patient, neutral" Shelleyans has generally been to show, in great detail, that Shelley's "actual", the "objects" in which he is interested, are not of the concrete kind in which critics like Leavis are interested: and that therefore Shelley's methods, or "grasp", could not be of the kind which Leavis approved either. In this way Eliot, Leavis, Tate and others have repeatedly and successfully been shown to have misread Shelley's poems and misunderstood his images.

Accusations of sensory weakness, however, have hurt Shelley's defenders far less, have been much easier to rebut at length, than accusations of moral weakness: most notoriously in Leavis's verdict that "criticism of Shelley has something more important to deal with than mere bad poetry".[10] This was, it should be emphasised, still in some sense an attack on the poetry: not, that is, on Shelley's behaviour, for example his treatment of Harriet (and there can be no denying his vulnerability there); but on his character as it is displayed in the very making of the poetry. Leavis saw "viciousness" and "corruption", "radical disabilities and perversions";[11] but he saw them revealed in the use of language and in the manner in which emotion is represented in the poetry. Shelley scholarship has dealt with this aspect of the attack chiefly by claiming that Leavis, Eliot and company disapproved of Shelley's behaviour and his beliefs, especially his religious and political beliefs, but disguised this disapproval as literary criticism. As Everest puts it, the "substance and explicit or unstated motives of these attacks, and of their subsequent elaboration by an impressive array of respected scholars and critics, were in essence sophisticated academic inflections of the political and religious objections to Shelley that had often been voiced".[12] The

New Criticism often claimed to be dealing *only* with the poetry; the New Historicism counter-claims that that is *always* impossible. Leavis's reference to "something more" than poetry apparently vitiates his purist insistence in the same essay that "it is strictly the 'poetry' one is criticizing". Still, may there not be something in the idea that poetry displays, represents or creates a "self" which is not the poet's everyday self but which is nevertheless open to criticism, or at least evaluation, in some of the ways in which everyday selves are? In any case it seems that there is a difference of views here which no amount of "patient, neutral description" could resolve.

Another reason for the defensive tone, detectable again in Everest's remarks above, is that Eliot, Leavis and their contemporaries were by no means the first to say things of this kind about Shelley's poetry. Allott notes the "uncanny resemblance" between what she terms the "prominent formalist critics" of Shelley from the 1930s to the 1950s and "certain critics of that first phase in the 1820s and 1830s",[13] particularly William Hazlitt. Donoghue complains, justifiably, that the "case against Shelley has been stated so insistently by modern critics that you would imagine they had invented it". In fact, he says, they "have merely refined what Hazlitt said in 1821 and Mary Shelley said, among more laudatory things, in 1824".[14] "Merely refined" may be doing a disservice to some original thought, and neither Eliot nor Leavis could be called a "formalist" critic, but Donoghue and Allott are right to point to Hazlitt as an important source and precursor of the modern attack on Shelley. Even Matthew Arnold's "ineffectual angel", writing his *"bête"* letter to Harriet,[15] arrived on the scene as long ago as 1888, bearing the same adversarial relation to Shelley scholarship of the late nineteenth century as the Shelley of Eliot and Leavis did to that of the mid-twentieth. So the case against Shelley is at least a longstanding one, deserving exploration to see if it amounts to anything more than political, religious and moral prejudice. Thomas McFarland wrote in 1976 that "modern Shelley scholars . . . simply ignore the fact that Hazlitt, Arnold and Leavis, that is, three of the half dozen or so greatest critics of English literature since Shelley's time, all call into severest question Shelley's poetic quality and importance".[16] Modern scholars do not all ignore this fact any more: Michael O'Neill, who quotes McFarland's remark, refuses to "take for granted Shelley's status as a great poet",[17] and has written a valuable book in defence of that status. So have Leighton, Richard Cronin and (in the 1970s) Timothy Webb; so, before them all, did Harold Bloom, as long ago as the 1950s. There are others too who have occasionally confronted their readers with the matter of the poetry's value. But too many Shelley scholars have contented themselves with volumes of "neutral" description, not only of the poetry but of anything or anyone remotely connected with it. Academics may be content to go on writing for the *cognoscenti* alone, but how many other people nowadays use the name "Shelley" to refer principally to the husband of the author of *Frankenstein*?

This book assumes that the two-hundred-year disagreement over the value of Shelley's poetry, which in its modern phase Pottle called "the case of Shelley", ought to be taken seriously. Unlike the few other books which assume this, however, it also argues that Hazlitt and his successors were, broadly speaking, right. This first chapter looks at both "sides" of the "case" (the forensic language is unhappily reductive), before attempting in its final section to go beyond the arguments about Shelley to some more general claims about the nature of poetry. The second chapter discusses Shelley's own arguments about poetry in his essays and letters, not because his poetry ought to be somehow measured against his theories of poetry (far from it) but because any poet is owed the primary hearing in a conversation about his own work. The remaining four chapters of the book offer a series of readings of major poems, with some references to a number of others. Throughout the book occasional references are made to Shelley's life: his circumstances, and his reflections upon them. This is not to "explain" the poetry in terms of the life, to dissolve those boundaries between two selves which the act of writing proposes. The references are intended, on the contrary, to shed an intermittent light on that very process of creating a *poetic* self, that best or wisest self which the poetry would have its readers attend to. The poetic wisdom displayed by the teller of a tale in his telling is not the same as the practical wisdom displayed, or not, by the teller in his everyday life; but the practice of attending to the former must still be informed by the reader's own practical wisdom. This is part of what Iris Murdoch means, I take it, when she says that art may be more "a case of morals" than an "analogy of morals".[18] Our business is with the complex personality or self discovered in the relational act of reading poetry. If this act evokes deep reservations as well as, or even instead of, admiration, then sometimes it is important to register those too, and to keep on registering them.

"COBWEBS OF THE BRAIN": THE CASE AGAINST

The nineteenth century

A tactic frequently employed by defenders of Shelley is to attribute the arguments of his detractors entirely to some theory or prejudice, sometimes cunningly concealed and sometimes crudely displayed, sometimes concerning Shelley's life, beliefs and behaviour rather than his poetry, but in any case as if the detractors were already determined to dislike the poetry before reading it. Those making a case against Shelley's poetry often do have such theories or prejudices, but sometimes that is not all they have. Besides, the defenders frequently have theories or prejudices too, which merely happen to coincide more closely with Shelley's own. They have also been known to agree with or even inadvertently develop parts of the opposing case; Mary Shelley is the outstanding example. We shall hear more about the defenders, however, in the next part of this chapter. This section, on the detractors, begins with four representative contemporary criticisms: those of John Taylor Coleridge, John Gibson Lockhart, William Sidney Walker and William Hazlitt.

No-one could accuse *The Quarterly Review* of concealing its prejudices. Shelley "has loosened the hold of our protecting laws, and sapped the principles of our venerable polity; he has invaded the purity and chilled the unsuspecting ardour of our fireside intimacies; he has slandered, ridiculed and blasphemed our holy religion":[19] so spluttered J. T. Coleridge in his notorious attack on *The Revolt of Islam* for the *Quarterly* of April 1819 – an attack which deeply angered and depressed Shelley himself (although he long thought Robert Southey had written it). The review, like many favourable accounts of the poem, treats it as a prolonged exposition of its author's political, sexual and religious opinions; he "has a theory of course respecting the government of the world". The *Quarterly* was a Tory journal; 1819 was a year of considerable political disturbance; no poetry by a known and self-confessed radical could expect a fair hearing in these circumstances. Leigh Hunt, Shelley's friend and first defender in print, followed this line of defence when responding to Coleridge's attack in *The Examiner*, Hunt's own liberal-radical journal, in September and October of the same year; the "reviewing Scribes and Pharisees beg the question against Mr. Shelley's theories because he does not believe in their own creed".[20] This was true, on both sides, and both sides knew it. To make matters worse in Hunt's eyes, however, Coleridge had gone on to hint disingenuously at the "disgusting picture" of Shelley's "private life" which he could have drawn, but of course would not stoop to drawing. Hunt was furious, and not without reason. "What is the argument of this? or what right have they to know any thing of the private life of an author? or how would they like to have the same argument used against themselves?"

Shelley and his poetry have provoked this kind of shouting-match ever since. The poetry *does* bear some kind of relation to "theories", or doctrines, whose truth or falsehood has become an issue overshadowing everything else about it; the life *did* include episodes, behaviours, whose rightness or wrongness have also become such an issue. So persistent has the shouting been, indeed, that one is driven to ask what it is about this poetry which provokes, or at least does not discountenance, these two kinds of criticism. Is the very self, or personality, which is projected in and by the poetry, of a kind which attracts such criticisms instead of deflecting or disarming them? Perhaps the most significant moments in Coleridge's review are the one where he refuses to comment on Shelley's life, and the one where he condescends for a moment to be a literary critic, distinguishing between "the freight" and "the 'build' of the vessel", and commending the latter as being "not without beautiful passages"; the "language is in general free from errors of taste, and the versification smooth and harmonious". Again and again readers of Shelley have wanted to praise his language, his rhythms, his music, his imagery, whilst tactfully witholding judgement, or censoriously passing it, on his ideas, opinions, theories or beliefs, and on his conduct or behaviour. On the one hand these look like two familiar critical procedures, both usually (but not always) erroneous: distinguishing between a poem and its ideas, between truth and beauty, between the logical, and the aesthetic or rhetorical, qualities of a work; and not distinguishing between the events in or character of a person's life and the events in or character of the work or works which that person has written. On the other hand these procedures are not always erroneous, and they seem to be undertaken more often with Shelley than with any other major English poet. He deserves to be protected from false criticism, but one wonders why he attracts so much. Coleridge's was undoubtedly one of the harshest as well as one of the earliest public attacks on Shelley, but in its harshness it is representative of a whole class of Shelley criticism called forth by the poetry's own doctrinal and confrontational purposes.

The next two criticisms are less deeply engaged ideologically, but more so critically. J. G. Lockhart was no liberal; but in a review of *Rosalind and Helen* for the Tory *Blackwood's Edinburgh Magazine* in June 1819 his disapproval of the poem's "creed", "opinions" and "principles", which he was among the first to attribute to the influence of William Godwin, were modified by his admiration of its "strong feeling, and strong passion, and strong imagination".[21] Shelley is a "true poet" of "masterly genius", but his poem "exhibits at the same time a strange perversion of moral principle". He "writes like a man angry and dissatisfied with the world, because he is angry and dissatisfied with himself". His Godwinian "opinions" have been "adopted" out of "waywardness and caprice ... and, perhaps, as a vain defence against the reproaches of his own conscience", so they "carry no authority along with them to others". The "finer essence of his poetry never penetrates them – the hues of his imagination never clothes them with attractive beauty. . . . Accordingly there is no great moral flow in his poetry". As an exploration of the contiguities and adherences of "vessel" and "freight", and of life and work, of the constant exchanges between them, this is much more challenging than Coleridge's criticism. Lockhart was as distressed as Coleridge by Shelley's hatred of priests and Christianity, and by his interest in incest. But he says nothing about the poet's private life, and tries not to confuse the man's behaviour with the poetic personality; Shelley *"writes like* a man dissatisfied". More importantly still, Lockhart tries to say how it is that the "opinions" seem to sit uncomfortably in this poetry. Not only does he not like them; the poetry does not, as he puts it, "penetrate" them. He still wants to keep the "poetry", the "attractive beauty", distinct from the "opinions" which it "clothes"; but he is also searching for a conception of poetic thought as something which must operate through and in both "feeling", or "passion", and "opinion", or "principle": in each case taking full possession of them, not just clothing them with "attractive beauty". Lockhart wants a smooth ride from "characters" to "lesson" unspoiled by all these dogmatic bumps, and yet his phrase "moral flow" registers his dislike not so much of the poem's moral direction (although he does dislike that) but of its texture of thought: of how it *feels*.

Another *Quarterly* reviewer, W. S. Walker, writing in October 1821, carefully distances himself from *ad hominem* criticism; of "Mr. Shelley himself we know nothing, and desire to know nothing".[22] He also confines his assault on Shelley's reformist opinions to the final paragraphs of his review, where he regards them with some justice as fair game, since the poet "professes to write in order to reform the world". But Walker spends most of his time putting another case argued many times since, most notoriously but not only by Leavis, Eliot and Tate: that the "predominating characteristic of Mr. Shelley's poetry . . . is its frequent and total want of meaning". All is "brilliance, vacuity, and confusion"; "fragments of images pass in crowds before us" but leave "not a trace" of meaning behind; everywhere there is "exaggeration, copiousness of verbiage, and incoherence of ideas". There are few passages of alleged "confusion" in Shelley's poetry which have not, 170-odd years later, also been praised as minutely organised and deeply coherent. Still, this is the sort of criticism which has provoked careful attention to the poetry, and which is hard to dismiss as political prejudice. Looking closely at the "train of thought", including the imagery, in several passages, Walker complains that the words and ideas are often "connected by slight and accidental associations, among which it is impossible to distinguish the principal object from its accessory". A related and equally "characteristic trait" of the poetry is that in Shelley's descriptions "he never describes the thing directly, but transfers it to the properties of something which he conceives to resemble it by language which is to be taken partly in a metaphorical meaning, and partly in no meaning at all". These fundamental charges of arbitrariness and metaphorical carelessness in Shelley's poetic thought have been impressively answered in many cases, but they still carry some weight, as we shall see in later chapters.

Our fourth contemporary detractor is William Hazlitt: in two essays of 1821, for *The London Magazine* and his own volume, *Table-Talk*; and in a review of 1824, for *The Edinburgh Review*. The Whig *Edinburgh* was the doyen of the reviews; the *Quarterly*, its great Tory rival, was founded in an attempt to challenge its immense authority. *The London Magazine*, like the *Examiner*, was regarded by the Tory press as a nest of liberal-radical "Cockneys"; it also numbered Charles Lamb, Hunt and Thomas De Quincey among its contributors. So Hazlitt was not of a company whose political or literary views were likely to be regarded with much favour by the Walkers, Coleridges and Lockharts. If the political groupings of the period are loosely identified as Tory, Whig and Radical, Hazlitt belonged in the third group. He was not primarily a political writer, however, but a literary critic and journalist. This makes his criticisms of Shelley something of an embarrassment to many of the poet's defenders. Here was a radical writer sympathetic to many of the causes Shelley espoused, who was nevertheless also a critic antipathetic to the poetry. The crudely historicist or politicising solution to this quandrary is to argue that the pragmatic Hazlitt objected to the visionary extremism with which Shelley put his views, believing that his manner, rather than the views themselves, was likely to harm the radical cause. But this is to concede that the poems *are* primarily political statements, read as such by fellow-travellers. This surely entitles the *Quarterly* reviewers and their allies to their own political responses. In any case, Hazlitt's objections to Shelley's poetry are not primarily pragmatic; they are nevertheless radical in the proper sense, and fundamental to all adverse criticism of Shelley's poetry.

Hazlitt's particular readings of poetry, whether Shelley's or Shakespeare's, arise out of a general critical constitution or temper which it is impossible to abstract from any passage much shorter than a complete essay, or to render properly in much less than a book. Indeed, Hazlitt's great strength as a critic lies precisely in this resistance to abstraction or re-description: a resistance of principle but also, admirably, of practice. He does not have a critical position so much as a critical *dis*position; he is a moralist, but he is the least homiletic, theoretical and condescending of moralists – or of critics. He has accordingly been unfashionable for most of this century, when literary criticism in English has been dominated by the clerisy of systematisers and theorists whose progenitors are Coleridge, Kant and Descartes; Hazlitt's precursors, on the other hand, were Johnson, Hume, and Montaigne. That is to say, he conceived a self, a person, as aggregated, both passional and reasoning, instead of as disaggregated, with a central windowless reasoning core controlling, or failing to control, an outer crowd of unruly passions. For Hazlitt the entire self is saturated with both passion and reason. Continuity of identity, the consistency (in both senses) of the self, is provided not by a central quasi-impersonal or objective "reason", with a neutral standpoint or view from nowhere, but by the self's capacity for inhabiting its own aggregated past-and-present dispositions – or another's. The name Hazlitt sometimes uses for that inhabiting capacity is "imagination", and in its aspect as explorer or discloser of another self, including, importantly, its own future self, he calls it "disinterestedness".[23] Self-constitution and perceptiveness about others are related aspects of the same power. So too are moral and aesthetic activity, at least in so far as the latter is concerned with the representation of the human.

For Hazlitt, the striking common feature of the great writers of his own age was that they were predominantly egotistical, rather than disinterested.[24] Byron, Wordsworth and Godwin (as novelist) were by no means deficient in "intensity", in the force and interest with which they felt their own small range of feelings, but they seemed to lack "variety",[25] a dramatic sense of the reality of thousands of other possible selves and *their* feelings. Walter Scott seemed to Hazlitt to be the significant converse Romantic case, various but not intense. Only in the work of the Elizabethan dramatists, Hazlitt thought, could the two qualities of intensity and variety be found in combination. The egotistical imagination can probe deeply into a few passions, but it is not widely *experienced*, and in the end this lack of experience will colour and limit its self-discovery. Meanwhile, contemporary thinkers such as Bentham and Godwin (as philosopher), "deep logicians and enlightened legislators", "persons of the most precise and formal understandings", seemed to Hazlitt to be "cut off from human sympathy and ordinary apprehension", and to possess "the loosest and most extravagant imaginations".[26] In their case reason and passion are disaggregated, and the imagination is again inexperienced and egotistical. Hazlitt was as contemptuous as Burke had been, or as Hume would have been, towards those who, as he thought, took "decisions of abstract reason" as if "passion were a mere nonentity in the government of the world",[27] but his antipathy towards those who ignored all the passions extended, in diluted form, to those who were interested in only a few. In both respects he saw the leading thinkers and writers of his age as the victims or prisoners of what we might now call an Enlightenment conception of the central reasoning self: of what Hazlitt thought of as the egotistical imagination.

We have already begun to read the first of the two 1821 essays mentioned above, "On People of Sense".[28] The phrase is used sarcastically; Hazlitt is referring to "the self-conceited wise", the "modern Panoptic and Chrestomathic School of reformers and reconstructors of society".[29] As an attack on Benthamite utilitarianism the essay ranks with Peacock's *The Four Ages of Poetry*, except that Peacock is ironical, oblique and mannered, while Hazlitt is scornful and direct. But like Hazlitt's other 1821 essay, "On Paradox and Commonplace", this one shows as concisely and accurately as anything he wrote how his thinking about literature was continuous with his moral and political thought. In both essays the writer most implicated in that continuity is Shelley. Hazlitt does not make Lockhart's explicit connection between the poet and his intellectual mentor, Godwin, but the two are clearly bracketed together by the essay as "people of sense". Hazlitt's implied objection to Shelley is that he too is a person of precise and formal understanding and of intense feeling, but of loose and extravagant imagination; that he too is thus "cut off from human sympathy and ordinary apprehension". We should note that this is an objection to Shelley as a poet, to the self of the poetry. Hazlitt has nothing whatever to say about Shelley's life, behaviour or personal character. His passage of explicit criticism, slightly shortened, is as follows:

> Poetry . . . is nature moralizing and *idealizing* for us; inasmuch as, by shewing us things as they are, it implicitly teaches us what they ought to be; and the grosser feelings, by passing through the strainers of this imaginary, wide-extended experience, acquire an involuntary tendency to higher objects. Shakespeare was, in this sense, not only one of the greatest poets, but one of the greatest moralists that we have. Those who read him are the happier, better, and wiser for it. No one (that I know of) is the happier, better, or wiser, for reading Mr. Shelley's

Prometheus Unbound. One thing is that nobody reads it. And the reason for one or both is the same, that he is not a poet, but a sophist, a theorist, a controversial writer in verse. He gives us, for representations of things, rhapsodies of words. He does not lend the colours of imagination and the ornaments of style to the objects of nature, but paints gaudy, flimsy allegorical pictures on gauze, on the cobwebs of his own brain.... He assumes certain doubtful speculative notions, and proceeds to prove their truth by describing them in detail as matters of fact. This mixture of fanatic zeal with poetical licentiousness is not quite the thing.... The poet describes vividly and individually, so that any general results from what he writes must be from the aggregate of well-founded particulars: to embody an abstract theory, as if it were a given part of actual nature, is an impertinence and indecorum. The charm of poetry, however, depends on the union of fancy with reality, on its finding a tally in the human breast....[30]

A modern reader of this passage will have trouble making sense of Hazlitt's claim that poetry teaches us how things "ought to be" by showing us how they "are". Our moral and critical thought is deeply conditioned by a supposedly hard-and-fast distinction between fact and value. The Gestapo officer enjoys Mozart; art cannot teach us how to live. But Hazlitt was a critic who believed that poetry is a form of thought in which statements of fact are also judgements of value. For him, "things as they are" are value-soaked facts, just as selves are passion-soaked thoughts. To read poetry is to extend the feelings, which is to say the moral capacities, by reflecting upon a rich or (as the cultural anthropologists say) "thick" linguistic representation of human experience, of the passional self, its stresses, strengths and collapses. This self is what Hazlitt calls "the human breast"; what it experiences are the "objects of nature". "The grosser feelings" are those which conceal from us our whole or better selves (Hazlitt is clearly indebted to Wordsworth's conception of poetry, regardless of what he may have thought of the poetry itself). Theory, controversy, speculative notions, brain-cobwebs: these too stand between us and ourselves, so to speak. Illustrating these notions will not deepen or broaden the grosser feelings. If poetry is a form of moral thought which concerns itself chiefly with "actual nature", with the passions and reason as generally combined in "the human breast", then *Prometheus Unbound* is not poetry. It is not a matter of Hazlitt's disliking the theories themselves; he simply believes Shelley is mistaken about the nature of his mode of thought. But the result is not just a mistake; it is an unpleasing mistake, a discordance.

The essay "On Paradox and Common-Place"[31] categorises lovers of "paradox" with the companion essay's "people of sense" as lovers of the new, of any heterodox position, for its own sake. Hazlitt has little time for the "common-place", or "vulgar opinion", either; those who are guided entirely by "custom and authority" are dismissed as scornfully as those who are "equally under the influence of novelty and restless vanity".[32] He examines one case of each at length. The common-place example is George Canning, the Tory statesman. The lover of paradox is Shelley.

> The author of the Prometheus Unbound . . . has a fire in his eye, a fever in his blood, a maggot in his brain, a hectic flutter in his speech, which mark out the philosophic fanatic. . . . As is often observable in the case of religious enthusiasts, there is a slenderness of constitutional *stamina*, which renders the flesh no match for the spirit. His bending, flexible form appears to take no strong hold of things, does not grapple with the world about him, but slides from it like a river. . . . He is clogged by no dull system of realities, no earth-bound feelings, no rooted prejudices, by nothing that belongs to the mighty trunk and hard husk of nature and habit, but is drawn up by irresistible levity to the regions of mere speculation and fancy, to the sphere of air and fire. . . . There is no *caput mortuum* of worn-out, threadbare experience to serve as ballast to his mind; it is all volatile intellectual salt of tartar, that refuses to combine its evanescent, inflammable essence with any thing solid or any thing lasting. . . . Curiosity is the only proper category of his mind, and though a man in knowledge, he is a child in feeling. Hence he puts every thing into a metaphysical crucible to judge of it himself and exhibit it to others as a subject of interesting experiment, without first making it over to the ordeal of his common sense or trying it on his heart. This faculty of speculating at random on all questions may in its overgrown and uninformed state do much mischief without intending it, like an overgrown child with the power of a man. . . . With his zeal, his talent, and his fancy, he would do more good and less

harm, if he were to give up his wilder theories, and if he took less pleasure in feeling his heart flutter in unison with the panic-struck apprehensions of his readers. Persons of this class. . . . have at no time any particular cause for embarrassment and despondency because they have never the least chance of success . . . by including whatever does not hit their idle fancy, kings, priests, religion, government, public abuses or private morals, in the same sweeping clause of ban and anathema, do all they can to combine all parties in a common cause against them, and to prevent everyone else from advancing one step farther in the career of practical improvement than they do in that of imaginary and unattainable perfection.[33]

This is the passage which may be taken to mean that Hazlitt disliked Shelley's poetry chiefly because he saw it as standing in the way of moral and political reform, of "practical improvement". It would be truer, however, to say that here Hazlitt sees Shelley's poetry, but not all poetry, as incompatible with any achievable moral cause, because it is defective as poetry. Poetry must, he implies, concern itself with "the world": the shocks of accident, the weight of authority, "realities", "earth-bound feelings", "rooted prejudices", "nature and habit", "experience", "solid" and "lasting things", "common sense". So must reform; the spheres of poetry and of reform intersect, even if they are not co-extensive, and their segment of intersection, in Hazlitt's terms, is not "knowledge" but "feeling". In Hazlitt's writing an underlying metaphor is often to be found where Coleridge would have a system. Here the underlying metaphor is one of substance and weight, grappling and gravity, the flesh, contrasted with insubstantiality, volatility and levity, the spirit. Judgement in Shelley is seen as a matter of scientific analysis ("he puts everything into a metaphysical crucible"), of the centrifugal separation of fact from value. For Hazlitt judgement is a matter of assay, of weighing experience on the heart and the "common sense". In the end the perceived poetic inadequacies and the moral ones stem from the same source; it is not that the latter cause the former.

Hazlitt's fullest consideration of Shelley's poetry was in his review[34] for the *Edinburgh* of the 1824 volume entitled *Posthumous Poems*, edited by Mary Shelley. By now, presumably only partly out of respect for the dead, Hazlitt is ready to declare in the general and introductory part of the review that Shelley, "with all his faults", was "a man of genius", "a remarkable man" and "an honest man". The predominant tone of the personal passages is one of praise rather than of blame. Shelley is still one of the people of sense, still a lover of paradox in whom "the rage of free inquiry and private judgment amounted to a species of madness", but his "nature was kind, and his sentiments noble".

> There was neither selfishness nor malice at the bottom of his illusions. He was sincere in all his professions; and he practiced what he preached – to his own sufficient cost.... He thought and acted logically, and was what he professed to be, a sincere lover of truth, of nature, and of human kind. To all the rage of paradox, he united an unaccountable candour and severity of reasoning.... An Epicurean in his sentiments, he lived with the frugality and abstemiousness of an ascetick.

Shelley's best friends were hardly more generous; no "chatter about Harriet" here. Only when Hazlitt's emphasis shifts back to Shelley's *thought* do the old reservations reappear.

> His fault was, that he had no deference for the opinions of others, too little sympathy with their feelings (which he thought he had a right to sacrifice, as well as his own, to a grand ethical experiment) – and trusted too implicitly to the light of his own mind, and to the warmth of his own impulses.... Whatever shocked the feelings of others, conciliated his regard; whatever was light, extravagant, and vain, was to him a proportionable relief from the dulness and stupidity of established opinions. The worst of it however was, that he thus gave great encouragement to those who believe in all received absurdities, and are wedded to all existing abuses: his extravagance seeming to sanction their grossness and selfishness, as theirs were a full justification of his folly and eccentricity.... The martello-towers with which we are to repress, if we cannot destroy, the systems of fraud and oppression should not be castles in the air, or clouds on the verge of the horizon, but the enormous and accumulated pile of abuses which have arisen out of their continuance.... To be convinced of the existence of wrong, we should read history rather than poetry: the levers with which we must work out our regeneration are not the

cobwebs of the brain, but the warm, palpitating fibres of the human heart. . . . By flying to the extremes of scepticism, we make others shrink back, and shut themselves up in the strongholds of bigotry and superstition. . . . To this consummation, it must be confessed that too many of Mr. Shelley's productions pointedly tend. He makes no account of the opinions of others, or the consequences of any of his own; but proceeds – tasking his reason to the utmost to account for every thing, and discarding every thing as mystery and error for which he cannot account by an effort of mere intelligence – measuring man, providence, nature, and even his own heart, by the limits of the understanding. . . .

Is this anything more than the radical realist's distrust of the Utopian extremist's effect on public opinion? Shelley's admirers can only dismiss this kind of criticism if that is all it is; but Hazlitt is surely also saying that poetry is not at its best when it is trying to be either an instrument of reform or a product of pure reason, and that "mere intelligence" is not the best instrument of reform. Shelley's reformism took the shape of a poetry of "mere intelligence"; Hazlitt therefore chastises him as both poet and reformer. The "levers with which we must work out our regeneration are not the cobwebs of the brain, but the warm, palpitating fibres of the human heart". We may work out our regeneration partly, but not entirely, through poetry, and then only if it is a poetry of the heart. Reform is not the same as regeneration.

The nature of this objection is clearer still in the first three paragraphs of the review, where Hazlitt describes Shelley's poetry as "a straining after impossibilities":

. . . he had no respect for any poetry that did not strain the intellect as well as fire the imagination – and was not sublimed into a high spirit of metaphysical philosophy. Instead of giving a language to thought, or lending the heart a tongue, he utters dark sayings, and deals in allegories and riddles. . . . He mistook the nature of the poet's calling, which should be guided by involuntary, not by voluntary impulses. He shook off, as an heroic and praiseworthy act, the trammels of sense, custom, and sympathy, and became the creature of his own will. . . . Almost all is effort, almost all is extravagant, almost

all is quaint, incomprehensible, and abortive, from aiming to
be more than it is. . . . He has single thoughts of great depth
and force, single images of rare beauty, detached passages of
extreme tenderness; and in his smaller pieces, where he has
attempted little, he has done most. . . . but give him a larger
subject, and time to reflect, and he was sure to get entangled
in a system. . . . The success of his writings is therefore in general
in the inverse ratio of the extent of his undertakings; inas-
much as his desire to teach, his ambition to excel, as soon as
it was brought into play, encroached upon and outstripped
his powers of execution. . . . he was crushed beneath the weight
of thought which he aspired to bear, and was withered in the
lightning-glare of a ruthless philosophy![35]

Hazlitt anticipated by more than a century Allen Tate's criticism
of the "Ode to the West Wind": that it is a manifestation of "the
will trying to do the work of the imagination". In other terms,
Hazlitt is regretting the entry into poetry of systematic Enlightenment philosophy. He thinks that in Shelley the philosophy, or
"voluntary" intellectual impulse, comes first, and the poetry, or
"involuntary" passional impulse, second. The images and subjects seem "quaint, incomprehensible, and abortive" because they
are in the service of the difficult philosophical system which Shelley
is trying to illustrate. This is a poetry divisible into "vehicle"
and "freight", or perhaps symbol and doctrine. To such a criticism the multitude of later attempts to render the poetry com-
prehensible, and even enjoyable, by explaining the systems, will
seem absurd. Philosophy has its ways of "giving a language to
thought", its own kinds of thought to give a language to, but so
has poetry: specifically, its ways of "lending the heart a tongue".
One of the most important of these ways, exemplified but not
theorised in Hazlitt's own criticism, is metaphor. Hazlitt finds
that Shelley is metaphorically lax and unthoughtful; that his images
illustrate but do not extend or question his doctrines; that his
language does not metaphorically inhabit or search itself.

Hazlitt's treatment of particular poems in the second half of
the review, in the fashion of the time, contains far less comment
than quotation. "Julian and Maddalo" is "full of that thoughtful
and romantic humanity", in "Mr. Shelley's best and *least mannered* style", but too often unintelligible and obscure.[36] "The Witch
of Atlas" and "The Triumph of Life"

abound in horrible imaginings, like records of a ghastly dream;
– life, death, genius, beauty, victory, earth, air, ocean, the trophies of the past, the shadows of the world to come, are hud-
dled together in a strange and hurried dance of words. . . .

The "Triumph" is "filmy, enigmatical, discontinuous, unsubstan-
tial", yet "full of morbid genius and vivifying soul"; parts of the
"Witch" are "the very height of wilful extravagance and mysticism". In the "Ode to Naples", on the other hand, "immediate
and strong local feelings have at once raised and pointed Mr.
Shelley's style"; the result is "a fair specimen of [his] highest
powers". Hazlitt's greatest praise is reserved for Shelley's translations; if the volume contained only these "the intellectual world
would receive it with an *All Hail!*" Hazlitt is plainly uncomfortable with those complex and allusive mythopoeic structures of
symbol and imagery which later criticism has taken such pains
to explicate; yet he is consistent in his dislike of a poetry which
needs such explication. The direct language, strong feeling and
topical political theme of the "Ode to Naples" find his approval;
the translations draw their strength from the work of other poets. What Hazlitt dislikes is the appearance of abstraction ("life,
death, genius . . ."), or the absence of an apprehensible foundation in the quotidian world.

   Hazlitt's objections to Shelley as a poet arose out of his inter-
related conceptions of the self and of poetry. His Shelley criticism is not so much the dislike of a gradualist for an extremist
reformer as that of an experiential and metaphorical critic for an
idealist and symbolist poet. This is a deep and enduring post-
Romantic disagreement, much in need of fuller articulation. No
such articulation can be offered here, although this book may
perhaps serve as a kind of preliminary case study. What is of
importance here, however, is that notwithstanding his archaic
and apparently impressionistic terminology Hazlitt did express
some of the fundamental objections to Shelley's poetry. His was
not a criticism founded on something called "a theory of poetry"; it was not *founded* at all, in the quasi-scientific certainty-
seeking sense of the term. Hazlitt's practice assumes that criticism
is not founded on anything more certain than the self of the
poetry it reflects on and reflects, along with the responding self
of each critic: each party to the transaction being an imaginatively aggregated passional person partly constituted by a

metaphorically aggregated language, not a disembodied brain, a
set of intellectual ideas, plus a quivering jelly of emotions and a
disaggregated symbolising imagination. Hazlitt is a critic outside the systematising Coleridgean-Kantian, and ultimately Platonic, tradition that has dominated English-speaking literary
criticism, and especially theory, this century. He belongs within
another tradition, less interested in first principles and more
in individual responses, which is Johnsonian and, ultimately,
Aristotelian.

Little was added to Hazlitt's position in the rest of the nineteenth century, as Shelley's reputation grew, and as adulation
set in – especially of his lyricism but also, in different circles, of
his political views. A persistent strain of character criticism, reminiscent more of J. T. Coleridge than of Hazlitt, dwelt unforgivingly
on Shelley's treatment of Harriet. Matthew Arnold's 1888 essay
on Shelley, a review of Edward Dowden's *Life* and a reaction to
what Arnold saw as its excessive hagiography, is remembered
now chiefly as a monument of Victorian censoriousness: "What
a set! what a world! is the exclamation that breaks from us as
we come to an end of this history of 'the. occurrences of Shelley's
private life'".[37] Yet Arnold still preferred to remember Shelley's
generosity, delicacy, forbearance and tact, his "reverent enthusiasm for the great and wise", his "high and tender seriousness".
Of even more significance, however, is Arnold's practice of carrying over the terms of character judgement into criticism of the
poetry; the terms, furthermore, are very similar to Hazlitt's. Where
Hazlitt wrote of the poet's "slenderness of constitutional *stamina*"
and "bending, flexible form", of his "person" as "a type and
shadow of his genius", Arnold wrote, in the most famous of all
descriptions of Shelley, that "in poetry, no less than in life, he is
'a beautiful *and ineffectual* angel, beating in the void his lumi-
nous wings in vain'". His fault was "unsubstantiality", Arnold
thought, "the incurable want, in general, of a sound subject
matter";[38] one recalls Hazlitt's complaint at the way Shelley seemed
to him to slide away from the "mighty trunk and hard husk of
nature and habit". Neither critic read the poetry in the light of
his disapproval of Shelley's behaviour or beliefs; both held that
as a general matter poetry and personal character can be evalu-
ated in similar terms.

Other Victorian men of letters made similar observations. "Weak
in genius, weak in character" was Thomas Carlyle's judgement

of Shelley, "a man infinitely too *weak* for that solitary scaling of the Alps which he undertook in spite of all the world".[39] Coventry Patmore thought his lack of "natural affection" and insensitivity to "ties of relationship" made Shelley "almost wholly devoid of the instincts of the 'political animal' which Aristotle defines a man to be", adding that "these "deficiencies were the cause of [both] the abnormal phenomena of his life [and] the imperfections of his poetry".[40] Leslie Stephen in 1879 outdid both Hazlitt and Lockhart in his description of Shelley's debt to Godwin: "the two seem to be related as the stagnant pool to the rainbow-coloured mist into which it has been transmuted". Stephen found in Shelley the poet, the man and the political theorist a "flightiness and impulsiveness inconsistent with real depth of sentiment"; an expression, on the contrary, of a "pathetic sentiment" caused by his despair at the "great gulf" between the "transcendental world of joy, love and pure reason", and the "actual world of sin, and sorrow, and stupidity".[41] J. M. Robertson argued in the 1870s that in Shelley's "longer works his thought, such as it was, is quite inadequately meditated for purposes of beautiful expression";[42] the terms recall Lockhart and anticipate T. S. Eliot. Alexander S. Kinnear brought *The Quarterly Review* up to date in 1861 with an appreciative article on Shelley, but he still insisted that the poet's "capital defect was that he understood nothing so little [as] human nature".[43]

The balance of power in the Shelley debate shifted markedly in his favour during the nineteenth century, but the substantial case against him remained uncontroverted. This case was not *ad hominem*, morally, politically or religiously. Instead its proponents assumed that poetry has a kind of self or personality, which in Shelley communicates itself as "weak", frail, slender, flexible; words such as "shrieking" or "shrill" are often used to describe his poetic "voice". This "weakness" had to do, they implied, both with the manner in which feeling or passion was manifested or thought, and with how philosophical, political or ethical ideas were treated. There are undoubted "beauties" or "brilliance" of sound and imagery, but these are extraneous to the main flow of the poetry, in which metaphorically arbitrary associations of words and subject seem to go hand in hand with an intensity of emotion made unpleasing by its singleness or abstraction from human complexity, and also by its frequent source in equally single and abstracted principles of pure reason. In either case the self of the poetry is disturbingly childish, shrilly monomaniac. This is not simply a sensory or "concretist" criticism. The chief "weakness" of the poetry, on this view, isn't that the imagery is ethereal or symbolist, but that the self of the poetry, in its language, and especially its metaphoricity, is "thin", disconnected from other selves and unintegrated within itself. In Hazlitt's terms, Shelley's is a particularly "egotistical" imagination. The self of this poetry is not only unusually "thin", but especially hard to distinguish from some positable self of Shelley's own.

The twentieth century

The main objections to Shelley's poetry in this century were stated between the late 1910s and the late 1930s, since when the popular tide has run the other way, as it did for the same period of the last century. The modern case is essentially the same as the one we have just explored, with the addition of some helpful new terms. We can summarise it relatively briefly.

Irving Babbitt, the classicist and "New Humanist", was T. S. Eliot's most influential teacher at Harvard. His polemical book *Rousseau and Romanticism* (1919) was the manifesto of Aristotelian anti-Romanticism for a generation of American students; its closest equivalent on the other side of the Atlantic was T. E. Hulme's *Speculations* (1924). As far as Babbitt's general (and impassioned) case against Romanticism is concerned we need only notice his notion of the "ethical imagination".[44] The "only rule, if we are to achieve art that has an ethical soul, is to view life with some degree of imaginative wholeness". As for Shelley, he expresses in his poetry a "morality" that "becomes a matter of mood", an "infinite indeterminate desire" for, later falling into disappointment with, an unattainable Romantic Arcadia.

> ... the quality of [Shelley's] imagination is on the whole not ethical but Arcadian or pastoral. In the name of his Arcadia conceived as the "ideal" he refuses to face the facts of life. I have already spoken of the flimsiness of his "Prometheus Unbound" as a solution of the problem of evil. What is found in this play is the exact opposite of imaginative concentration on the human law. The imagination wanders irresponsibly in a region quite outside of normal human experience. . . .

Hazlitt's "disinterested" imagination has become Babbitt's "ethical" imagination. Both critics notice in Shelley egotism and irresponsibility, a poetic personality which does not fully inhabit and recognise either itself or what is not itself. In this poetry, says Babbitt, "the landscape is not only a state of the soul but the soul is a state of the landscape; just as in Shelley's Ode, Shelley becomes the West Wind and the West Wind becomes Shelley". Babbitt's friend and fellow New Humanist, Paul Elmer More, had already expressed in 1910 the then unfashionable view that for all Shelley's "genius", which was "fine and impressionable", he was unusually susceptible to the influence of current moral doctrines, especially the view that "man is naturally and inherently virtuous" but oppressed by an external evil. He was also liable, said More, to attach his emotions to those doctrines, not seeing the need for any other context or use for the emotions, or for any further reflection upon them. "Revolution", for Shelley, "meant the fluttering of an opaque and dizzying flag between the poet's inner eye and the truth of human nature". His opinions became "chiefly unliterary, destructive, that is to say, of that self-knowledge out of which the great creations . . . of literature grow". More saw "the same force at work in his conduct", incidentally, but the criticisms of the poetry stand alone.[45] More is in effect reviving Hazlitt's claim that Shelley's love of novel "theory" or "paradox", combined with his intensity of thin or unexplored feeling, often attached to the theory, prevented him from "disinterestedly" inhabiting or imagining himself.

T. S. Eliot's novel and influential critical concepts, the "objective correlative" and the "dissociation of sensibility", were first deployed in 1919 and 1921 respectively. His broader conceptions of poetry and the self, however, were remarkably close to Hazlitt's, especially in the importance they assigned to the passions, which Eliot also called "emotion".

The only way of expressing emotion in the form of art is by finding an 'objective correlative'; in other words, a set of objects, a situation, a chain of events which shall be the formula of that *particular* emotion; such that when the external facts, which must terminate in sensory experience, are given, the emotion is immediately evoked. . . . The artistic 'inevitability' lies in this complete adequacy of the external to the emotion.[46]

... the more perfect the artist, the more completely separate in him will be the man who suffers and the mind which creates; the more perfectly will the mind digest and transmute the passions which are its material. . . . Poetry is not a turning loose of emotion, but an escape from emotion; it is not the expression of personality, but an escape from personality. . . . And the poet cannot reach this impersonality without surrendering himself wholly to the work to be done. And he is not likely to know what is to be done unless he lives in what is not merely the present, but the present moment of the past, unless he is conscious, not of what is dead, but of what is already living.[47]

The poets of the seventeenth century, the successors of the dramatists of the sixteenth, possessed a mechanism of sensibility which could devour any kind of experience. . . . In the seventeenth century a dissociation of sensibility set in, from which we have never recovered. . . . The possible interests of a poet are unlimited; the more intelligent he is the better . . . our only condition is that he turn them into poetry, and not merely meditate on them poetically. A philosophical theory which has entered into poetry is established, for its truth or falsity in one sense ceases to matter, and its truth in another sense is proved. [All great poets] have the same essential quality of transmuting ideas into sensations, of transforming an observation into a state of mind.[48]

The elegant language is also programmatic, categorical and quasi-scientific: "only way", "the formula", "must terminate", "sensory experience", "will be", "cannot reach", "mechanism of sensibility", "never recovered", "transmuting". Eliot and Pound were initiating a post-Georgian revolution in literary taste; this was also, we should remember, the time of Rutherford and Bohr, Einstein and Planck. But Hazlitt would have recognised that poetry is still conceived here as a kind of metaphorical thought in which "emotion" is the agent as much as the material; in which "sensory" and not intellectual experience is the court of last appeal; in which "impersonality" (read "disinterestedness") is achieved not by abstracting from the self but by utterly inhabiting it. Read in this light, Eliot's particular criticisms of Shelley look familiar rather than novel. He notices, as Hazlitt did and as many of

Shelley's admirers still do, the omnipresent "zeal for social and political reforms",[49] or more generally the centrality in many of the poems of a "doctrine, theory, belief, or 'view of life'": of "ideas".[50] Shelley "seems to have had to a high degree the unusual faculty of passionate apprehension of abstract ideas. . . . abstractions could excite in him strong emotions". But this is, in Eliot's terms, precisely what it is to be "dissociated". One is emotional about the ideas, but unthoughtful about the emotion. There is certainly a stumbling-block, for Eliot as for Hazlitt, if the ideas in question are abhorrent or repellent. But "a poet may borrow a philosophy or he may do without one"; he may even "propagate a doctrine", concedes Eliot, as Dante and Lucretius did. A deeper problem is encountered when the ideas seem "puerile", "repellent" and "shabby", "childish" and "feeble", rather than "coherent, mature, and founded on the facts of experience"; when, as here, they are the "ideas of adolescence". In Hazlitt's words, Shelley is "a child in feeling"; he "does not grapple with the world about him". But even though Eliot does say at one point that this can set up "an almost complete check" on a reader's capacity to appreciate a poetry, the general logic of his position takes him further. The real problem is not that the ideas (free love, revolution, vegetarianism) are repellent, but that they are "bolted whole", so that they, and the poet's attitude to them, become the object of the reader's attention. On the one hand there are poets such as Shelley "who employ their verbal, rhythmic and imaginative gift in the service of ideas which they hold passionately"; on the other, there are those who "employ the ideas which they hold with more or less settled conviction as material for a poem". Eliot found in "one or two passages" of "The Triumph of Life", Shelley's last poem, some "traces of a struggle towards unification of sensibility",[51] traces of the second kind of poetry, and in general he thought Shelley's "poetic gifts", presumably of eye and ear, "were certainly of the first order". Hazlitt too had found "morbid genius and vivifying soul" in the otherwise "filmy" and "enigmatical" "Triumph"; he too thought Shelley "a man of genius". Neither was motivated primarily by prejudice against Shelley's beliefs or his behaviour, although Eliot admitted his distaste for the latter too. Eliot, like Hazlitt, articulates a general conception of poetry with which Shelley's poetry is ill-assorted: a "conception", not a "theory", because for all Eliot's quasi-scientific metaphor there is, happily, none of the pseudoscientific methodology so often associated with a "theory" of poetry. Eliot, like Hazlitt, notices in the poetry an absence of full self-possession.

A great many critics adopted similar views of Shelley between the 1920s and the 1950s.[52] Nowadays defenders of Shelley dismiss these critics collectively as "New Critical formalists" or "Leavisites", but many of them would have been horrified or uncomprehending at being called "New Critics"; the criticisms often had little to do with the forms of Shelley's poems; and Leavis was not the originator of the views (not even Eliot was, as we have seen). Thus T. E. Hulme, for example, wrote in *Speculations* (1924) that poetry is a "visual concrete" language which "always endeavours to arrest you, and to make you continuously see a physical thing, to prevent you gliding through an abstract process".[53] William Empson in 1930 noticed Shelley "discovering his idea in the act of writing, or not holding it all in his mind at once, so that, for instance, there is a simile which applies to nothing exactly, but lies half-way between two things, when the author is moving from one to the other". An "extreme case" of this "transitional simile" can be found "when not being able to think of a comparison fast enough" Shelley "compares the thing to a vaguer or more abstract notion of itself".[54] Yvor Winters (1947) thought the "Ode to the West Wind" a good example of poetry which expresses a feeling not "in terms of its motive, but in terms of something irrelevant or largely so, commonly landscape".[55] Cleanth Brooks (1949) claimed that the "characteristic fault of Shelley's poetry is that it excludes on principle all but the primary impulses".[56] These are all, like Eliot's, sophisticated versions of views expressed in Shelley's own lifetime, not about his beliefs or conduct but about his poetry, which for all its concern with ideas and its use of symbol seems to these critics not to think sufficiently about, or with, the senses and the passions. Again, a criticism of Shelley's metaphorising is implied.

F. R. Leavis's criticisms of Shelley stung not because they went deeper or were more original, but because they were angrier and apparently more *ad hominem* than Eliot's. Much of the chapter on Shelley in *Revaluation* (1936)[57] might be seen as a forceful restatement of Eliot's arguments about the objective correlative, impersonality and dissociation, themselves re-expressions of much older conceptions of poetry. According to Leavis, Shelley has a "weak grasp upon the actual. . . . there is nothing grasped in the poetry – no object offered for contemplation, no realised presence. . . . Shelley, at his best and worst, offers the emotion in itself, unattached, in the void". In his poetry feeling "is divorced from thought"; it "does not inhere in a concretely imagined particular situation, but is a general emotion pumped in from outside". Here and elsewhere Leavis's formulations are vivid and pugnacious, but they are not especially novel. As he says himself, "the essential observations . . . in the reading and appreciation of Shelley's poetry. . . . would seem to be obvious enough". What is less obvious is where Leavis stands on the perennial question of Shelley's "beliefs", of the relation of the character of the man to the self of the poetry. Leavis begins his essay by insisting, *contra* Eliot, that "when one dissents from persons who, sympathising with Shelley's . . . 'beliefs', exalt him as a poet, it is strictly the 'poetry' one is criticizing". He is unhappy about Eliot's suggestion that Shelley's untenable beliefs may set up a "complete check" to the reader; he quite properly wants to say that the "repellent" quality inheres not in the beliefs but in the way the poetry thinks and feels about them, a position implicit but not fully brought out in Eliot's argument. Shelley's unattached or "high-pitched" treatment of emotion, for Leavis, was what gave the poetry its effect of "vanity and emptiness"; the treatment of emotion indicated an absence of thought in places where to think is a responsibility of the poet, and not to is a sign of self-indulgence. This is what has made Leavis's criticism of Shelley's poetic "weakness" almost impossible for most readers to separate from a criticism of moral failure in the man. Leavis says in the same essay that "criticism of Shelley has something more important to deal with than mere bad poetry; or, rather, there are badnesses inviting the criticism that involves moral judgments". In this "transition from the lighter concerns of literary criticism to the diagnosis of radical disabilities and perversions, such as call for moral comment", we come to the heart of what has so annoyed admirers of Shelley ever since. Leavis is saying both that the man and the poet should be separated more effectively than Eliot separated them, and that the poet is subject to "moral judgments". This looks like an inconsistency. But if moral thought is about not just philosophical theories of good and bad, fact and value, right and wrong, but about whole lives, whole selves; if poetry involves thinking about whole selves, and especially thinking with the passions: then poetry must often be a kind of moral thought, and failings of one will be failings of the other. Leavis is more honest than most critics in facing up to the possibility that a created poetic self may be as objectionable as some people may be. "Shelley's characteristic pathos is self-regarding, directed upon an idealized self", narcissistically dwelt upon, rather than that best self which the poet has it in him to be. A "weak grasp upon the actual", when "the actual" is a human situation involving several people or characters, can look like a failure of feeling, of humanity. "Belief", the poet's moral philosophy, has on this view nothing to do with the "moral" strength of the poetry. René Wellek once put to Leavis the counter-argument so often employed by Shelley's admirers, arguing that the poet's "philosophy is astonishingly unified, and perfectly coherent", and that Leavis is simply a moral realist who finds the Platonist and idealist traditions unsympathetic. Here is Leavis's response:

> If, in reply to my charge that Shelley's poetry is repetitive, vaporous, monotonously self-regarding and often emotionally cheap, and so, in no very long run, boring, Dr. Wellek tells me that Shelley was an idealist, I can only wonder whether some unfavourable presumption has not been set up about idealism.[58]

In other words, no amount of exegesis of a poet's beliefs or "philosophy", no library of scholarly books showing his debts to Godwin or Plato or Hume, will defend him against this sort of charge, because Leavis, like Eliot and Hazlitt, is repelled by the very texture of Shelley's mind as it is discernible in the poetry.

Leavis's American contemporary Allen Tate, writing in the Eliot tradition, thought that Shelley's metaphor "the thorns of life", in the "Ode to the West Wind", was of some historical significance. Its appearance might be seen, Tate said, as a "landmark in the history of poetry", a clue to that "moment of dissociation in modern poetry" when "poets lost control of the literal significance of their metaphors". Shelley's was "the way of the unliteral imagination";[59] he believed in Godwinism and Platonism more than in poetry. His poem, according to Tate, was an example of what Yeats called "rhetoric", namely "'the will trying to do the work of the imagination'".[60] Tate turns to another famous Shelleyan metaphor in order to amplify his point. The lines from *Adonais*,

"Life like a dome of many-coloured glass/ Stains the white radiance of eternity", are "not poetry";

> . . . they express the frustrated individual will trying to compete with science. The will asserts a rhetorical proposition about the whole of life, but the imagination has not seized upon the materials of the poem and made them into a whole. Shelley's simile is imposed upon the material from above; it does not grow out of the material. It exists as explanation external to the subject: it is an explanation of "life" that seems laden with portent and high significance, but *as explanation* it necessarily looks towards possible action, and it is there that we know that the statement is meaningless. . . . If the simile of the dome were an integral part of a genuine poem, the question of its specific merit as truth or falsehood would not arise.

Tate contrasts Shelley's figure with Edgar's "Ripeness is all" from *King Lear*, a statement which "rises from the depths of Gloucester's situation" and constitutes an *"experienced statement"* whose "specific merit . . . as general truth or falsehood is irrelevant".

The truth or falsity of Shelley's figure is the only issue that it raises. This bit of Platonism must be accepted before we can accept the material of the poem *Adonais*; for it must be a true idea to afford to the poet a true explanation. He must have an explanation for a material that he cannot experience. The idea of the dome is asserted to strengthen a subject that the poem has not implicitly imagined.

Crucially for Shelley studies, this "forcing of the subject, which is abstractly conceived, not implicitly seized upon . . . excites the 'curiosity' of the reader, who dwells on the external details of the poem or pities the sad poet". Readers, like the poet, fall into the search for information or explanation. Poetry is "dissolved into biography and history", instead of resisting dissolution by retaining an identity separate from the poet's own behaviour and beliefs. Tate wants poetry in which the figures, the metaphors and images, are so positioned and developed that an immensely complex concept, such as "life", is attended to without being directly confronted, explained or invoked. When it *is* directly confronted, and described as "thorny" or "domed", then the inadequacy of his figure beside his sense of the complexity of the concept disappoints both the poet and, eventually, the reader. The poet's very personality becomes implicated in his failure to impose his abstraction on experience, and thus the reader is also drawn into the poet's life, instead of staying in the poetry. So both the philosophical and the biographical approaches to Shelley's poetry are occasioned by the same flaw in the poetry itself. Tate has no interest in what Shelley's beliefs or behaviours actually were, but he has strong views about what it was in the poetry which made Shelley's critics unable to avoid an obsession with those things. He thinks, furthermore, that poetry which does compel such an obsession is unsatisfactory: a view shared by many adverse critics of Shelley since Hazlitt and his contemporaries.

In summary, we may regard the "case against" Shelley as essentially Hazlitt's, with important embellishments by T. S. Eliot. It has been put chiefly in two periods, roughly 1819–40 and 1919–40, but it has been a minority critical case; most writers on Shelley since his lifetime have been admirers (this does not mean, of course, that most readers of literature in English have: they probably have not, which may partly account for his admirers' defensiveness). Philosophically and personally this minority case at its strongest is generally unprejudiced, resting on a view of poetry and of the self rather than on any dislike of Shelley's beliefs or behaviour – although it is true that the critics we have noticed do regard Shelley as having exposed himself to such prejudices by writing the kind of poetry he did. The "view of poetry and of the self" in question is not sufficiently derived from agreed first principles, or sufficiently monolithic, to be described as a "theory", or even as "a" view. Still, in the fourth section of this chapter we shall try to sketch a broader framework within which to understand it, or them; for now we can say that these critics all seem to perceive a kind of disconnection in Shelley's poetry between feelings, emotions or passions on one hand, and ideas, beliefs or doctrines on the other. An appearance of verbal arbitrariness or metaphorical thinness is created for the ordinary reader, they believe, because connections are made *via* the "cobwebs of the brain", as Hazlitt called them, rather than the "warm, palpitating fibres of the human heart". Shelley may be a person of "precise and formal understanding", but he is a "child in feeling". His passions are aroused by his beliefs, his doctrines, but these passions are not themselves subject to reflection, to metaphorising imagination, to the pressures and possibilities of other selves, to the consequent reconstitution into a fully inhabited self.

SYMBOLISING THE TRUTH: THE CASE FOR

There are only a few essays making "the case" against Shelley; there is a whole library of books, articles and journals making many cases for him. Perhaps it is not eccentric, given this imbalance, to state the favourable side of the argument more briefly than the unfavourable. A few synoptic claims can and must be made about several thousand pieces of criticism, which may seem by their number alone to constitute overwhelming evidence of the breadth of the poetry's appeal; some of the leading names in Shelley scholarship can only be perfunctorily treated. There is another reason for brevity, however: relatively few of Shelley's army of admirers in print have attempted anything like a direct answer to the kinds of criticisms just mentioned – have attempted to justify their valuation of Shelley as a poet. This omission has become even more glaring since Shelley's transformation into yet another canonical object of the twentieth-century literary-academic industry. Michael O'Neill commented some years ago on the "tendency shown in much recent criticism to take for granted Shelley's status as a great poet"; there "is still scope", he said, "for a book that grapples with the issue of the poetry's worth".[61] His was such a book, and there have been others: very few, however, in proportion to that library of Shelley appreciation.

Referential defences

The vast majority of these appreciations could be called "referential". They assume, more often than they argue, that the poetry draws its value from – that its value is *in* – the system or systems of reference in terms of which it is to be understood. The referential position has two main variants: the biographical-historical and the philosophical-intellectual; more simply, Shelley's life and times, and his ideas and beliefs. As with the "case against", there is a marked continuity of assumption and even methodology amongst the referentialists across the years.

The first variant of referential Shelley criticism originated with Mary Shelley. Hunt may have been the first admirer into print, but it was Mary who laid the foundations for all Shelley scholarship, and especially for the biographical approach to it, with her editions of the poems and prose. The 1824 *Posthumous Poems* provoked the first wave of general notices of Shelley's work, but it was the full 1839 edition of the poems and the 1840 collection of essays and letters that really turned the tide in Shelley's favour after the more controversial period before: despite Mary's near-treacherous expressions of regret that Shelley did not more fully develop "human interest and passion" in his poems. In hindsight these two editions can be identified as the original sources of that often unthinking biographicalism which dominated Shelley criticism last century and most of this, and which created the "Shelley myth". Mary's framing notes to the poems, wrote Sylva Norman in 1954, "everywhere supply a biographical and spiritual clue to the poems, besides rendering Shelley's tragedy forever inseparable from his writings".[62] For a J. T. Coleridge or an Arnold the tragedy was Harriet's, but the approach was the same; and Coleridge and Arnold, Carlyle, Stephen and Patmore, even in the end Eliot and Leavis, were in any case all but swept away in a flood of biographicalist appreciation. There were the memoirs of Shelley by those who knew him – Hogg, Trelawny, Peacock, Medwin, Horace Smith and Thornton Hunt; there were the substantial biographical essays prefixed to those doorstop Victorian editions of his work by W. M. Rossetti, H. Buxton Forman and George Woodberry; there were the monumental landmark biographies by Edward Dowden (1886), Walter Edwin Peck (1927), Newman Ivey White (1947) and Richard Holmes (1976). White, arguably the principal restorer of Shelley's reputation this century, acknowledged that in his 1400-page book he "said little . . . about Shelley's greatness as a poetic artist";[63] he simply assumed it. The same could be said about all the others just mentioned except Holmes, not only the finest writer of all Shelley's biographers but the only one to attempt genuine criticism of the poetry. Biographers, by the nature of their undertaking, looked in the poems for traces of the life; furthermore they accepted, again in White's words, that of "few writers more than Shelley can it be said that his works are the man himself".[64] Robert Browning anticipated this thought, and likewise reflected this dominant tendency in Shelley appreciation, when speaking of "the work

'Shelley'", and claiming that "in our approach to the poetry, we necessarily approach the personality of the poet"[65] – rather than the personality of the poem, one might say. Whether in the vapid panegyrics of Francis Thompson, the sardonic condescension of André Maurois or the sober erudition of White, biographicalism continued to dominate Shelley scholarship into this century, so that not only the biographers themselves but many of the major mid-century critics placed much of the weight of their interpretations on the poet's life. The "Shelley myth",[66] the idea of Shelley as an angel, an ineffectual angel, or a devil, has clogged criticism of his poetry ever since his lifetime, and blocked, for admirers and detractors both, the path to the self of the poetry.

The other major variant of referentialism, the philosophical-intellectual, often takes issue with its biographical-historical fellow. Timothy Webb's *Shelley: A Voice Not Understood* (1977), for example, is among other things a pugnacious and telling attack on biographicalism.[67] For scholars and critics in this category (which of course often overlaps with its fellow) the explanatory web or framework within which to make sense of Shelley's poetry should be his ideas, his mind, as distinguished from his life or events affecting him. G. H. Lewes opined in 1841 that Shelley was "eminently virtuous . . . eminently sincere". But he was one of the "two most memorable men of the nineteenth century" (the other was Bentham) not so much because of these qualities of character as because his philosophy of "progression, humanity, perfectibility, civilisation, democracy" had become "the dominant Idea . . . throughout Europe".[68] The poet Mathilde Blind, writing in 1870, thought Shelley's poems were collectively "the poetical interpretation of a life", but that the real meaning of that life was to be found in Shelley's "impetuous passion for reforming the world".[69] John Todhunter argued in 1880 that Shelley "never degenerates from a man into a mere poet" because he is "full of the new wine of modern ethical ideas".[70] Shelley the political radical was a hero to Richard Carlile and Robert Owen; his early poem *Queen Mab* was widely known as "the Chartists' Bible". Karl Marx himself reportedly believed that Shelley "was essentially a revolutionist and . . . would always have been one of the advanced guard of socialism".[71] George Bernard Shaw mocked the genteel Shelley Society types of the eighteen-nineties, those for whom, he said, the poet was "nothing more than a word-jeweller". Had Shelley been born fifty years later, said Shaw, "he

would have been advocating Social-Democracy with a view to
its development into the most democratic form of Communism
practically attainable".[72]

These nineteenth-century admirers of Shelley's political ideas
promoted both his activism and his reformism, and thus in a
sense his life as well as his ideas, over his poetry. As the political issues at stake lost their immediacy, or at least changed their
terms, critics of this cast were able to set Shelley's ideas in broader
and less charged contexts. Thus Crane Brinton in 1926, Gerald
NcNiece in 1969, Carl Woodring in 1970, P. M. S. Dawson and
Michael Scrivener in 1980 and Terence A. Hoagwood in 1988 all
published books or chapters of books showing the influence of
political events and ideas on Shelley's poems, rarely asking
whether a poem is the kind of thing which is best or even well
understood in these terms. Paul Foot claimed in *Red Shelley* (1980)
that poetry, like every other form of thought, is principally a
means of social and political change, and that that was Shelley's
view too. We must, said Foot, "pass on Shelley's political enthusiasms
to today's socialists, radicals and feminists".[73] Foot's instrumen-
talism is unusually blunt, but it is not eccentric. The doyen of
this modern school of political referentialism, Kenneth Neill
Cameron, has been publishing since the early 1950s what amounts
to one long continuous account of Shelley's life and work in a
series of books and studies, arguing throughout that the "core
of Shelley's poetry" was "his philosophy of social revolution",
and that his objectives were "not aesthetic but agitational".[74]

Political referentialists often stray into biographicalism, perhaps because theory, practice and personality are hard to separate in politics. Political referentialism also makes it hard for
Shelley's defenders to claim that his detractors are motivated by
political prejudice. After all, if some of the most distinguished
Shelley scholars argue, frequently on the poet's own explicit
authority and frequently from a standpoint of obvious sympathy for the causes he espoused, that in his poetry he was primarily motivated by political considerations himself, why should
not those of opposing persuasions attack that same poetry on
equally political grounds? Besides, as we have seen, this is not
the heart of the case *against* Shelley. His defenders are more extensively, more centrally and often more prejudicially interested
in his politics than his detractors are. Political referentialism has
been a most influential category of Shelley scholarship, and it

has not always been as "neutral" (to recall Pottle's word) as its practitioners may think. Let us regard this as a distracting subvariant of philosophical or intellectual referentialism.

Referentialism's wider and less tendentious goal has been to "demonstrate the genuinely great importance of Shelley as a thinker and the intelligible order of his intellectual development".[75] The words were Carl Grabo's, from his seminal book *The Magic Plant: The Growth of Shelley's Thought* (1936). Grabo, with White, relaunched Shelley scholarship as a respectable activity this century. During the next thirty to forty years many scholars produced accounts of Shelley's "thought" in terms of one system or another, one theme or another, one version or another of the history of ideas: not only reformism or radicalism, socialism or communism, but desire, restraint, religion, death, Platonism, scepticism, science, Godwinism, mysticism, realism, perfectibilism, auto-eroticism, materialism, utilitarianism, the Enlightenment and the Greek revival. Two dominant Shelleys emerged from this welter of single-thesis or history-of-ideas studies: the Platonist model, advanced chiefly by J. A Notopoulos in 1949, popular in the 1950s and 1960s but nowadays looking a touch frenzied or rhapsodic, and an urbane Humean model, first proposed by C. E. Pulos in 1954. This Enlightenment-to-Regency sceptic has become *the* modern Shelley, readily conformable to various other recent theses, especially about language. The peculiarity of both models, however, as well as of their many variations and combinations, is first that their proponents are always seeking, in the words of Pulos, "a possible clue to the unity of [Shelley's] thought in all its variety";[76] and second that their proponents' very erudition, so powerful an instrument in the diagnosis of intellectual influence, lures them ever further away from "the issue of the poetry's worth". An obsession with unity in variety, ultimately Coleridgean and Kantian, can blind the seeker to diversity, uncertainty, dilemma, luck, or disguise the absence of serious thought about or in terms of these conditions of humanity. An obsession with philosophical influence may produce a sense of enormous variety, but always of *philosophical* variety. Hazlitt's objections remain unanswered; indeed, the more philosophically sophisticated Shelley can be shown to be, the more weight Hazlitt's objections have.

Even the three modern masters of referentialism, Earl R. Wasserman, G. M. Matthews and Donald H. Reiman, cannot fully protect Shelley from the case against him; indeed one is tempted to say that they are especially unable to do so. Matthews argued that to understand the poems "one must reckon with the whole of Shelley – and not with his texts alone, but also with his science, his politics, his theories of literature, his medical record",[77] his social context, the literary genres and coteries within which he worked. Wasserman's massive *Shelley: A Critical Reading* (1971), the formidable culmination of the Pulos tradition, argued that the system of reference for each poem is no less than the entire "poetic corpus", the whole "structure of Shelley's mind". Each poem is a "newly created thought" made up of the combination of inter-animating ideas.[78] Reiman, also working in the Pulos tradition, and the most indefatigable of all modern Shelley scholars, believes that Shelley will never be properly appreciated until *all* his symbols, *all* the references, are elucidated.[79] All three, Wasserman in one magisterial text and Matthews and Reiman in long series of definitive scholarly studies, implicitly claim that the poetry is precisely as valuable as its range of reference and its various intellectual positions, to all of which it gives unique expression. But as another redoubtable modern scholar, Kelvin Everest, has recently conceded, the poet's specificity and range of reference can be "a real problem for even attentive and sympathetic readers"; his meaning can be "in practical terms just about impossible to grasp without the assistance of detailed academic commentary".[80] And referentialism alone, no matter how sophisticated, will never convince those who dislike not just the reference but the texture of the poetry's thought, the projected self with which the reader comes into conversation. One may find a philosopher's precision or a reformer's commitment to the cause impressive without liking either as a person. In combination with pure textual and bibliographical scholarship, of course, referentialism has by now supplied a helpful gloss, and often more than one, on every difficult passage in Shelley; it has made unanswerable objections to attacks based on poor texts, wilful misreadings or insufficient information; and in the hands of its more responsive practitioners it has even suggested that defences of Shelley's poetry should sometimes be more concerned with how it thinks than with what it thinks about.

Symbolist and stylist defences

This is an extract from a review of *Prometheus Unbound* in *The London Magazine and Monthly Critical and Dramatic Review* for September–October 1820. Reiman thought the piece was a "triumph of Romantic critical theory"; White said it represented "the summit of contemporary admiration of Shelley as a poet":[81]

... the deliverance of Prometheus, which is attended by the dethroning of Jupiter, is scarcely other than a symbol of the peaceful triumph of goodness over power; of the subjection of might to right; and the restoration of love to the full exercise of its benign and all-penetrating sympathies. To represent vividly and poetically this vast moral change, is, we conceive, the design of this drama, with all its inward depths of mystical gloom, its pregnant clouds of imagination, its spiry eminences of icy splendour, and its fair regions overspread by a light "which never was by sea or land," which consecrates and harmonises all things.[82]

What looked to Hazlitt the next year like "flimsy allegorical pictures", futile attempts "to embody an abstract theory", looked to this anonymous reviewer like successful *symbols*: of triumph, subjection, restoration and moral change. This old difference of views lies at the heart of the "case of Shelley"; the central defence of his poetry may be called "symbolist". It is not necessary for our purposes here to connect this defence to the Symbolist tradition of Poe, Baudelaire, Laforgue, Arthur Symons and others, or to their Modernist successors, but a book might certainly be written on Shelley's place in this tradition. Another one might be written on the connections betwen Symbolism and nineteenth-century Idealism; certainly the "symbolist" defence of Shelley grew stronger as British Idealism developed during the century. We shall return briefly to this wider subject in the final section of this chapter; our business here is only to identify a central line of thinking in Shelley criticism.

The chief progenitor of British Idealism was Coleridge (S. T., not J. T.), who remarked in 1830 that Shelley's "Atheism would not have scared *me* – for *me*, it would have been a semi-transparent Larva, soon to be *sloughed*, and, through which, I should have seen the true *Image*; the final metamorphosis".[83] Behind all ideas lies the true Image, the final Symbol of the One Idea. The poet Swinburne concluded in his 1869 "Notes on the Text of Shelley" that the earlier poet's "aim [was] rather to render the effect of a thing than a thing itself; the soul and spirit of life rather than the living form".[84] Hazlitt wanted poetry to show us "things as they are"; this, says Swinburne, is poetry which shows us the effect and the spirit of things as they are. As Todhunter put it,

> Shelley's subtle intellect delighted in the thought that behind the universal mind, behind even that life of its life which he calls spirit, there was some more recondite principle, some more essential substance, the nature of which we cannot imagine or find a name for.[85]

Our inability to find a name or image for this "essential substance" or "spirit" is the very thing out of which Shelley makes poetry, according to Todhunter. The literary historian Oliver Elton, in his classic *Survey of English Literature 1780–1830* (1912), placed Shelley in an idealist spiritual tradition; in his poetry the "things seen are not the reality, they are the metaphor: the reality is Shelley's own soul".[86] The idealist philosopher George Santayana, writing about Shelley in a volume published in 1913, conceded that the poet displayed "a certain moral incompetence" in his human judgements: but "is life . . . the same thing as the circumstances of life on earth? Is the spirit of life, that marks and judges those circumstances, itself nothing?"[87] Where Babbitt at about the same time was deploring the fact that in Shelley's poetry the landscape is represented as a *state* of the soul, Elton and Santayana were praising his use of it as a *symbol* of the soul. This general line of defence had already been renewed for the twentieth century by W. B. Yeats, a poet with close affiliations of his own to the Symbolist tradition, in his influential essay "The Philosophy of Shelley's Poetry" (1900). The essay is in two complementary parts, significantly entitled "His Ruling Ideas" and "His Ruling Symbols". In the first part Yeats attempts to explain, as any good referentialist would, "the system of belief that lay behind"[88] the poems. In the second part he isolates a few characteristically Shelleyan symbols – river, cave, star, moon, tower – and argues that while much of the poetry derives its strength from its reference to the ruling ideas, it is these "ancient symbols", which do *not* have a meaning exhaustible by such reference, that give Shelley's poetry its power:

> It is only by ancient symbols, by symbols that have number-less meanings besides the one or two the writer lays an emphasis upon, or the half-score he knows of, that any highly subjective art can escape from the barrenness and shallowness of a too conscious arrangement, into the abundance and depth of nature.[89]

Indeed, Yeats elsewhere said that he could only enjoy Shelley by "massing in [his] imagination his recurring images of towers and rivers, and caves with fountains in them and that one Star of his, till his world had grown solid underfoot and consistent enough for the soul's habitation".[90] In these criticisms we can see how the symbolist defence both resembles and transforms referentialism. Yeats thinks that most of Shelley's images are referentially explicable. A resonant few are not, however; they have "numberless meanings", can be dignified by the term "symbol", and defy articulate admiration. Yeats's own poetry, of course, contained many such "symbols": too many, some would say.

The mid-century Shelley revival was predominantly referential, but a few critics engaged with the "case against" by returning to this symbolist defence. In 1939 C. S. Lewis commented that in *Prometheus Unbound*, "the greatest long poem in the nineteenth century", the "events . . . seem to become the symbols of the spiritual process [Shelley] is presenting without effort or artifice or even consciousness on his part". There is thus "no strain between the literal sense and the imaginative significance". The "events", which become "symbols", do still refer to a "spiritual process", but in doing so they give the process a new and unfamiliar form.[91] G. Wilson Knight claimed in 1941 that "the real business of poetry" was "symbolism"; agreement or disagreement with Shelley's "moral or political ideas must be allowed only a minor emphasis". In "Shelley more nearly than elsewhere image is event and event highly imaginative . . . objective imagery *is* inward thought or feeling".[92] To the objection that feeling and belief are ill-matched, and that abstract poetic images are randomly associated with both, the response is that belief should be left out of consideration entirely, and that images should be seen not as sensory vehicles for exploration of familiar feelings but as abstract instruments for the creation of new and strange ones. R. H. Fogle mounted one of the most sustained exposi- tions of this view in the late 1940s and early 1950s. In that fa- mous image of life as a dome from *Adonais*, so disliked by Allen Tate, Fogle found that Shelley was "offering to the reader a va- riety of relationship" between a simple and basic shape, the dome, and an abstraction, life. The abstraction and the shape are on the same existential level, as it were. *Contra* referentialism, the image is not "exhaustible in terms of abstract ideas"; it "take[s] on a life of [its] own from the imagination of the poet, difficult to define because entirely unprecedented and original".[93] The innovation and the poetic value lie not so much in the countless abstract meanings of the shape, as Yeats had it, but in the *rela- tionship between* a shape and a complex abstraction. As Peter Butter said in 1954, the image is "a sort of shorthand", a "good bridge for the reader from his own experience" to Shelley's "sometimes rather exotic ideas and emotions". No "explanation can ever exhaust [the image's] possible meanings"; the "deepest truths are to be found within the cave of the mind and can be expressed only in symbols".[94]

The Coleridge-Yeats-Fogle defence of Shelley regards his im- ages as "symbols", unique shapes referring to complex ideas and evoking unfamiliar feelings in the reader. Ideas and feelings alike are otherwise inexpressible, including by the critic. Nevertheless they exist in the poetry as those "deepest truths" which the symbol still in a sense refers to, or at least stands in some relation to. The Humean, ironist Shelley who emerged after Pulos could not be allowed to accept even this degree of referentialism, how- ever, and a new variant of the symbolist defence appeared. By 1959 Milton Wilson was claiming that Shelley's poems "aspire to a unity and finality which is beyond them". They are "more allied to becoming than being"; they are "not whole poems, be- cause oneness must necessarily be outside them".[95] This is a version of the symbolist defence which can make a conscious ironist vir- tue out of what Shelley's adversaries see as metaphorical care- lessness or incapacity. Shelley's metaphors, according to James Rieger in 1967, "are at best the hierophants of an inspiration which remains unapprehended", but only because he consciously set out to examine the limits of metaphor, to doubt "the adequacy of a trope".[96] Still, both Wilson and Rieger seem ill at ease with the kind of poetry they are defending. This is really "potential poetry", says Wilson; it is only metaphorically effective at the very end, in "The Triumph of Life", says Rieger, sounding like T. S. Eliot.[97] Harold Bloom puts this newer symbolist case far more confidently. He is the strongest of all the non-referential defenders of Shelley, both in his seminal 1959 book, *Shelley's Mythmaking*, and in his later attempts to demonstrate the poet's "continuous effort to subvert the poetic image, so as to arrive at a more radical kind of verbal figure, which [he] never altogether achieved". Everything "vital in Shelley's poetry", claims Bloom, "deliberately strains away from the minute particulars of experience". Shelley "chants an energetic becoming that cannot be described in the concrete, because its entire purpose is to modify the concrete, to compel a greater reality to appear".[98] For Bloom, as for Fogle, Shelley's images are principally a struggle to convey relationship. On Bloom's reading the poet seeks relationship between himself and a nature through which he glimpses a transcendent, eternal "Thou", but he struggles vainly to escape being absorbed into a nature experienced as an inanimate "It".[99] Bloom's version of the symbolist defence is abstract to the point of obscurity (what does "chants an energetic becoming" mean?), anti-experiential to the point of dogmatism (there must be a "greater reality", a "more radical kind of verbal figure", an attempt "to modify the concrete"), over-programmatic (Shelley must be a "mythmaker", and his myths must be explicable using Martin Buber's "Thou/It" terminology), and still at times reliant on the obliquely referential assumptions of the earlier symbolist defences (the "verbal figure" pointing to a "greater reality"). But Bloom is exemplary in his repudiation of referentialism proper ("Shelley is an original religious mythmaker rather than a secondhand philosopher"[100]) and in his concern for the self of the poems rather than for the life of the poet. His argument is also underpinned by extensive and perceptive close reading. This, and not a referential case such as Wasserman's, is the best model for a modern defence of Shelley.

The post-Bloomean symbolist defence has been complemented and reinforced, especially in recent years, by a thinner and shorter (but still distinctive) strand of criticism concerned with Shelley's style. We may regard Wordsworth as its great originator, just as with Coleridge for the symbolist case. Shelley was "one of the best *artists* of us all: I mean in workmanship of style",[101] commented Wordsworth in his later years. Edmund Gosse, in a centenary address half a century later, said that the "poetry is of the highest and most classical technical perfection".[102] In his *History of English Prosody* (1910) George Saintsbury found Shelley's prosodic virtuosity unequalled in the language.[103] Donald Davie's *Purity of Diction in English Verse* (1952) chimed in nicely with the contemporary Pulos Shelley, pointing in a chapter entitled "Shelley's Urbanity" to an Augustan control of tone and deployment of the familiar style, especially in the late poems to Jane Williams and in "Julian and Maddalo";[104] the latter, indeed, has sincè become one of Shelley's most-discussed poems (Hazlitt liked it too). These earlier hints and suggestions have grown into received opinion among modern scholars, who now unanimously proclaim Shelley's tonal urbanity and technical virtuosity.

A predominantly American sub-variant of this stylist case is the deconstructionist argument, popular in the 1980s, although the familiar Derridean metaphors are now beginning to sound worn and over-professionalised. Paul de Man's "Shelley Disfigured" (1979) played at length with "The Triumph of Life", indeed with Romanticism itself, as a fragment "in a process that now includes us within its horizon". The status of language and of texts was de Man's concern; the "repetitive erasures by which language performs the erasure of its own positions can be called disfiguration". Shelley's last poem "warns us . . . that nothing, whether deed, word, thought, or text, ever happens in relation . . . to anything that preceded, follows, or exists elsewhere, but only as a random event".[105] There are discernible affiliations between de Man's purely linguistic, stylist concept of "disfiguration" and Bloom's symbolist, significatory "radical kind of verbal figure", but in de Man's essay Shelley's poem is serving mainly as a convenient illustration of the author's idiosyncratic theses about Romanticism, language and "texts". Several of the essays in G. Kim Blank's collection, already mentioned, are similarly preoccupied with what they see as Shelley's self-referential and self-effacing language. Ronald Tetreault's "Shelley: Style and Substance", for example, observes unsceptically the "affinity between deconstruction and scepticism" and meditates unplayfully on "the extravagance" of the poet's "play with language".[106] Tillotama Rajan's "The Web of Human Things" represents *Alastor* as "a text which presents the process by which the Narrator tries to represent the Poet and discloses to himself the inevitable functioning of language as difference".[107] Tetreault's book *The Poetry* of Life: Shelley and Literary Form (1987) suggests that Shelley wants "the reader to participate in the endless pursuit of meaning through the play of différance".[108] Jerrold E. Hogle's daunting Shelley's Process (1988) attempts in the same remote academic terminology to "dethrone the center-at-one-with-itself . . . and replace it with this centerless displacement of figural counterparts by one another"; "Shelley" is "the name attached to a series of writings".[109] Hogle attacks, and argues that Shelley's language attacks, a supposedly essential, unchanging and repressive central self. Shelley was singularly conformable to this 1980s Derridean-Marxist, sceptical-idealist view of language and politics. But even in the most political of these readings a sceptical theory of language is ascribed to Shelley and posited as the central fact about his poetry. The Wordsworth-Davie stylist tradition sees Shelley's style as the register of an urbane poetic self; the deconstructionist variant sees it not even as the register of a disturbed and fragmented self, but as the only reality.

There are some less self-erasing accounts, mainly British, of the relation between self and style in Shelley, accounts which also preserve Bloom's case. Timothy Webb's Shelley: A Voice Not Understood, mentioned above, has some of the characteristics of such an account; so does Timothy Clark's Embodying Revolution: The Figure of the Poet in Shelley (1989). Four other recent books responsively and accessibly opposed to the case against Shelley on symbolist-stylist lines are those by Richard Cronin, William Keach, Angela Leighton and Michael O'Neill. In Shelley's Poetic Thoughts (1981) Cronin considers the ways in which Shelley's techniques, his verse forms, syntax and styles, "are not vehicles of the poem's meaning but expressions of it";[110] he focuses chiefly on how the poetry thinks on a formal, generic and stylistic level, rather than on how it thinks locally, verbally and emotionally. This is an admirable example of the modern symbolist-stylist defence. Where the case against Shelley demands that poetic language be constantly and perspicuously engaged in experiential thought about and with feeling, with the engagement taking place in a recognisable and full human context, the symbolist defence asserts that the overall shapes of the poems, their orientation, their relation to an indiscernible tertium quid, constitute Shelley's chief means of reflection on an abstracted feeling, and on a possible correspondent to that feeling which is beyond sensory apprehension. As Donald Davie put it, a Shelley poem often "has

no meaning except as a whole. It is one half of a vast metaphor
with the human term left out; and this, its meaning for human
life, emerges from the shape of the whole or else it is lost for
ever".[111] To those who want "meaning" to inhere in local or tex-
tural qualities of thought as well as overall shape, of course, the
Cronins and Davies have less to say, but they do cause the essential disagreements to stand out clearly, which is no mean
achievement. Keach is a subtle stylist defender who sets out in
Shelley's Style (1984) to represent as one of Shelley's characteristic successes what many of his adversaries regard as his principal failing. Where William Sidney Walker and his successors have
seen verbal and metaphorical confusion, Keach sees an entirely
conscious scepticism about the limits of language. For Shelley,
he argues, language is both "fully and precisely expressive
of thought" and an "inherently imperfect sign of thought". The
"indeterminacy in Shelley's similes"[112] is not muddle, but a way
of thinking about the indeterminacy of the world, which itself
often turns out to be a matter of language. What Empson
condemned as "short-circuited comparisons" in which a thing
is compared to a "vaguer or more abstract notion of itself",[113]
Keach praises as "reflexive imagery" in which Shelley figures
the troubling reflexiveness of "the self's relation with the world
and with other people".[114] Such a disagreement must be tested
against the poetry itself, and we shall return to Keach in Chapters
3 and 5 to see whether this stylist defensive manoeuvre is as
credible as it is ingenious. Leighton's *Shelley and the Sublime* (1984)
is philosophically referential in structure, although not in disposition. Leighton uses an account of the Lockean-empiricist
and Longinian-Kantian sublime traditions as the basis for an
interpretation of Shelley's poetry, which she sees as torn
between "religious scepticism and poetic need".[115] Shelley is
sceptical about the existence of a transcendent power, and yet
he needs to believe in one. But Leighton's deft touch with her
referential material and her sense that the poetry remains itself
rather than the instrument or product of its "ideas" allow her to
avoid the dogged and obtrusive schematism of so much referential
scholarship, enabling some refreshingly direct readings of the
major poems:

> It is not surprising, therefore, that a poet whose frequent con-
> cern is with the failure of the creative mind to reach its object

should not measure up to Leavis' standard [i.e. of "grasp upon the actual"]. Shelley's own descriptions of the working of creativity are essentially anti-tactile. They emphasise a failure either to arrest or to apprehend the Power of inspiration as it passes. Those 'large gestures' which Leavis derides in fact beautifully describe a characteristic of the Shelleyan sublime: that its language generously reaches towards its object, but also fails to grasp it. Such a language both promises and loses its object. Its gestures. . . . are a measure of the poem's movingly inadequate reach. . . . what Shelley celebrates in his odes [is] that insuffiency of language which, in his version of the sublime, goes unrewarded, and which thus acknowledges failure and loss as the ever-present potential of poetry.[116]

This is one of the clearest statements of the symbolist-stylist defence of Shelley. On this account, as on Bloom's and Keach's, the poet's detractors disvalue his central undertaking, which is to suggest the unrepresentable in language which is necessarily and consciously inadequate. "Failure" is not culpable but moving. Again, the only proper test of this defence is against the poetry itself, as we shall see in Chapter 4. In *The Human Mind's Imaginings* (1989) O'Neill is exemplary in his refusal to take Shelley's status for granted, in his insistence that criticism be evaluative, concerned above all with "the poetry's worth". His book has the same misgivings as this one about Wassermanian referentialism, which O'Neill calls a "self-fulfilling" criticism that "identifies poetic achievement with thematic coherence", subordinating the poetry to "some overall quasi-metaphysical design" and depriving it of its "capacity to move, affect, disturb or excite". Post-structuralist and deconstructionist readings of Shelley also seem "critically unpersuasive" to O'Neill; they seem to "slight the particularity of poems, to see them as exemplifying certain theories about language". Keach agrees, and O'Neill finds his particularised discovery of "analysable ingenuities" in Shelley's language impressively unburdened by theories of language.[117] But Keach is less alive, O'Neill thinks, to the frequent obtrusiveness of "the writing's design on us", its "will-driven" quality, its deliberate derivation from abstractions. O'Neill wants to explore how poetic language tests and experiences ideas and emotions, "ways of knowing and feeling", in non-philosophical ways.[118] Like Leighton, Cronin and Bloom, he believes that "Shelley offers . . . comparisons which implicitly comment on their own figurativeness, underscoring the extent to which the poem's subject defeats language"; that Shelley writes "out of a sense of a gap as well as alliance between sensory experience and evoked emotion, a gap which [his] similes both try to bridge and acknowledge".[119] This attractive symbolist-stylist defence of Shelley has a good deal in common with the case against him, agreeing in general terms about what poetry and criticism should be, and conceding that Shelley's poetry is vulnerable to some of the arguments brought against it. On the central issue of the relations in the poetry between feelings, ideas and sensory experience, however, this defence asks us to admire the very phenomena which its adversaries dislike: particularly that "gap" between "evoked emotion" and "sensory experience", or in other words a derivation of emotion from an idea rather than from an experience; and an analogous "gap" between language and reality, such that language is an always-inadequate representative instrument, a symbolical gesture towards a reality which it can never fully apprehend. O'Neill believes that the "best poetry deals profoundly . . . with what it means to be 'human'".[120] The sense of these two "gaps" is an important part of being human, on his account, and Shelley's poetry is full of that sense.

The "symbolist" defences of Shelley are the best responses to the case against him. They fall into two groups: the earlier Coleridge-Yeats-Fogle group, linguistically more confident or perhaps just less sophisticated, according to which Shelley's poetic symbols point to a reality which is ultimately stateable, even if only in highly abstract terms ("the peaceful triumph of goodness over power"); and the later post-Bloomean group, more sceptical, stylist and symbolist, according to which Shelley's poetry realises that language itself is an important part of what prevents us from grasping reality. Both groups, however, have a similar, roughly Platonist conception of some "more essential substance", as Todhunter put it, some transcendent Idea beyond the ordinary world, which language has only a limited capacity to capture or represent. The existence of that substance or Idea has the effect of making not just language but the whole representable world into a symbol of the true reality which is beyond it. The deepest meanings of emotions will therefore lie not in ordinary human situations but in transhuman, unfamiliar ones; the meaning, or what we might call the "self", of a poem will be constituted principally in its relation to some greater Being, not in an exploration of that self for itself.

POETRY: THINKING ABOUT LIVES OR THINKING ABOUT LIFE?

In the case of Shelley, there are on the one hand those who admire poetry which appeals beyond the sensory realm and the feelings as familiarly embodied to a transcendent realm and a more rarefied conception of the feelings; poetry which is primarily self-regarding, but regards the self primarily in relation to that transcendent realm, and its feelings as things to be thought *about* in so far as they intimate that relation; poetry in which language is treated as an inadequate means of pointing towards that realm and the relation between it and the self. On the other hand, there are those who dislike such poetry, preferring an alternative in which the self and its feelings are conceived at least partly in relation to other selves and feelings, in which feelings are thought *with*, and in which language is ameliorable but is also what we have to think with (especially if we are poets): so that extending it is extending the self. On the one hand are those who like poetry which thinks about Life; on the other, those who prefer it when it thinks about lives.

This difference of views goes far beyond the case of Shelley, of course, and even beyond poetry. If we suppose the practice of literary criticism principally to involve a sustained and responsive attention to various works of poetry, drama or the novel, to constitute a reflection or representation of their distinctive qualities and modes of thought in and through criticism's own expository and evaluative medium, then in English the practice is about 250 years old, originating with Dr Johnson. But whereas during that period some critics – Johnson himself, Hazlitt, Arnold, Eliot, Leavis – have carried on without offering any systematic, fully theorised accounts from first principles of the nature of these various works and of their own critical activity, other critics, particularly Coleridge and those latter-day Coleridgeans who have dominated much modern academic criticism and theory, have frequently tried to offer such accounts of both matters. Coleridge and his followers want both criticism and its subjects, which collectively have come since Coleridge himself to be called

"literature", eventually to be grounded in some great system or
set of principles, resting in turn on a Truth or an Idea, a certainty, discernible to a trained clerisy but not to the ordinary
reader, in the literary representation of which opposites are reconciled or held in a synthetic tension, and symbol often plays a
key revelatory role. A critical disposition such as Hazlitt's, on
the other hand, needs no founding principle, no systematic theory,
no single Truth or Idea for symbols to refer to, no certainty, and
no reason why opposites should be reconciled. Such a disposition recognises, however, that ordinary readers matter more than
a clerisy, and that they do not need to have a theory about something called Literature, about its supposedly systematic foundations, in order to recognise or respond to poems, plays and novels
– or short stories, autobiographies and letters, come to that. In
their very efforts at definition and categorisation (even canoni-
sation), Coleridgeans turn such works into disguised systems of
one sort or another: quasi-religious revelations, quasi-homiletic
conduct books, quasi-philosophical epistemologies or language
games, and quasi-political power struggles. The works dissolve
into their "real" subjects, purposes or motivations. But there are
also readers who regard these various works as distinctive practices, special ways of thinking about or attending to human lives;
who may even regard lives as themselves untheorisable without
important epistemic and affective loss.[121]

For much of this century, but especially during the last twenty-
five of those 250 years, academic literary criticism has been mesmerised by two of those conceptions of literature: as language
game and as power struggle. Few critics or theorists of literature have been able or willing during those twenty-five years to
offer the ordinary reader any other view of the subject; fortunately, however, several moral philosophers have. Impelled by
a related crisis in their own discipline, these philosophers have
been trying, again roughly since the 1960s, to re-articulate ideas
of the self as passionate and substantial, and of language as a
store of value. They have often turned to works of "literature"
(the term has become almost indispensable, and we must dis-
pense instead with the quotation marks) as an exemplary manner of attending to and partly constituting human reality. Modern
moral philosophy has thrown off almost as a by-product of its
own enterprise a rejuvenated version of a "moral" conception of
literature not just as old as Dr Johnson, but as old as Aristotle.

Raimond Gaita, for example, resists both identifying the "moral" with the "deliberative or imperatival" and identifying moral thinking with moral theory. Moral thought, he says, is both revelatory and constitutive of the self in its relation to whatever it attends to; this revealing and constituting, rather than rule-making, applauding or condemning, are the primary functions of moral thinking. "Vital responsiveness" is required of the self in its relation to others; this responsiveness arises out of an indissoluble union between the moral understanding, which has to do with the passions such as love or remorse as much as with the reason; and moral language, which is to be regarded as the rich and various catalyst and facilitator of the understanding, not as its dispassionate and often inadequate instrument. To criticize someone's thought or behaviour as "sentimental" is not to claim in an unnecessarily obscurantist, rhetorical or censorious way that the thought or behaviour are "simply" false or wrong, nor is it to diagnose an abstraction called "sentimentality" as the cause of the wrong thought or behaviour; it is to "mark a distinctive way in which" that thought or behaviour "can fail", can falsify or misprize its object. For Gaita, it seems, "moral" speech is something more like poetry than like science or even philosophy.[122]

Iris Murdoch refers to art in general as something between an "analogy" and a "case" of morals, and to "the study of literature" – criticism, in other words – as "the most essential and fundamental aspect of culture", not least because of literature's unique capacity to disclose the "fabric" or "texture" of human being. Murdoch is both a philosopher and a novelist; she sees literature as a manner of moral thinking which is as indispensable as moral philosophy, although she properly insists on the differences between the two. She believes that what is importantly "moral" about literature, indeed about any art, has nothing to do with doctrines, codes of behaviour or finger-wagging, but everything to do with clarity of vision, unselfish attention to the reality of others, detachment and self-transcendence; with a conception of "the soul" as a "substantial and continually developing mechanism of attachments"; with metaphors as "fundamental forms of our awareness of our condition" which often carry a "moral charge"; with moral growth as a simultaneous attention to or deepening of both language and feeling; and with language as a medium of thought to be explored and extended seriously and non-reductively.[123]

Cora Diamond also insists on the importance of literature as moral thought about not just behaviour, conduct or action, but about the entire "texture of being"[124] in individual human beings and in forms of social life. Like Murdoch, Diamond wants to fit her understanding of the function of literature into a bigger picture of the moral life, or just of human life. Both think that we "have suffered a general loss of concepts, the loss of a moral and political vocabulary";[125] that "we need an enriched vocabulary", and that "this is a task for literature".[126] Literature contributes to the "human good of articulateness, of having the words one needs".[127] Diamond uses passages from Tolstoy and Primo Levi as examples of "the *recognition* of a human being", full instantiations of "the concept of a human being", as opposed to the partial or "dissociated" uses of the concept (her term recalls Eliot) by many moral philosophers and other writers of a theoretical disposition, for whom it is merely "the concept of a member of a particular biological species, *Homo Sapiens*". The work of writers like Tolstoy and Levi "illuminate for us the concept of a human being and at the same time can elaborate and deepen it". Literature "shows us forms of thinking about life . . . which philosophical requirements . . . may lead us to ignore";[128] it can "enlarge the moral imagination"; it can "appeal to the intelligence" without using philosophical arguments. If one takes "as the root of morality in human nature a capacity for attention to things imagined or perceived", then one "is likely to regard imaginative literature as of the greatest importance in developing and strengthening our moral capacities".[129]

Martha Nussbaum makes broadly the same case, buttressing it by numerous rich and powerful readings of Greek tragedies and of modern novels. She finds these to be works of "ethical reflection in their own right", and argues that our "cognitive activity . . . centrally involves emotional response"; indeed "emotional response can sometimes be not just a *means* to practical knowledge, but a constituent part of the best sort of recognition or knowledge". Perception "is both cognitive and affective at the same time". "Passional reaction", suffering for example, is "a kind of knowing", a kind disclosed above all in tragedy. Poetry works by "hovering in thought and imagination around the enigmatic complexities of the seen particular"; this is a kind of practical understanding, of knowledge by acquaintance, which is not like philosophical or intellectual knowledge. The passions, "passional responsiveness", play an essential role in this practical wisdom; recognition of the "morally salient" is often "accomplished by and in appropriate emotional response as much as through intellectual judgement". Above all, judgement or *krisis*, in Aristotle's phrase, lies in the act of perception or *aesthesis*. You cannot make an "objective" criticism in this moral realm. How you grasp the event determines how you judge it.[130]

These are only four of the better-known contemporary moral philosophers out of many who are turning to literature at crucial points in their work. Others include Stanley Cavell, Charles Taylor and Alasdair MacIntyre, all in recent major works. Of these philosophers, it is true, only Nussbaum offers readings of works of literature as sustained, responsive and unschematic as literary criticism should be, which is to say as the works themselves deserve. These are, after all, still philosophers, albeit philosophers whose conceptions of the human self and of language might have been expected to render them in practice as well as in principle much more explorative than they are of the ways in which poems, novels or plays think about lives and with language, as opposed to containing ideas and decorating them persuasively or rhetorically: of the ways in which these works are precisely those which resist assimilation into systems built upon prior principles or purposes. Still, these philosophers' general approach to literature puts to shame a good deal of modern criticism and theory, including that of various European and American philosophers popular in theoretical circles who enthusiastically extol the canny autonomy of some unfortunate work, or of literature in general, while remorselessly assimilating its language and purposes to their own. Of course the lack of any responsive richness of reading shared by most of these philosophers, which is the real problem, is not confined to them. Even the few critics who are neither theorists nor contextual explicators, who are able and willing to conceptualise literature in unapologetically non-philosophical and non-historical terms – critics such as Wayne Booth, Charles Altieri or Tobin Siebers – can sound disappointingly programmatic when actually reading works of literature, so insidious is the systematising post-Coleridgean atmosphere we all have to breathe. The atmosphere, of course, could just as easily be called "Kantian" or "Cartesian", "Lockean" or "Benthamite", "theoretical" or "rationalist". Among modern moral philosophers one thinks of Hare and Stevenson, Nagel, Rawls

and Dworkin; in literary theory of Heidegger and his successors, Derrida, Foucault and Habermas. "The genus is not scarce
in population", as Keats said; in the intellectual population it
is more plentiful still. But for others, for Murdoch, Diamond,
Nussbaum and Cavell, for Bernard Williams and Annette Baier,[131]
for Wittgenstein before them and Hume before him, morality is
not to be seen as "rational only insofar as it can be formulated
in, or grounded on, a system of universal principles". The "intellectual virtues of theorizing, such as universality, explicitness,
consistency, and completeness" are not for them "essential to
the moral life". For "morality" and "the moral life" read "moral
thinking", or "literary criticism". "Anti-theorists"[132] in criticism,
including for example Johnson and Hazlitt, see or treat both poetry
and reading poetry as kinds of moral thought and moral language which are more like evaluative description within a shared
sense of life than theorising from outside one. For them, and for
this book, poetry and criticism are kinds of practical wisdom,
ways of asking questions about a life, or lives, or passages of a
life, without wanting to know answers, or already knowing them;
ways of asking those questions from within a life, rather than
from that principled viewpoint outside any practice, any life, which
is the theorist's.

Too few contemporary critics both conceptualise and actually
read literature as practical wisdom.[133] Those who do are usually
saying something not about "theory" but about language and
about the self. Language, and especially metaphorical language,
they are saying, is both a constituent and an instrument of thought:
not just one or the other. The language of literature, so often
metaphorical, they describe as language at its "richest" or "thickest"; as that state of language in which judgement most completely coincides with apprehension, in which fact and value can
least easily be separated. Here language is not "content" plus
"style", but an undissociated medium of life. The forms and genres
of literature are likewise constituents, not containers, of its thought.
A life, meanwhile, or a "self" in the current jargon, is to be seen
as both "substantial" and "continually developing", in Iris
Murdoch's terms: not a hard unchanging core of reason surrounded by fickle and fluctuating passions, but a permeable coa-
lescence of affiliations, of affection and reflection, of desires and
considerations, in which the passions (affections, emotions, feelings) play a central cognitive role as agents and media of thought,

rather than a peripheral but distracting role as impediments to thought. The self is infiltrated and partly constituted both by language and by everything else, by "reality"; but the individual self, a life, is no more dissolved in or completely determined by language and reality than they are entirely created by it. Both language and the self are transcended by reality, but not entirely, and extending the limits of language extends the self's grasp of reality. Intuitions of a metaphysical super-reality or unity which transcends all the senses are most impressive when attained after such an effort at extension, not when simply declared and then imposed on a physical and moral reality whose richness and complexity has not been demonstrably grasped.

This account of language and the self, and of literature, can serve as a broader framework for the case against Shelley outlined in the second section of this chapter. Hazlitt and his successors see the same disconnection between passions and ideas in Shelley's poetry that modern moral philosophers deprecate in dissociated Enlightenment accounts of the self. Hazlitt and his fellow-critics dislike what they see as Shelley's "thin", metaphorically complacent language, just as the philosophers disapprove of moral language that is separated into fact and value, or content and style. Critics and philosophers alike want ordinary moral and physical realities to be given due consideration, even when metaphysical Reality is being invoked. Those with serious reservations about Shelley's poetry will also be able, in the light of this account, to respond to the two principal kinds of defence of it as outlined in the third section of this chapter. The referential defences argue that the great bulk of Shelley's work has to be exhaustively explicated in terms of the ideas and events it refers to; this explication *is* the defence, and the poetry in so far as it is poetry is a matter of elegant decoration, of the economical or memorable expression of separable philosophical and historical truths. This kind of defence seems, on the view of literature outlined in this section of the chapter, simply wrong about how poetry distinctively thinks, about how it is poetry and not something else.

According to the much subtler symbolist defences, only some of Shelley's work is poetic, and that because it evokes not these little truths but a greater transcendent Truth, in a way which is essentially inexplicable by discursive means. The function of this poetry is to find mysterious ways of intimating the unrepresentable, the inaccessible. This is a thoroughly Coleridgean conception of poetry, and Coleridge was heavily influenced by German, and especially Kantian, notions of an abstraction called "the poetic imagination". Here is Mary Warnock's elegant summary of Kant's theory of the poetic imagination as expressed in his *Critique of Judgement*:

> Briefly, we may say that the role of the imagination here is to lead us beyond what is present to our senses towards the realization that there is something *signified by* the things before us, something which we can grasp in a way, but cannot express. . . . Creative genius, then, consists in the ability to find expression, although inevitably not complete expression, for the ideas which are to be apprehended in, or glimpsed beyond, objects in the world. . . . It is through such symbolism that we seem to be able to breach the otherwise impenetrable wall between ourselves and the world of ideas. . . . in Kant's vocabulary an idea in the technical sense was the product of the highest faculty of the mind, but something so far removed from sense-perception that it could never find exemplification in the world of sense.[134]

This is remarkably close to the conception of Shelley's poetry, when it is *really* poetic, held by his best defenders. As we shall see in the next chapter, his own view of poetry did not always correspond with this Coleridgean-Kantian conception; but this conception has clearly won modern Shelleyans over. This poetry's meaning, as the theorists would say, is always deferred, because it is always *ref*erred: beyond the senses, beyond ordinary language, beyond that rich and complex reality which presses upon us, beyond the self and its familiar feelings, to a deeper truth, a more real reality which we will in the end have to take on trust because it is by definition inaccessible, ungraspable by language. This Truth is inaccessible despite being – also by definition – determinative of the self, reality and language. The self, for its part, principally consists of its own intuition of the Truth; its other affections, other selves, ordinary reality, are peripheral. Poetry's evocation or symbolising of the Truth must be finally unevaluable; either it "works" for the reader, or it doesn't.

To a non-Coleridgean this seems to make the task of the literary critic very limited indeed in the case of Shelley. There is, to be sure, the enormous preliminary scholarly or explicatory task, the referential task, but what is left after this, the residue or added poetic value, is both small and beyond comment. In important respects the language is above criticism. It may be elegant, concise and mellifluous, it may be ironical, sceptical and self-doubting, but its metaphorical richness, its deepening or otherwise of the passions and of the self, its power to extend our grasp of moral and sensory reality, must be beside the point, since its characteristic virtue is gracefully and self-effacingly to refer beyond these things to a greater Reality, which cannot be grasped or described. If literature must refer beyond reality to Reality, beyond lives to Life, moral philosophers like those discussed above, critics like Hazlitt, would prefer that it do so without palpably disvaluing that which is transcended, and if possible that it do so after, indeed *in*, showing the value of what is transcended. Poetry striving principally to transcend the human may well look impatient with or indifferent to the human. Poetry searching for a subtler language must still use, still *be*, the language that we have. An art which constantly expresses despair at the limitations of its own materials, which indeed makes the expression of that despair one of its chief functions, is unlikely to appeal to lovers of that art who look to it as exemplary in what it can do with, discover in, those materials. Besides, many of those who believe Shelley's poetry neglects lives think that even its pursuit of Life is often a matter of doctrine or *credo* as much as of successful practice: that the poetry can sound chiefly like an assertion of the value and difficulty of its own enterprise.

Readers must decide for themselves whether the moral and linguistic case sketched here against Shelley's poetry and its defenders is sustained by, or rather derivable from, the particular readings which follow in Chapters 3 to 6. But first we should pay some attention to Shelley's own views of poetry, not as determinative of his poems, but to see what light they may shed on the poems; and to see how Shelley's views, as opposed to his poems, may have influenced this controversy.

2

Shelley's Views of Poetry

INTRODUCTION

Shelley developed no systematic and consistent understanding of poetry's formal principles and rules, nor of its underlying psychological and historical causes, nor of its metaphysical and epistemological foundations. He was not what we would nowadays call a "theorist" of poetry, or of language more generally: not even in the senses in which Herder, Schlegel, Sainte-Beuve, or Arnold, let alone Heidegger or de Man, were theorists of these things. The closest he came to a full statement of what he believed poetry and the poet to be was in his late essay "A Defence of Poetry", but, as we shall see, his subject even there was only "poetry" in a rather unusual sense, and the view of poetry expressed there was inconsistent with his earlier views. Studies of Shelley's "theory" of poetry tend therefore to be somewhat forced:[1] readings of his other works in the light of a foundational account of the "Defence"; tracings of the influence on Shelley of other theorists, with more or less persuasive suggestions as to his theoretical affiliations (Aristotelian or Platonist, Lockean empiricist, Humean sceptic or Longinian enthusiast, primitivist or progressivist, neo-Kantian or proto-deconstructionist); even statements of the author's own theory of poetry. The more helpful studies[2] also give consideration to Shelley's theories of language in general, of the mind and of knowledge; they point out that his reading both in the classics (Plato, Locke) and in the popular philosophical and critical literature of his day (Godwin, Monboddo, Stewart, Drummond, Horne Tooke) led him in various theoretical directions and into various intellectual fields (metaphysics, moral philosophy, rhetoric, linguistics) at the same time. Even here, however, there is a tendency to intellectualise, to separate Shelley's thinking about language from his thinking about everything else, as if he were not what all his admirers must claim him to be, or else have little reason to write about him at all: a poet. There is also a tendency to "explain" what he thought by reference to his "sources", as if he were constructing systems to compete with other systems: as if he were an academic, perhaps.

In this chapter we shall consider a number of Shelley's remarks about poetry, including his own, in their own terms, referring only occasionally to their possible intellectual affinities, taking them more or less in the order in which he made them (where this is known), and not trying to abstract any "poetic theory" in them from what they also reveal of Shelley's attitude to inseparably connected matters, including the "self" (as even he termed it), other human beings, natural landscapes, moral, political and metaphysical beliefs, and language in general. In this way we may expose both the texture and the tendency, the life-direction, of Shelley's mind in its thinking about poetry and the things poetry thinks about, as opposed to its thinking in poetry about these things. We shall take as much account of his letters as of his essays and prefaces, and we shall come to the "Defence" as the late outgrowth of his thinking, rather than as its hypostasised core.

For much of his life Shelley had two views of poetry (especially his own): that it was the servant of the reason, the vessel of the ideas, beliefs and doctrines which reason conceives; and that it was the uncontrollable emanation of the passions or feelings. Although these two views, which might be termed "utilitarian" and "expressionist", may seem incompatible, Shelley often voiced them almost simultaneously and tried to reconcile them. Generally, he liked poetry best when it could be described as reason's servant, rather than when it seemed to be only passion's outlet. But he increasingly believed that in expressing certain passions poetry might be intimating or recommending a higher Idea or deeper Truth. The same sort of double vision underlies his views of language, or "words", in general. Furthermore, these two views of poetry, and of language in general, went hand in hand with two views of the self (especially his own): that as a purely passional entity it was solitary and selfish, while as a reasoning and idealising entity it could escape from or channel the passions through contact with another ideally attuned self. For much of his life Shelley saw most human beings as brutish and distasteful creatures of passion unless and until they were transformed in the light of an ideal or a doctrine. Similarly, he

saw natural landscapes principally as occasions and vehicles for
doctrinal and metaphysical speculation. Only occasionally, though
increasingly towards the end of his life, did he show a partiality
for feeling over reason and ideas, a regard for other people and
for natural objects, and a sense of poetry as a distinctive mode
of thought, the voice of a whole self. Shelley never developed
this rudimentary third view of poetry.

We shall consider Shelley's remarks on these subjects in chrono-
logical order, through three distinct phases: from his first observations in 1811 to his final departure from England in early 1818;
during his first two years in Italy (1818–19); and during the last
two years or so of his life (1820–2). In the first two phases Shelley
held his utilitarian and expressionist views in uneasy conjunction, surviving a shock to his utilitarianism in Italy; in the third,
which included the composition of the "Defence", he showed
signs of a radical shift in his understanding of poetry. This chrono-
logical approach, and the references we shall be making to events
in Shelley's life, should not be seen as examples of biographical
referentialism. This chapter is not concerned with how events in
his life determined either Shelley's views of poetry or the poetry itself, any more than it is concerned with how his views
determined his poetry. But if a certain style and cast of mind
are revealed in the letters, essays and prefaces, then perhaps
becoming attuned to that mind here, including in its responses
to life events, will help us make better sense later of how it rec-
reates and develops itself in the poems.

SHELLEY IN ENGLAND, 1811–17

Shelley's ambivalent attitudes towards poetry are discernible
from his earliest writings. These are extracts from two letters
written in 1811, when he was eighteen (i 98, 43–4):

> . . . my opinion is that all poetical beauty ought to be subordi-
> nate to the inculcated moral – that metaphorical language ought
> to be a pleasing vehicle for useful & momentous instruction.
> But see Ensor on the subject of poetry – Adieu.

> As to the stuff wch. I sent you, I write all my poetry of that
> kind from the feelings of the moment – if therefore it neither

has allusion to the sentiments which rationally might be supposed to possess me, or to those wch. my situation might
awaken, it is another proof of that egotizing variability whilst
I shudder when I reflect how much I am in it's power.

We have already seen that Shelley's defenders rarely advance
far beyond the utilitarian and doctrinal conception of poetry and
metaphor summarised in the first extract; they have taken their
cue, it now appears, from the poet himself. This conception, formulated so early, long retained its hold on Shelley. "Truth is *my*
God", he says in the same letter (i 98); Shelley long saw poetry
much more readily as the "subordinate" of God or the Truth
than as one of Their modes of being. His reference in this extract is to George Ensor's *On National Education* (1811), a book
critical of British institutions for their allegedly centralising tendency to inculcate a particular set of morals. Ensor was a popular reforming writer with close allegiances to William Godwin,
in this case to Book VI of the age's great work of philosophic
radicalism, the *Enquiry Concerning Political Justice* (1793). Notwithstanding his Godwinian objections to a national education system, Ensor proposed his own set of virtues to be generally
"inculcated", claiming that poetry was the best way to do this,
"the most powerful means of instructing youth", fit to be "used"
by "legislators" to "subdue the savage nature of the people".[3]
Shelley speculated in another letter a month later on what he
would do were he ever a "moral legislator" (i 126). His thinking, like Ensor's, is firmly in a dissociative Benthamite tradition
in its conception of the relation between metaphor and thought,
between utility and poetry.

Ensor says poetry can be used to subdue people's "savage
nature"; Shelley regards poetry as a subordinate and a subordinating instrument in the first of the two extracts quoted above.
In the second, on the contrary, it becomes the irresistible out-
flow of the very "feelings of the moment" which it is represented
as controlling in the first: the expression of the fickle ego, the
savage self, whose power over him leaves him shuddering. In
this guise his poetry can have no "allusion" to any "sentiments"
which reason might approve; Shelley even appears to distinguish
between the "feelings", which are irrational and "of the moment",
and "sentiments", those post-Enlightenment intellectualisations
of the passional realm. Earlier in 1811 Shelley had fervently wished

he "*were* the Antichrist", so that he could "crush the Demon" of Christianity; "I expect to gratify some of this insatiable feeling in Poetry", he added (i 35). Opposition to Christianity is here a matter of "insatiable feeling" rather than of rational belief, and poetry is now the gratification of insatiable feeling, not the instrument of divine reason. Early in 1812 Shelley told a friend to think of some poetry he had sent her "as a picture of my feelings not a specimen of my art", adding in another letter, "I sometimes can write poetry when I feel" (i 226, 254). He often referred to his poems of this time as "dementiae", "raphsody" [*sic*] or "maddened stuff" (i 91, 107–8). Again and again in these years his own poetry, which should be "subordinate to the inculcated moral", is represented almost shamefacedly by Shelley as insubordinate, the outcry of "savage nature", of those collectively variable and egotistical "feelings" or passions which dominate the small reflective "I" of reason, wilfully and randomly driving the self and the poet. The general Romantic conception of poetry as the wild voice of passion and of the primitive heart of humanity – common European coin since the middle of the eighteenth century, since Hamann and Herder in Germany, Diderot and Rousseau in France, Warton and Hurd in England – was already familiar to the young Shelley through the popular, derivative but synoptic work of Monboddo and Kames. So at the very inception of his career the poet held one view of his poetic practice in the teeth of another, quite contrary, Godwinite-utilitarian view, which he favoured in principle. To reconcile these views, or rather to begin to recognise that both rely on the same metaphor of the divided self, took Shelley most of his short life.

In another letter of early 1812, this time to Godwin himself, Shelley is once more the man of reason, criticising what he represents as a much earlier, pre-Godwinian disposition: "I was haunted with a passion for the wildest and most extravagant romances. . . . My sentiments were unrestrained by anything within me" (i 227). To the eminent Enlightenment philosopher Shelley speaks fashionably of "sentiments", not "feelings", but he does confess to a specific "passion" for wild romance; fortunately, however, this was a "weakness which is past". Reading *Political Justice* the year before had opened his eyes to the perils of "self", causing him to bid "adieu to egotism" and to become "sick to death at the name of *self*. . . . that *hateful* principle", unable to "endure the horror the evil which comes to *self* in solitude" (i 34, 77–8). In 1814, in a journal entry, he was still insisting that the "most exalted philosophy, the truest virtue consists in an habitual contempt of self".[4] Shelley is declaring his support for Godwinian arguments against self-love, and his opposition to Rousseauan arguments that, properly conceived, self-love is the foundation of virtue. But his "horror", his sheer revulsion, is not Godwinian. It arises from Shelley's own enduring sense of the passional self as something wild, frightening and recalcitrant. "Is it not then the business of reason to conquer passion?", he wondered in mid-1811 (i 128–9).

> I recommend reason. – Why? is it because since I have devoted myself unreservedly to its influencing, I have never felt *Happiness*. I have rejected all fancy, all imagination. I find that all pleasure resulting to self is thereby completely annihilated. (i 101)

Fancy, imagination, pleasure, happiness itself: all these must, as if for sanity's sake, be annihilated by reason. Shelley's formal essays of 1811–13 – attacks on Christianity, proposals for political reform, vindications of vegetable diet, none of them about poetry – were all written from the vantage point of this tyrannical empirico-rational "I". Reason itself is represented in these essays as reassuringly "founded on the evidence of our senses", while "belief" is merely an involuntary "passion", denied any sensory confirmation.[5] The very myth of Prometheus, later to be the stuff of Shelley's greatest poem, was now easily dismissed in rationalising terms:

> How plain a language is spoken by all this. – Prometheus, (who represents the human race) effected some great change in the condition of his nature, and applied fire to culinary purposes. . . . From this moment his vitals were devoured by the vulture of disease. . . . Tyranny, superstition, commerce, and inequality, were then first known, when reason vainly attempted to guide the wanderings of exacerbated passion.[6]

The reasoning and as it were selfless centre of the self, in touch with reality through the senses, must strive to control the passionate, selfish and empirically disconnected provinces. Shelley's philosophical prose and his ideal of poetry always belonged in the first camp, his actual poetry sometimes in the second. Language "is only useful as it communicates ideas";[7] "words are only signs of ideas" (i 215); "the science of things is superior to the science of words" (i 318); and yet the passional self also tries to speak, and its language is poetry. The young Godwinian is solemnly determined to eliminate all traces of his own weakness. His "pleasure" in a Welsh mountain landscape must be investigated, he says, until it "ceases to exist"; "*once* [he] was tremulously alive to tones and scenes", but now he despises "the slaves of passion & sickly sensibility" who "will not analyse a feeling" (i 119–20, 127). He prefers reading Erasmus Darwin, the popular writer of versified natural science, to "exploring this scenery" (i 129). Either quiver with mindless sensibility or analyse natural pleasure completely away: there is no middle course. Not that suppressing this pleasure was very difficult for Shelley. The countryside around Keswick, in the Lake District, provided in late 1811 the creative trigger for the composition of Shelley's first major work of poetry, *Queen Mab*, and yet his imagination, like the poem itself, was full of "ideas millions of ideas" (i 185) derived from Volney, Holbach, Condorcet, Hume, Godwin and Wollstonecraft.

These gigantic mountains piled on each other, these water-falls, these million shaped clouds tinted by the varying colours of innumerable rainbows hanging between yourself and a lake as smooth and dark as a plain of polished jet, – oh! these are sights admirable to the contemplative. I have been much struck by the grandeur of its imagery. Nature here sports in the awful waywardness of her solitude; the summit[s] of the loftiest of these immense piles of rock seem but to elevate Skiddaw and Helvellyn; Imagination is resistlessly compelled to look back upon the myriad ages whose silent change placed them here, to look back when, perhaps this retirement of peace and mountain simplicity, was the Pandemonium of druidical imposture, the scene of Roman pollution, the resting place of the savage denizen of these solitudes with the wolf. – Still, still further! – strain thy reverted Fancy when no rocks, no lakes no cloud-soaring mountains were here, but a vast populous and licentious city stood in the midst of an immense plain, myriads flocked towards it; London itself scarcely exceeds it in the variety, the extensiveness [or] consummateness of its corruption! Perhaps ere Man had lost reason, and lived an happy

happy race. – No Tyranny, no Priestcraft, no War. – Adieu to the dazzling picture. (i 189)

This "dazzling picture" has little to do with the mountain landscape actually before Shelley, everything to do with the "millions" of Enlightenment "ideas" in his mind. His imagination is "resistlessly compelled", at that crucial moment in the centre of the passage, not by "cloud-soaring mountains", by Skiddaw and Helvellyn, but by outrage at urban "corruption", "druidical imposture" and "Roman pollution", or by Romantic primitivist enthusiasm. Shelley is far less ready to question these "ideas" than he is to analyse his feelings of pleasure, but the ideas nevertheless easily displace the pleasures in his mind. Shelley believes in the senses as the underwriters of reason, but he cannot recognise them as constituents of the passional self. Nothing could be further from a Wordsworthian interaction with the landscape than this almost wilful displacement by "ideas" of both the landscape and the "pleasure" found in regarding it: a displacement which is the central manoeuvre not just of this passage but of *Queen Mab* itself. So when we hear Shelley confessing to Godwin in 1812 "I either *am* or fancy myself something of a Poet", and calling poetry "an attachment ... which has characterised all my wanderings and changes" (i 260, 303), we should not conclude that he is about to disavow "ideas". When he refers in 1811 to the "power which made me a scribbler" (i 101) he is not considering the possibility that this power may yield a self-knowledge inaccessible to reason alone. His opposition to Christianity is a more urgently a matter of "insatiable feeling" than one of doctrine, but the feeling derives more from doctrine than from anything else about either Christianity or Shelley, and the poetry which "gratifies" the feeling does so by venting it on ideas, not by using it to explore the self which holds those ideas. Shelley insisted repeatedly that *Queen Mab* itself was not "didactic", not a systematic propagation of his "principles", but a "sincere overflowing of the heart & mind", a beautiful embodiment of his principles (i 350, 566–7). Those principles are what he feels passionately about, what for the time being constitute himself. But he will not use the poem as a way of exploring what there is of himself or any other self lying outside, and thus showing the limits of, the principles. Passion seems to be an attribute or quality of thought, not a mode of thought. Poetry likewise seems to be a way of expressing ideas, not a way of modifying them. Shelley knows that there is a power driving him to poetry, that there is savage and variable passion outside the world of ideas, but connecting that power to that passion is just what he recoils from. Other selves, we must now observe, were generally as alarming and unfamiliar to Shelley as his own. For all his pamphleteering advocacy of the cause of the people in 1812 and 1813, he was fastidious when he actually encountered them. At Keswick, he said, "tho the face of the country is lovely the *people* are detestable" (i 223). In Ireland, where Shelley went in 1812 to advance the cause of the Catholic oppressed, he found that the "*mob*" was "one mass of animated filth"; he found the "uninteresting details" of their "ordinary life" as tedious as he had found the scenery at Keswick (i 267–8, 277). Shelley was to say similar things all his life about ordinary people, the "mob", when he met them on his travels. Even those he befriended often lost their lustre with real intimacy. Elizabeth Hitchener, the "dearest friend" of so many excited letters of this period, became the "Brown Demon" soon after she came to live with Shelley and his first wife, Harriet Westbrook (i 191, 336). Shelley's intellectual mentor Godwin later became his father-in-law and finally left the poet with "ruined hopes" (i 459), although here Shelley had good reason for disillusionment. As for Harriet, he married her in 1811, when she was sixteen, intending to "mould a really noble soul into all that can make its nobleness useful and lovely" (i 163). Only three years later, however, he was saying this:

> In the beginning of spring, I spent two months at Mrs. Boinville's without my wife. If I except the succeeding period these two months were probably the happiest of my life. . . . The contemplation of female excellence is the favourite food of my imagination. Here was ample scope for admiration. . . . I suddenly perceived that the entire devotion with which I had resigned all prospects of utility or happiness to the single purpose of cultivating Harriet was a gross and despicable superstition. . . . I saw the full extent of the calamity which my rash and heartless union with Harriet: an union over whose entrance might justly be inscribed
> Lasciate ogni speranza voi ch'entrate!
> had produced. I felt as if a dead & living body had been linked together in loathsome & horrible communion. (i 401–2)

The "female excellence" was that of Mrs Boinville's accomplished daughter, Cornelia Turner, with whom in April and May 1814 Shelley had been reading Dante, as his images and his quotation imply: reading Dante being quite beyond Harriet, of course. In this company, said Shelley, "I have escaped . . . from the dismaying solitude of myself. . . . I have felt myself translated to a paradise" (i 383). In escaping the "loathsome & horrible communion" with Harriet Shelley was also escaping from himself, translating his feared passional self, in its different failures of understanding with both Harriet and Cornelia, into an ideal paradise. In terms strongly anticipatory of *Alastor*, written a year later, he elsewhere describes a waking dream of an ideal woman, partly Cornelia, partly a kind of portent of Mary Wollstonecraft Godwin, whom he met for the first time in June 1814. "Manifestations of my approaching change tinged my waking thoughts. . . . A train of visionary events arranged themselves in my imagination until ideas almost acquired the intensity of sensations. Already I had met the female who was destined to be mine" (i 402). Ideas acquiring the intensity of sensations: the phrase aptly registers what we have seen so far of Shelley's moral condition, his habits of mind and heart. When he met the real Mary, Shelley said, he realised at last "the integrity of [his] nature, its various dependencies, & learned to consider [himself] as an whole accurately united rather than an assemblage of inconsistent and discordant portions" (i 403). But this is a rare recognition by the younger Shelley of integrity and affiliability as vital qualities of the self, and of his own fragmented affections as best united in and by a personality, rather than an idea. After he and Mary had escaped to France, where incidentally Shelley found "the inhabitants the most unamiable inhospitable & unaccommodating of the human race" (i 392), he wrote to Harriet, left behind with their two children, telling her "I am united to another; you are no longer my wife", but urging her to join them, or failing that to "send quick supplies" of food or money (i 410). In one of Shelley's favourite books, Sir James Lawrence's *The Empire of the Nairs: Or, the Rights of Women* (1811), the narrator informs us that the fictional Nairs believed the "word fidelity should never be used in matters of love; love is an exhalation of the soul".[8] Godwin writes in *Political Justice* of the "evil of marriage"; no "ties ought to be imposed upon either party".[9] Mary Wollstonecraft even ventures to suggest in *A Vindication of the Rights of Woman* that "the neglected wife is, in general, the best mother".[10] And now Shelley had found in Mary the very child of Godwin and Wollstonecraft, his own utopian romantic vision made flesh. The reality of Harriet, a person, was twice displaced by Shelley's own vision of Woman, an idea: the first time when he took her up, and the second when he let her drop.

The question that arises in reflecting on Shelley's expressed attitudes to other people, both intimates and the "mob", is this: what quality of thought about the human, and especially the passions, is such a mind likely to be capable of, especially in poetry? This is not a biographicalist irrelevancy, not a question of whether our knowledge of Shelley's behaviour, or even of his thinking outside his poetry, should affect our sense of the poetry's worth. Clearly Shelley himself wanted to think in poetry about ideal displacements of the passions very like the ones we have just been considering: hence *Alastor*. The "youth" described in the preface to the poem is happy while thinking about "objects infinite and unmeasured", but he "images to himself the Being whom he loves" (p. 69), ignores a real woman who loves him, and seeks this image in vain until his solitary death. Shelley's account of himself in 1814 also discloses a conception of the self as fragmented and unaffiliated unless it succeeds in finding the embodiment of its ideal. *Alastor* is not to be read "merely" as an attempt by Shelley to reflect on his circumstances or remedy his personal deficiencies, but it does display in its thinking about the self those qualities and habits of mind with which the letters of 1811–14 have now begun to make us familiar.

Those patterns of dissociated thought are no less discernible in and constitutive of the writings of 1816–17. The places occupied in 1811–13 by Godwin, the Keswick mountains, the long doctrinal poem *Queen Mab* and its attendant political essays, are now taken by Rousseau, Mont Blanc, the even longer doctrinal poem *The Revolt of Islam*, and *its* attendant essays:[11] as if a cycle were being repeated. Even the retrospective self-questioning of the *Alastor* period, 1814–15, finds its later counterpart in the poetry of 1818–19, as we shall begin to see in the second section of this chapter.

Shelley travelled in Switzerland during July and August 1816, describing what he saw in letters to Thomas Love Peacock, then a classicist and poet, later a satirical novelist, and probably the best and most understanding friend Shelley ever had. Shelley thought Peacock's poetry was "exact & superficial" (ii 126), scholarly but not politically *engagé*. For his part, Peacock found a "want of reality" in Shelley's dramatic characterisations. He thought the poet sometimes "built a fabric of romance" around himself in his life, and ascribed this habit partly to Shelley's self-confessed fondness for romance novels, which, Peacock believed, "had the strongest influence in the formation of his character", and thus contributed to a deficiency in his poetry of any "clear development of what men were".[12] The romances Peacock singles out for special attention are those of the American Gothic novelist Charles Brockden Brown; "nothing so blended itself with the structure of his interior mind as the creations of Brown".[13] In 1816 Shelley had been reading Brown for about two years. There are marked coincidences of plot between the novels and some of Shelley's poems, but what he apparently found most congenial was the combination of "horrid" and apparently supernatural effects with simple, if contrived, scientific causes (ventriloquism, sleepwalking). The characters, meanwhile, are either entirely evil or entirely noble. Again, quoting Peacock on Shelley and Brown is not just reductive referentialism. Peacock is describing what he sees as the crucial shaping influence on one artist's mind of another's creations, which is a different matter entirely from the kind of influence that may have been exerted on Shelley the poet by the philosophy of Locke, Hume, Godwin and the rest. Peacock is also making a connection between Shelley's lack of any consistent sense of himself and his difficulty in creating convincing representations of other selves. He found in Shelley a chronic inability to think fully about ordinary lives. Shelley, meanwhile, sent Peacock from Switzerland long descriptions of the countryside: of villages and castles, forests and groves, rivers and waterfalls, glaciers and mountains, storms and avalanches, flowers, animals and birds (i 480–8, 495-502). The people, of course, were the "degradation of the human species", "wretched, diseased and poor", "half deformed or idiotic" (i 482, 499). But with a few noteworthy exceptions even his descriptions of the countryside have an air of neutrality, of the guide book. As at Cwm Elan and Keswick, there is rarely much sense of an affective participating self in Shelley's accounts of these natural objects. Two years later Peacock told Shelley that he should publish his letters from Italy about pictures and scenery; they would be best-sellers in England.[14] No, said Shelley, he did not wish to interest "ordinary men", "the many", and he did not believe his letters actually would do so (ii 70). His travel letters do indeed lack the wit and human perception of those of his neighbour and companion Byron, whom Shelley met for the first time in Switzerland, but they do sometimes catch fire:

> This journey has been on every account delightful, but most especially, because then I first knew the divine beauty of Rousseau's imagination, as it exhibits itself in Julie. It is inconceivable what an enchantment the scene itself lends to those delineations, from which its own most touching charm arises. . . . I read Julie all day; an overflowing, as it now seems, surrounded by the scenes which it has so wonderfully peopled, of sublimest genius, and more than human sensibility. Meillerie, the Castle of Chillon, Clarens, the mountains of La Valais and Savoy, present themselves to the imagination as monuments of things that were once familiar, and of beings that were once dear to it. They were created indeed by one mind, but a mind so powerfully bright as to cast a shade of falsehood on the records that are called reality. (i 480, 485)

The sentimental novel called *Julie, ou La Nouvelle Héloïse* (1761), of all Jean-Jacques Rousseau's works the one which had the widest popular appeal in the later eighteenth and early nineteenth centuries, intervened between Shelley and the countryside around Lake Geneva far more effectively than Erasmus Darwin's couplets had at Cwm Elan, or than those "millions of ideas" had at Keswick. Rousseau's wonderful people utterly outshone the deformed wretches of Evian and Chamonix; he "made nature even lovelier than itself" (i 487); his "sensibility" seemed "more than human". Rousseau himself said of the book in his *Confessions* (1781), which Shelley had read much earlier: "ignoring the human race, I created for myself societies of perfect creatures celestial in their virtue and in their beauty, and of reliable, tender, and faithful friends such as I had never found here below".[15] Shelley's turn from Godwin to Rousseau was not so much a way of discovering "the human race" and "human sensibility" as a new way of ignoring them.

Another exception amidst Shelley's generally dispassionate travel letters from Switzerland was a long excited description of Mont Blanc and its surroundings; Shelley's famous poem on the mountain was being written at the same time.

I never knew I never imagined what mountains were before. The immensity of these aerial summits excited, when they suddenly burst upon the sight, a sentiment of extatic wonder, not unallied to madness – And remember this was all one scene. It all pressed home to our regard & to our imagination. . . . All was as much our own as if we had been the creators of such impressions in the minds of others, as now occupied our own. – Nature was the poet whose harmony held our spirits more breathless than that of the divinest. . . . One would think that Mont Blanc was a living being & that the frozen blood forever circulated slowly thro' his stony veins. (i 497, 500)

No ideas, no other mind, can intervene between the observer's senses and *this* scene. External reality for once refuses to be displaced, and it is poetry which seems the only proper mode of response to it, the only conduit for the observer's feelings of "wonder" and "madness", the only mode of appropriation and recreation of these "impressions". Nor will poetry overshadow this reality: merely echo it. Shelley's own responding poem could only be called "Mont Blanc", and his admission that it was "an undisciplined overflowing of the soul" issuing from "the deep and powerful feelings excited by the objects"[16] it describes has far less of that suggestion of apology for the poem's lack of doctrine than such an admission would have had in earlier years. The power that made Shelley a scribbler had found an answering power in the world: or rather a Power. For while Mont Blanc had prompted, and "Mont Blanc" registers, a recognition on Shelley's part that poetry need be neither doctrinal like *Queen Mab* nor self-absorbed like *Alastor*, the letter and the poem both reveal that he was trying to reconcile his utilitarian and expressionist views of poetry by regarding deep and powerful feeling as the self's response to an ideal Power transcending the sensory and human world, which can thus still be ignored. When a natural landscape finally forced itself through the veil of ideas which customarily intervened between Shelley and the world, he immediately started looking, in Platonic and Kantian manner, for those greater Ideas which could be discerned through it.

In any case, this modification of Shelley's old sense of poetry's deeper power took place within an unchanged overall conception of its utility, as the phrase "undisciplined overflowing" hints. He still felt, as he always had, that poetry should be subordinated to "the inculcated moral". Harriet's suicide in December and Shelley's subsequent marriage to Mary having made his social position tenable, especially with Mary's father Godwin, Shelley re-entered radical literary and political circles in London in early 1817, re-asserting the "doctrines" of *Queen Mab* and telling Leigh Hunt: "I am undeceived in the belief that I have powers deeply to interest, or substantially to improve, mankind" (i 517). In Switzerland in August 1816 he had begun to read Rabaut's *Histoire de la Révolution Française* (1792). A month later he told Byron, by whom he had felt a little overshadowed in Switzerland, that "the master theme of the epoch in which we live" was "the French Revolution", and that only Byron was fitted to compose the "Epic Poem" that this theme required (i 504, 507). Of course Shelley was talking to himself; this was a Shelleyan undertaking, not a Byronic one. A year later he told Byron that he himself had "completed a poem. . . . in the style and for the same object as 'Queen Mab', but interwoven with a story of human passion" (i 557). This was Shelley's longest poem, the 5000-line *Laon and Cythna*, published late in 1817 and re-issued early in 1818, with suppressions of incestuous and atheistic passages, as *The Revolt of Islam*. Shelley called it "the *beau ideal* as it were of the French Revolution", a "tale illustrative of such a Revolution as might be supposed to take place in an European nation, acted upon by the opinions of what has been called (erroneously as I think) the modern philosophy" (i 563–4). Rousseau and Mont Blanc had shaken the Godwinian, and Shelley was determined to humanise his doctrines, to write a poetry of passion as well as of ideas. Where *Queen Mab* had employed supernatural machinery and, in its notes, long harangues expounding "the modern philosophy" (Enlightenment scepticism and materialism), *The Revolt of Islam* was meant to be a "mere human story", appealing to "the common & elementary emotions of the human heart" (i 563), confining its machinery to a few framing passages, and leaving any didactic harangues to the separate prose essays published earlier. But Shelley did not feel at home with "common emotions". He also called the poem a "genuine picture of [his] own mind" and an example of his own peculiar "power", which was, he said, "to apprehend minute & remote distinctions of feeling", and to "communicate the conceptions which result from considering either the moral or the material universe as a whole" (i 577). Apprehension of minute and remote feelings and consideration of the whole moral universe hardly sound like matters of common emotion; indeed Shelley himself sounds distinctly uneasy, in the preface to the poem, about his "power of awakening in others sensations like those which animate my own bosom", which power he acknowledged as "an essential attribute of Poetry".[17] The poem still enlists "metrical language" and "human passion" in "the cause of a liberal and comprehensive morality"; the "reader should see the beauty of pure virtue" and understand the author's "political and moral creed".[18] Reviewing Godwin's novel *Mandeville* in December 1817, Shelley remarked on how well its "enchanting melody of language" clothed "the genuine doctrine of 'Political Justice'".[19] After six years' thought about poetry Shelley still believed that feeling and language were things to be enlisted in the service of doctrines and creeds.

SHELLEY IN ITALY, 1818–19

Impelled by fears of consumption and prosecution, Shelley left England for Italy in March 1818. The next four and a half years brought with them repeated and increasingly radical challenges to his tenacious utilitarian conception of poetry: mainly artistic challenges in 1818 and 1819, countered by a renewal political fervour late in 1819; more intimate, personal and professional challenges from 1820 to 1822, with signs of a real change of heart in 1821 and 1822. In this section of the chapter we shall see Shelley under the influence of Italian art accommodating an increasingly expressionist view of poetry, but one in which the passions are tolerated, as they were in Switzerland, only in so far as they can be isolated and thought about, not combined and thought with: one in which, therefore, the artist's various feelings all in the end point towards and rest on a single ideal Truth or Beauty.

The "emblem of Italy", Shelley told Peacock, was "moral degradation contrasted with the glory of nature & the arts": on the one hand "the green earth & transparent sea and the mighty ruins of antient times ... the most sublime & lovely contemplation that can be conceived by the imagination of man"; on the other "the Italians of the present day ... the most degraded disgusting & odious" (ii 94, 67). It was art, rather than nature or the Italians, which in 1818 and 1819 enlarged Shelley's conception of what poetry might be. The "green earth", with its "green banks", certainly gave him his "chief pleasure in life", and was even a moral necessity: "I depend on these things for life" (ii 15–16, 3). He sent his friend, once more, detailed descriptions of various popular scenes: Como, Vesuvius, the Baths of Caracalla.[20] As in Switzerland, however, or in Keswick or Cwm Elan, these accounts seldom seem to have come from his heart, or stirred his imagination. Mont Blanc had been a rare message from the natural world; Italy's only equivalent was a single storm near Florence in October 1819. Shelley's attitude to "the modern Italians" (ii 22), as he called his hosts, is entirely consistent with his earlier responses to the inhabitants of Keswick, Ireland, France and Switzerland: although it must be said that a contrast between the glorious Italian past and its depraved present was a commonplace in nineteenth century travellers' tales and guidebooks, including the ones Shelley used, published in 1813 by Joseph Forsyth and J. C. Eustace. From his letters, and Mary's journal, issues a barrage of contempt and dismay at the condition and character of these wretched people, this "miserable race . . . without sensibility or imagination or understanding" (ii 9, 22). Here were "pollution-nourished worms",[21] "the deformity & degradation of humanity", "barbarian ferocity", "filthy modern inhabitants", "puny generations" (ii 60, 69, 59). The women were "particularly empty", a "kind of gentle savages" (ii 22, 92); and the Venetians outdid all other Italians in "avarice, cowardice, superstition, ignorance, passionless lust, & all the inexpressible brutalities which degrade human nature" (ii 43). Shelley saw all these people, in Italy as on his earlier travels, as effects of despotism, evidences of the need for universal political reform, rather than as *people*. He described "the human part of the experience of travelling" as "a thing of which I see little and understand less, and which if I saw and understood more I fear I should be little able to describe" (ii 15): a self-criticism echoing the comments of his best friend about his human perception, and suggesting that "the human part of the experience" was not what he thought it his competence to explore in his poetry.

So neither Italian nature nor the Italian people did much in 1818 or 1819 to enlarge or disturb Shelley's views of poetry, or of himself as a poet. The omnipresent examples of the Italian plastic arts, however, did bring about some important rethinking, reproducing on a larger scale the change of ideas occasioned in Switzerland by Rousseau and Mont Blanc. The architecture, especially, seemed to reflect and complement, although only rarely to overshadow, the "shapes of nature" (ii 55), and thus to be neither a matter of utility nor an intimation of disturbing passions. Architecture seemed to have nothing to do with either political reform or "the human part of the experience", but only with higher and more abstract ideas. The sculpture and painting, meanwhile, seemed to express and idealise single feelings, not complex webs of feeling. These conceptions of art owed a good deal to Shelley's contemporary reading, especially in the enormously influential *History of Ancient Art* (1764, French translation 1802) by the eighteenth-century German neoplatonic aesthetician, J. J. Winckelmann. His influence on Shelley's sensibility, like Brockden Brown's, is generally given far less weight by historians of ideas than that of Hume, for example; and yet Winckelmann and Brown informed Shelley's conception of poetry's possibilities much more fully than Hume could have.

To begin with architecture: the buildings of Pompeii demonstrated to Shelley that the ancients "lived in a perpetual commerce with external nature and nourished themselves upon the spirit of its forms". Their "incomparable columns" were "that ideal type of a sacred forest", "portals as it were to admit the spirit of beauty which animates this glorious universe" (ii 73–4). At Spoleto the "shapes of nature are of the grandest order", but "the creations of man sublime from their antiquity & greatness seem to predominate" (ii 55). The "effect" of Milan Cathedral, "piercing the solid blue with those groupes of dazzling spires relieved by the serene depth of this Italian Heaven . . . is beyond any thing I had imagined architecture capable of producing" (ii 7–8). The Pantheon in Rome "is as it were the visible image of the universe; in the perfection of its proportions, as when you regard the unmeasured dome of Heaven, the idea of magnitude is swallowed up & lost. . . . at night the keen stars are seen through the azure darkness" (ii 87–8). At Paestum the "effect of the jagged outline of mountains through groupes of enormous columns" was "inexpressibly grand"; the symmetry of the building "overpowers the idea of relative greatness" (ii 79–80). Over and over again Shelley was confronted with art which appeared to him to co-exist with "external nature", and even to abstract its formal secrets, such that the art became nature's "visible image", its "ideal type", the "spirit" of its beauty. In 1812 at Keswick Shelley had ignored nature completely in his thinking about poetry; in

1816 in Switzerland he had begun to see poetry as nature's analogue; in 1818 Italian art was suggesting to him that poetry might
by capturing nature's ideal spirit actually *become* that spirit, and
thus be transformed from the servant of ideas into the embodiment of an Idea.

In sculpture Shelley found a way to rethink his other view of
poetry: that it was the emanation of the passions. He found that
his old conglomerate horror, "the self", could be broken up or
abstracted into single passions, individually representable. "In
art", according to Winckelmann, "the term *expression* signifies
imitation of the active and passive states of the mind and body,
and of the passions as well as of the actions".[22] "Expression" is
Winckelmann's term for the Greek *êthos*, more commonly translated "character" or "disposition"; Shelley duly found in classical sculpture the "expression" of individual or dominant passions,
not of whole characters. A Mercury "expresses an imperturb-
able and god-like self-possession" and is "the animation of swiftness";[23] a Venus "expresses . . . voluptuousness without affectation",
and her tongue and lip "express love, still love";[24] a Minerva is
"Wisdom . . . pleading earnestly with power", the image of a
"nameless feeling";[25] the parted lips of the winged Victories on
the arch of Titus in Rome "express the eager respiration of their
speed", while the figures as a whole express "that mixture of
energy and error which is called a Triumph" (ii 89, 86). The Niobe
in Florence and the Laocoon in Rome, made much of by
Winckelmann and others, became two of Shelley's favourite
groups. Laocoon's "predominant and overwhelming emotion" is
"Intense physical suffering", whilst his children's "features and
attitudes indicate . . . filial love and devotion". The Niobe was
"probably the most consummate personification of loveliness"
surviving from "Greek Antiquity".[26] For Winckelmann, too,
Laocoon was "an image of the most intense suffering"; Niobe
was "beautiful according to the highest conceptions of beauty".[27]
Shelley found in these works and in an authoritative modern
theory of them an argument that art can work by isolating single feelings, making abstract ideas out of them, and then "expressing" the ideas. His responses to the works are studded with
individuated references to self-possession, voluptuousness, wisdom, power, joy, sorrow, dignity, desire, suffering, despair, injustice, destiny, nobleness, majesty, devotion, torment, surprise,
pain, grief, horror, loveliness, beauty, innocence, purity and

strength.[28] Shelley had told Godwin in 1812 that words were "merely signs of . . . inexpressible ideas" (i 317); here he found that sculptures *were* expressible ideas. Where Hazlitt looked at the Elgin Marbles and saw "casts from nature . . . from real, living, moving nature; from objects in nature, answering to an idea in the artist's mind, not from an idea in the artist's mind abstracted from all objects in nature",[29] Shelley looked at these sculptures and saw them as casts from abstracted ideas, rather than from objects in nature. As we saw in Chapter 1, this is a difference essential to their respective views of poetry and of the self. Shelley had now come to accept art as legitimately expressive of the passions, as well as subordinate to ideas, but he had done this by seeing a passion as a kind of idea. For Hazlitt, art is precisely the mode of thought in which a passion is not a kind of idea.

Of course, from Shelley's other, utilitarian point of view it was congenial to think of the passions in this way, and that point of view was still paramount with him. The artist can think of "liberty" or "injustice", of "pain" or "resistance", and then "express" them, so as to advance the cause he believes in. He can "analyse" the self into its constituent "feelings", such as love, grief or suffering, and then find images for them. What he need not do is think about whole selves, whole lives. Furthermore (and this is a matter of some importance in Shelley's view of poetry) if "suffering" can be thought of as an abstract idea of exactly the same kind as "liberty", for example, then art can be regarded as a way of reforming and saving the very self, not just as a kind of legislative instrument: certainly not as a way of merely disclosing the self. The Greeks, said Shelley, were "alone capable of combining ideal beauty and poetical and abstract enthusiasm with the wild errors from which it sprung", and of turning "all things, superstition, prejudice, murder, madness – to Beauty".[30] Here was a way to bring his old utilitarian conception of poetry to bear on that equally old horror, the self. Poetry's reforming function need not be only political; it could be ethical too, even spiritual. Where formerly Shelley had seen poetry both as a way "to subdue the savage nature of the people" and as the voice of the savage self, now he could see it as a way of turning the self "to Beauty". One of his "chief aims in Italy", he wrote to his friend Maria Gisborne, was "the observing in statuary & painting the degree in which, & the rules according to which, that

ideal beauty of which we have so intense yet so obscure an apprehension is realized in external forms" (ii 126). It is a small
step from government by "inculcated moral" to seduction by "ideal
beauty"; indeed, one might see this as a predictable fate for that
over-protected child, Shelley's view of poetry. His persistent dislike
of comedy, coarseness and mannerism in art reflected his reforming preference for this kind of "beauty". He hated a
Michelangelo Bacchus because it was "drunken, brutal, and nar-
row-minded" – rather like the modern Italians in general, in fact;
a clàssical Greek Bacchus, on the other hánd, had the "immortal
beauty" of "one who walks through the world untouched by its
corruptions".[31] The "human part of the experience" was alien to
Shelley; if he could not reform or subdue it then perhaps he
might redeem it, idealise it.

As with sculpture, so, even more, with painting. "The material part indeed of these works must perish, but they survive in
the mind of man. . . . opinion that legislator is infected with their
influence; men become better & wiser" (ii 53). Shelley echoed
Winckelmann's preference, and anticipated that of the Pre-
Raphaelites, for the earlier Renaissance over the later. Raphael's
St Caecilia "is most unlike any of those things which we call
reality. It is of the inspired and ideal kind. . . . it eclipses nature,
yet it has all its truth & softness" (ii 51–2). Michelangelo, on the
other hand, has "no sense of moral dignity and loveliness", "no
temperance no modesty no feeling for the just boundaries of art . . .
no sense of beauty". In the Sistine Chapel "the host of Heaven . . .
are in fact very ordinary people", when "they ought to have
been what the Christians call *glorified bodies*, floating onward, &
radiant with that everlasting light (I speak in the spirit of their
faith) which had consumed their mortal veil" (ii 80–1). The figure of Jesus "is in the attitude of common place resentment"
like "an angry potboy & God like an old alehouse-keeper looking out of window" (ii 112). Shelley has no time for the representation of "ordinary people", for potboys and alehouse-keepers.
He wants an art which will be "unlike . . . reality", which "eclipses
nature", glorifies bodies, purifies passion, influences opinion
towards Beauty and Truth. Rousseau is blended with Godwin;
ideal art produces the greater good.

In 1818 and 1819 Shelley was, of course, reading Italian and
Greek poetry, just as he was looking at Italian and Greek plastic
art. In the case of Dante he had to reconcile his admiration of

the poet's "exquisite tenderness & sensibility & ideal beauty" (ii 112) with his dislike of the *Commedia*'s medieval Christian doctrine. He did so by claiming that "the misty ocean of [Dante's] dark and extravagant fiction" was illuminated by "fortunate isles laden with golden fruit":[32] in effect, that Dante's grasp of "ideal beauty", of the nature of love, in his portrayal of Beatrice and of Paradise, redeemed his unfortunate doctrine and his rather unpleasant portrayal of the damned in the *Inferno*. Boccaccio, meanwhile, "possessed a deep sense of the fair ideal of human life considered in its social relations". His "more serious theories of love", Shelley adds solemnly, "agree especially with mine" (ii 122). As in Rousseau, Dante, Godwin and so many other writers, Shelley finds in Boccaccio *theories* of love, or rather of Love, rather than people loving. He finds "the fair ideal of human life", not human life. Ariosto was the Michelangelo to Boccaccio's Raphael; he "is so cruel too in his descriptions"; he "constantly vindicates & embellishes revenge". Shelley preferred the "delicate moral sensibility" of Torquato Tasso, but both Tasso and Ariosto were "the second-rate Poets of Italy" (ii 20, 122). Shelley explains this valuation with reference not to their poetry but to their times. When they were writing, in the sixteenth and seventeenth centuries, "the corrupting blight of tyranny was already hanging on every bud of genius". Boccaccio and Dante, however, in the fourteenth and twelfth centuries, were the "productions of the vigour of the infancy of a new nation". Innocent of political fetters, poetry may produce images of the ideal; imprisoned, its business must first be to loosen the fetters. So far this is very like the other things Shelley was saying about art in general. But as a poet he saw poetry rather differently. What he responded creatively to in Tasso was not the latter's poetry, his thought, but his situation, the plight of the mad and imprisoned Poet:

> There is something irresistibly pathetic to me in the sight of Tasso's own hand writing moulding expressions of adulation & entreaty to a deaf & stupid tyrant in an age when the most heroic virtue would have exposed its possessor to hopeless persecution. (ii 47)

> I have devoted this summer & indeed the next year to the composition of a tragedy on the subject of Tasso's madness,

which I find upon inspection is, if properly treated, admirably dramatic & poetical. – But, you will say I have no dramatic talent. Very true in a certain sense; but I have taken the resolution to see what kind of a tragedy a person without dramatic talent could write. (ii 8)

Tasso the mad prisoner was a figure for the poet in general. To write poetry about Tasso was, for Shelley, to think about what the poet is, what he himself was. The madness was a version of the old horror, "self"; the imprisonment was the proper subject of the utilitarian imagination. Shelley feared that he lacked this kind of "dramatic talent", but he was still fascinated by the spectacle of madness, the breakdown of the self under the assault of the passions. Political protest, on the other hand, was what he had always seen as his poetic task. To write about Tasso was to attempt in poetry simultaneously to redeem the self and reform the polity. Shelley never wrote his Tasso play, but the impulse to do so issued in "Julian and Maddalo" (1818) and *The Cenci* (1819), both of which are about imprisonment and madness. Meanwhile he remembered Tasso's own thought chiefly for one phrase which appears in none of his work, but is attributed to him in the various lives of the poet which Shelley read: "no-one deserves the name of Creator save God and the poet". Shelley quotes versions of this line in several places in his letters and essays.[33] His utilitarian conception of poetry now included an ethical and a spiritual as well as a political and social aspect; his expressionist conception now gave poetry an ontological and an epistemological pre-eminence. Poets could make "perfect creatures" themselves, or they could perceive the Reality behind God's creations. But to reconcile the two conceptions still involved subordinating the second to the first. Poetry must still serve the Idea.

Its idealising rather than its politicising aspect was what Shelley noticed when reading Greek poetry, more remote as it was from his own political concerns and circumstances. He had been reading Greek since Eton, but his real immersion in the literature began in mid-1817, just before he went to Italy. By late 1821 he was still reading "the tragedians, Homer & Plato perpetually" (ii 360). The *Iliad* "surpasses any other single production of the human mind", he wrote in 1817 (i 545); "as a poet", he added the next year, "Homer must be acknowledged to excel Shakespeare in the truth, the harmony, the sustained grandeur, the satisfying completeness of his images, their exact fitness to the illustration".[34] Homer was, in fact, the one poet whom Shelley appears to have admired chiefly for his exploration of "ordinary" humanity in images of "satisfying completeness" and "fitness". But Homer was not his preferred poetic model; even when he was moved to translate from earlier Greek literature he chose, not the *Iliad* or *Odyssey*, but the fantastic and idealising Homeric Hymns. The great tragedians were not ultimately his models either, although he translated Euripides and derived his own greatest poem from Aeschylus. That preferred model was Plato, a kind of amalgam of all that seemed admirable in Godwin, Rousseau and Homer, a thinker who exhibited "the rare union of close and subtle logic, with the Pythian enthusiasm of poetry".[35]

Plato was essentially a poet – the truth and splendour of his imagery and the melody of his language is the most intense that it is possible to conceive. He rejected the measure of the epic, dramatic, and lyrical forms, because he sought to kindle a harmony in thoughts divested of shape and action, and he forebore to invent any regular plan of rhythm which would include, under determinate forms, the varied pauses of his style.[36]

Harmonious thoughts divested of shape and action: together with "ideas acquiring the intensity of sensations" in 1814 the phrase is as good a description as Shelley ever penned of his own ideal of poetry. His greatest poetic undertaking was *Prometheus Unbound*, written in these same two years, and yet in the same breath as telling Peacock that the "1st Act of Prometheus is complete" he said:

I consider Poetry very subordinate to moral & political science, & if I were well, certainly I should aspire to the latter; for I can conceive a great work, embodying the discoveries of all ages, & harmonizing the contending creeds by which mankind have been ruled. (ii 70–1)

In the very preface to his *magnum opus* Shelley discounted poetry in the unreconstructed terms of 1812; what he really wished to produce, he said, was "a systematical history of what appear to me to be the genuine elements of human society". Let no-one imagine, he went on, that if he did so "I should take Aeschylus rather than Plato as my model" (p. 207). The Aeschylean *Prometheus* is less valuable than the Platonic "systematical history", the "great work" which will harmonize all creeds. It is as if Shelley wanted to be Hegel. His remarks on Plato in 1818 and 1819, and even as late as 1821, show that the ambitions and attitudes of 1812, although modified in Switzerland and Italy, remained essentially unaltered. Poetry is redefined to include Plato's work (this manoeuvre is central to "A Defence of Poetry"), but Shelley's current view of poetry as "subordinate to moral & political science" is hardly different from his old view of it as "subordinate to the inculcated moral". He may now see the poet as a God-like creator of perfect beings, a perceiver of divine Ideas, a redeemer of selves, as much as a social reformer or an outlet for selfish passion, but poetry is still fundamentally an instrument of thought, not a way of thinking.

Shelley often seems unaware, incidentally, of the Socratic ironies in Plato's dialogues. He accepts the poet Agathon's account of the madness of love in the *Symposium* as if it were endorsed by the dialogue as a whole, instead of criticised by Socrates; he understands Socrates' characterisation of the poet in the *Ion* as a passionate defence, rather than as a sly and magniloquent subversion; he reads the speech in the *Phaedrus* on divine and poetic madness as if Socrates had not gone on to expose the futility of any speech and writing which is not intended to instruct the audience in justice and goodness; he praises the *Republic*'s "speculations on civil society" without mentioning its treatment of poets.[37] In all these cases Shelley notices the descriptions of poetry as a madness of divine origin, but not the criticisms of it as socially destabilising. That is, he accepts Plato's account of poetry in so far as it answers to and assuages his own fears about poetry's mysterious power and source, but not in its contradiction of his utilitarian conceptions of poetry's social function. Poetry emanates from a mad self, but the madness may signify the presence of divinity, not just of wild passions. Shelley had found an affirmative restatement of one old view, but still no reason to doubt the authority of the other one.

His immersion in Plato and Homer in 1818 left Shelley in "despair of producing any thing original" and "totally incapable of original composition" (ii 22, 26). It was the Tasso idea, rather than these great models, which actually prompted him to write, rather than just translate, and which initiated what is now recognised as his *annus mirabilis*, from late 1818 to late 1819. That idea took two radically different forms, one congenial to Shelley, the other not, or at least not yet. The congenial form was *Prometheus Unbound*, a doctrinal but not didactic poem very much in the tradition of *Queen Mab* and *The Revolt of Islam*. Its imagery was "drawn from the operations of the human mind" without being exploratory of "ordinary" human life. Its hero was "the type of the highest perfection of moral and intellectual nature, impelled by the purest and the truest motives to the best and noblest ends". Its deepest sources were Shelley's old "'passion for reforming the world'"[38] and new belief that poets are the "companions and forerunners of some unimagined change in our social condition". Its rhetorical method was the deployment of "beautiful idealisms of moral excellence" in the service of "reasoned principles of human conduct" (pp. 133–5). Shelley thought of this poem as quintessentially his own, and his various comments on it in the preface and his letters show how utilitarian his conception of poetry still was. The other, less congenial form taken by the Tasso idea ultimately derived more from *Alastor* than from *Queen Mab*. Here Shelley meant, he said, to deal with "sad reality", not "dreams of what ought to be, or may be" (ii 96). He wanted "to represent . . . characters as they really were", to "lay aside the presumptuous attitude of an instructor", to suppress his own "peculiar feelings & opinions" or "conceptions of right or wrong", and to "express the actual way in which people talk with each other" (p. 240; ii 96, 102, 108). The major outcomes of these intentions were the conversation poem "Julian and Maddalo" and Shelley's only completed play, *The Cenci*, which is still successfully revived from time to time. In these works "moral error" (ii 190) remained the subject, Shelley claimed, while his passion for reform was suppressed, supposedly in the interests of exploring passion itself. In the case of *The Cenci*, however, as we saw above, Shelley felt some uneasiness about this undertaking. One can see why, when in the preface to the poem he calls imagination "the immortal God which should assume flesh for the redemption of mortal passion" (p. 241). This new foray into the "human part of the experience" assumes that mortal passion is a kind of aberration, and that poetry is a kind of salvation. In "Julian and Maddalo" Shelley felt that the "familiar style" had to be dispensed with in those passages "where the passion exceeding a certain limit touches the boundaries of that which is ideal" (ii 108). But if passion at its most excessive becomes an idea, and if poetry recognises this moment by dispensing with the familiar style and modulating into a higher one, then "the actual way in which people talk with each other", characters as they really are, will probably look like secondary concerns.

By the autumn of 1819 the energy of the Tasso idea had dissipated. Shelley frequently complained of lack of inspiration during 1818 and 1819. This was partly because of the uncongeniality of the "human part" of the Tasso idea, and its awkward relationship with the ideal and reformist part; partly because of personal unhappiness. The deaths of two children greatly exacerbated the growing estrangement between Shelley and Mary. But the real trouble was a lack of first-hand political inspiration; the Tasso idea was only second-hand. There was no stimulus corresponding to the discovery of the French Revolution as a theme for poetry in 1816, or that first excited discovery of politics in general in 1812. Shelley was in exile from his own country and circle, and Italian politics or art were no substitutes. He missed "public affairs" (ii 22) at home. What re-ignited the flame was the Peterloo affair of August 1819. Shelley called it "bloody murderous oppression", and thought that it portended "a crisis of approaching Revolution" in England (ii 117, 132). He heard the news on 5 September, and the "torrent of indignation . . . boiling in his veins" (ii 117) turned into a torrent of words pouring from his pen. He wrote an angry political ballad, *The Mask of Anarchy*, in September; a lengthy parodic criticism of Wordsworth, "Peter Bell the Third", and the resounding "Ode to the West Wind" in October; his longest prose essay, *A Philosophical View of Reform*, in November and December; an extra act for *Prometheus Unbound* and a metaphysical essay, "On Life", in December; and the sarcastic anti-Christian essay "On the Devil and Devils" in January: to say nothing of various shorter pieces of poetry. This was productivity on the scale of *Queen Mab* and its essays in 1812–13, or of *The Revolt of Islam* and *its* essays in 1817. Shelley's imagination was still fundamentally political, needing political inspiration to work at full capacity.

Still, its productions had by now become more metaphorically and emotionally sophisticated, more doctrinally restrained, than in 1812 or 1817. The interaction of Shelley's two views of poetry under the influences of Italy had had its effect. Certainly the

Mask opens with the claim that the speaker had been "asleep in Italy" until "a voice from over the Sea" led him forth to "walk in the visions of Poesy" (p. 301): as if only politics could awaken him, and as if poetry's "visions" were merely the servants of politics. Certainly "Peter Bell the Third" was prompted as much by dislike of Wordsworth's politics as of his poetry; Shelley had read his conservative *Addresses to the Freeholders of Westmoreland*[39] in 1818, and marvelled that such a "beastly & pitiful wretch" should be "such a poet" (ii 26). But the latter poem contains a genuine current of literary criticism, a sense that Wordsworth fails to imagine other lives besides his own. And for all Shelley's concern that in writing the *Philosophical View* he had "deserted the odorous gardens of literature to journey across the great sandy desert of politics" (ii 150), the essay extends those earlier insights about Dante, Boccaccio, Ariosto and Tasso to European history and literature at large in such a way as to give much more importance to the arts, and especially poetry, as constituents of culture than Shelley had ever given before. Great writers are represented as portents and proofs of the greatness of their peoples.[40] The argument rises to the peroration familiar from its later appearance in "A Defence of Poetry": the "most unfailing herald, or companion, or follower of an universal employment of the sentiments of a nation to the production of beneficial change is poetry. . . . Poets and philosophers are the unacknowledged legislators of the world".[41] Shelley had not yet turned his argument into a defence of poetry alone, and he wanted to think of poets and philosophers as alike, and as legislators, but in this supposedly political essay he was nevertheless elevating poetry far above the place it had held in his earliest conceptions of it.

The fragment "On Life", one of Shelley's best essays, is ostensibly about metaphysics rather than politics, but like the *Philosophical View*, and unlike so many earlier essays, it cannot stay away from poetry. Shelley sets out to examine the competing claims of Christianity, materialism and the Berkeleyan "intellectual system" (p. 476), modelling his argument on that of one of his favourite works of philosophy, Sir William Drummond's *Academical Questions* (1805). But unlike Drummond, who counsels his readers to "dread a trope as a snare",[42] Shelley talks freely of the "mist of familiarity", of artists imagining the world, of Tasso's remark about poets and God, of life as "the great miracle" to be perceived with "intense delight", of "all familiar objects as signs, standing not for themselves but for others" (pp. 474–7). Poetry thrusts itself into metaphysics as it had earlier into politics. The attack on Christianity in "On the Devil and Devils" contains some central paragraphs on *Paradise Lost*, in which Milton's "Devil as a moral being . . . [is] far superior to his God", and on hell and heaven in Dante, Raphael and Michelangelo, in whom it "requires a higher degree of skill . . . to make beauty, virtue and harmony . . . than to make injustice, deformity, discord and horror poetical".[43] There is something here, certainly, of the old Shelley, hostile to the doctrine of *Paradise Lost* and preferring "beauty" to "horror". But there is also a new one, more alive to "moral being" and poetic skill.

SHELLEY IN ITALY, 1820–2

During his two years in Pisa and his last few months at Lerici, Shelley's old utilitarian view of poetry seemed to be reaching something close to bankruptcy, as he despaired at his continuing public inutility. His other view was eventually almost forced into salience, by this despair and by developments in his human relationships, and as a result he started to write at the end of his life as if passion were an end, a way of thought, instead of just a means, an object of thought. But even Shelley's expressionist view of poetry was predominantly anti-passional and indeed anti-human. His recognition that it need not be was belated and against the grain, and there is no knowing how deep or lasting that recognition would have been. Still, growth is growth, and it is hard to see how even some new surge of reformist-idealist writing could not have been shaped by it.

Political and social reform continued to be uppermost in Shelley's thinking about and in poetry for much of the period. "I have confidence in my moral sense alone", he told Leigh Hunt in November 1819; "I cling to moral and political hope, like a drowner to a plank", he told Byron in mid-1821 (ii 153, 291). After Peterloo there were revolutions in Spain, Naples and Piedmont in 1820 and 1821, and the Greek revolt against Turkish rule in 1821; this was a time of resurgent liberalism and nationalism after the restoration of the old order in 1815. Shelley responded with odes for the Spaniards and Neapolitans and a longer dramatic poem, *Hellas*, for the Greeks, as well as the burlesque satire *Swellfoot the Tyrant,* on contemporary British politics, and the fragmentary historical drama "Charles the First": all in 1820 and 1821. Yet he was dissatisfied:

> I am, speaking literarily, infirm of purpose. I have great designs, and feeble hopes of ever accomplishing them. I read books, and, though I am ignorant enough, they seem to teach me nothing. To be sure, the reception the public have given me might go far enough to damp any man's enthusiasm. (ii 244–5)

Indeed it might. Those reviewers who noticed the poems at all were almost invariably hostile to *The Revolt of Islam,* the *Prometheus Unbound* volume, *The Cenci* and Shelley's favourite, *Adonais.* This was particularly discouraging in the case of *The Cenci,* which Shelley had intended to be popular, and *Adonais,* which he believed to be his finest work. But there was more to this literary infirmity of purpose than hostile reviews, or even exile and personal unhappiness. Shelley's "moral sense" had always been the basis not only of his personality but of his poetry. What if his confidence in it were misplaced? What if "moral sense" in poetry were something other than political and social indignation and ameliorism? All those revolutions had not cured this infirmity; what if "moral and political hope" were the wrong plank for this drowning poet to cling to?

Perhaps some version of the rival view of poetry might be the right plank. In the preface to *The Cenci* Shelley had written:

> In a dramatic composition the imagery and the passion should interpenetrate one another, the former being reserved simply for the full development and illustration of the latter. Imagination is as the immortal God which should assume flesh for the redemption of mortal passion. (p. 241)

A few months later, in November 1819, Shelley was telling Leigh Hunt that one of the latter's poems "affects the passions and searches the understanding", while another "appeals to the Imagination, who is the master of them both, their God, and the Spirit by which they live and are" (ii 152). Shelley had no doubt derived this abstracting and hypostasising manner of speaking about "the Imagination" from his German reading, and especially from that fecund Germanist Coleridge, whose *Biographia Literaria* (1817) he had read just before he left England.[44] In any case this manner of speaking, anticipating the style of "A Defence of Poetry" fourteen months later, is a far cry from that alarmed suppression of fancy and imagination by reason in 1811. But this is not the triumph of the self and the passions over reason and the "moral sense"; what the Imagination has triumphed over here is precisely the passional self. The process involved is the one we noticed earlier, in connection with sculpture. Shelley may speak of the imaginative "development and illustration" of the passions, or of searching the understanding, but clearly the true function of "the Imagination" here is redemptive, not exploratory. This is not a radical shift of allegiance from reformist utilitarian utopianism to experientialist humanism. Imagination as a redeeming Spirit, saving the self from its own passions, differs from poetry as a reforming instrument, subduing "the savage nature of the people", only in its metaphysical aspiration, its claim to divine authority. "As to real flesh & blood", Shelley told his friend John Gisborne in October 1821, "you know that I do not deal in those articles, – you might as well go to a ginshop for a leg of mutton, as expect any thing human or earthly from me" (ii 363). Shelley's talk of the Imagination was certainly a sign of his disenchantment with a purely utilitarian, politico-moral view of poetry. But it was a sign of a new faith in the expressionist view only in so far as that view was idealist and redemptive, not "human or earthly". In any case, the conversion in 1819 of moral and political enthusiasm into redemptive poetry was not so new in Shelley; it was exactly what had happened in *Queen Mab* in 1812 and *The Revolt of Islam* in 1817. The trouble was that after 1819 that enthusiasm, while undiminished, no longer seemed to feed Shelley's poetic energies. The "power that made him a poet", that deeper poetic energy which he distrusted, needed other fuel: namely "the human part of the experience", other people. And of course any immersion in the human would require Shelley to relinquish both the "moral and political" or utilitarian view of poetry, which he saw as the one plank temporarily saving him from drowning, and the idealist-expressionist view of the redemptive Imagination, which seemed to be the lifeboat on the horizon.

Thus Shelley could not write his political drama "Charles the First" in 1820–1 because his energy was sapped by the belief that he should have been attempting "a production of a far higher character" (ii 269): just as *Prometheus* had *not* been the "great work" of "moral and political science" he aspired to. He wanted the lifeboat and could not be satisfied with the plank. By early 1822 he was still worse off:

> I have written nothing for this last two months. . . . What motives have I to write. – I *had* motives – and I thank the god of my own heart they were totally different from those of the other apes of humanity who make mouths in the glass of the time – but what are *those* motives now? (ii 394)

Aping humanity was of course unthinkable for a poet with a view of Imagination as the immortal God sent to earth to redeem humanity, but even reformist political purposes paled in the light of this view. *Hellas* was composed, said Shelley, "in one of those few moments of enthusiasm which now seldom visit me" (ii 406). The enthusiasm was political, and therefore could only be "transitory" (ii 357): or so it seemed to Shelley now. "I try to be what I might have been", he laments, "but am not very successfull"; he quotes from Goethe's *Faust*, to the effect that the spirit's splendour is stifled in the foreign matter of the body (ii 364). Shelley thought he "might have been" the poet to achieve a transfiguration of moral and political passion into ideal images, but instead he found himself in danger of stifling in the human and earthly: in danger of drowning. Even *Adonais*, his brilliant performance on the occasion of the death of Keats, a poem which seemed to Shelley to achieve that transfiguration, to be "better in point of composition than any thing I have written" (ii 294), led to more disappointment. Shelley was convinced of its merits and at a loss to explain the unenthusiastic reviews. Perhaps the poem was still too political, insufficiently transfigured. "I have dipped my pen in consuming fire for his destroyers", he said at first (ii 300, 302): later he said, "I have been carried too far by the enthusiasm of the moment; by my piety, and my indignation" (ii 308). Perhaps this was after all only another Tasso poem about the situation of a poet, another stack of politico-moral kindling only half-consumed by idealising fire. "I wish I had something better to do than furnish this jingling food for the hunger of oblivion, called *verse*", said poor Shelley (ii 374); he even thought of joining the East India Company. He did not think of attempting to disclose in his poem about Keats's death that entirely different kind of meaning which is intrinsic to a life, rather than extrinsic to it.

Ironically, but not surprisingly, it was Keats himself who had put his finger on the problem the year before, in a letter to Shelley about *The Cenci*:

> There is only one part of it I am judge of; the Poetry, and dramatic effect, which by many spirits now a days is considered the mammon. A modern work it is said must have a purpose, which may be the God – *an artist* must serve Mammon – he must have 'self concentration' selfishness perhaps. You I am sure will forgive me for sincerely remarking that you might curb your magnanimity and be more of an artist, and 'load every rift' of your subject with ore. The thought of such discipline must fall like cold chains upon you, who perhaps never sat with your wings furl'd for six Months together.[45]

As we know, Shelley himself feared that the achievement of "dramatic effect", which Keats all but identifies with poetry itself, was not his forte as a poet. Indeed, on either of his two views of poetry that intrinsic effect was indeed the "mammon", the mere worldly or rhetorical appearance. The extrinsic "purpose" or Truth, the moral, political or ideal end, had always been Shelley's "God"; the Imagination was his new name for the power of apprehending it. Keats believes that the artist "must have 'self concentration'"; Shelley had always shied away from that very "selfishness". Even in "A Defence of Poetry", written early in 1821, Shelley was still saying that "Poetry, and the principle of Self . . . are the God and the Mammon of the world" (p. 503): borrowing Keats's imagery but reversing his sense. Exploration of "self" is what Keats recommends and Shelley abhors; subordination of poetry to moral and ideal purpose is what Keats disapproves and Shelley recommends. Curiously enough, Shelley's other great contemporary, Byron, had a similar lesson to teach. Shelley's creative depression from 1820 to 1822 was partly the result of watching Byron's extraordinary popular success from close range; the two were neighbours in Pisa for much of this time. "I despair of rivalling Lord Byron", Shelley told Mary in 1821, "and there is no other with whom it is worth contending" (ii 323). Simply put, Shelley found Byron's life and habits disgusting, but his poem *Don Juan*, on which Byron was then working, magnificent. He could not reconcile these judgements. On the first point he condemned his friend for associating "with wretches . . . who do not scruple to avow practices which are not only not named but I believe seldom even conceived in England"; his "Italian women are perhaps the most contemptible of all who exist under the moon" (ii 58). And yet the love letter from Julia to Juan at the end of Canto I of *Don Juan* [46] "is altogether a masterpiece of portraiture; of human nature laid with the eternal colours of the feelings of humanity. Where did you learn all these secrets? I should like to go to school there" (ii 198).

The answer to Shelley's question is that Byron learned his secrets in precisely the place where Shelley had all his life refused to go to school: among the "modern Italians", or Swiss, or Irish, or French; among "ordinary" people. Like Michelangelo, Byron found God in the face of old ale-house keepers, or seraglio women. Shelley never made the connection. He encouraged Byron nevertheless,[47] as he had in 1817, to write the great epic of the age, its *Iliad*, *Divine Comedy* or *Paradise Lost*; as *Don Juan* lengthened he became convinced that *this* was that epic, that it set "him not above but far above all the poets of the day". "Nothing has ever been written like it in English", he told Byron (ii 323). "You unveil & present in its true deformity what is worst in human nature. . . . We are damned to the knowledge of good & evil, and it is well for us to know what we should avoid no less than what we should seek" (ii 357–8). This was a new recognition: that disclosing the horrors of the "self" could be as much the function of great poetry as imagining ideal beauty; that the Michelangelo Bacchus might have its place next to the Greek one. Shelley still sees the disclosure, of course, in extrinsic moralising terms ("should avoid", "should seek"), but from here to a view of poetry as discovering the self intrinsically, without moralising purpose, is a short step. Shelley could see in Byron that "familiarity with the dramatic power of human nature" (ii 349) he felt himself to lack, that capacity for dramatic effect and human discovery which Keats had applauded. Byron "touched a chord to which a million hearts responded", said Shelley, "and the coarse music which he produced to please them disciplined him to the perfection to which he now approaches" (ii 436). He began not with Shelley's doctrinal kind of "moral sense", but with another kind, a sense of ordinary selves or lives. His discipline lay in perfecting that sense, not in looking outside the lives for their true meaning or value.

Shelley did in 1820–2 write his own poetry of the self, so to speak, and although it was not at all like Byron's or Keats's it evinced his growing need to think in a new way about lives and passions, especially his own. "The Witch of Atlas" was pure fantasy, Imagination at play; at the other extreme the "Letter to Maria Gisborne" was pure enumeration of everyday humanity, a lighthearted household conversation with almost no effort at imaginative redemption. Both were written in 1820; the next year brought the extremes together in *Epipsychidion*, a quintessentially Shelleyan love poem intended, he said characteristically, only for the "esoteric few", not for the "vulgar" (ii 263). This poem was, certainly, an idealisation of passion, and Shelley typically saw it as inferior to the Symposium he would have preferred to write. Still, it was his first sustained attempt since *Alastor* six years before to think poetically about his own passions and his own life in relation to another life. "Some of us have in a prior existence been in love with an Antigone, & that makes us find no full content in any mortal tie", he commented, in Rousseauan vein, with his poem partly in mind (ii 364): a sad and damaging admission, but also perhaps a sign of Shelley's growing appreciation of the value of mortal ties. The next year he said of the poem:

> The 'Epipsychidion' I cannot look at; the person whom it celebrates was a cloud instead of a Juno; and poor Ixion starts from the centaur that was the offspring of his own embrace. If you are anxious, however, to hear what I am and have been, it will tell you something thereof. It is an idealized history of my life and feelings. I think one is always in love with something or other; the error, and I confess it is not easy for spirits cased in flesh and blood to avoid it, consists in seeking in a mortal image the likeness of what is perhaps eternal. (ii 434)[48]

The old familiar Shelley: Mary was bitter about what she called his "Italian Platonics",[49] his friendship with the beautiful young Emilia Viviani, who seemed almost to displace her in his imagination as she had displaced Harriet. Shelley thinks of himself as a spirit cased in flesh, not a body which thinks; he seeks the eternal while ignoring a "person"; he describes the object of his love as "something or other", or "a mortal image". And yet this passage, like the poem it refers to, is still a piece of moral thought, a display of self-awareness, which exceeds the capacity of the Shelley of *Alastor*, and promises further growth. That promise is still more evident in the poems Shelley wrote at Lerici in 1822 for yet another woman, Jane Williams, the wife of his close friend Edward. Shelley had by now entirely given up on "moral and political hope"; he wished "utterly to desert all human society", he told Mary, except "you & our child". He thought his mind should be "withdrawn from the contagion" of public affairs (ii 339). He read *Faust* repeatedly, wondering if this were not "the right road to Paradise" (ii 406). He read Calderón, too, and listened to Jane singing, as once he had read the Italian of Dante and listened to Cornelia Turner. The poems for Jane have (to quote one of them) "a tone/ Of some world far from ours" (p. 451), but they also display a wry humanity, a sense of relationship and of the other person, which is rare in Shelley. His mood of political apathy and relational contentment was new and, for him, unusual:

> ... if the past and the future could be obliterated, the present would content me so well that I could say with Faust to the passing moment, 'Remain, thou, thou art so beautiful'. ... I feel too little certainty of the future, and too little satisfaction with regard to the past, to undertake any subject seriously and deeply. I stand, as it were, upon a precipice, which I have ascended with great, and cannot descend without *greater*, peril, and I am content if the heaven above me is calm for the passing moment. (ii 435–6)

Could thinking about "the passing moment", the human part of the experience, be more fruitful, bring more contentment, than thinking about "serious and deep subjects" such as ideal moral excellence or practical political reform? Even to entertain this thought was to think in a new way, neither utilitarian nor expressionist, about poetry. It was in this particular passing moment, his last, that Shelley produced his best work: the poems for Jane Williams, and his great unfinished dream-vision "The Triumph of Life", a criticism of humanity in general and, significantly, of Rousseau in particular.

"A Defence of Poetry", Shelley's most famous essay and his only extensive prose statement about poetry, occupies an ambiguous position in the evolution we have been considering. Written in early 1821, at the same time as *Epipsychidion*, it points in a few places in new directions: towards the human, the self, moral discovery. But in other places, including in some of its most famous passages, as well as in its general tendency and heightened, polemical tone, it points in old directions: towards the Imagination, towards moralistic purpose, towards *Adonais*, that other defence of poetry written a few months later. Shelley was stung into response by Peacock's *The Four Ages of Poetry* (1820),[50] an extraordinarily powerful ironical essay, simultaneously a quasi-utilitarian attack on poetry, actually expressing views which Shelley himself had held not so many years before, and a masterly *reductio ad absurdum* of the utilitarian case. Shelley noticed only the former aspect of the essay, and produced a defence of poetry inspired immediately by Coleridge and Wordsworth, and ultimately by German Romantic theory. This was a defence not of poetry narrowly defined, as Peacock defines it, but of the Imagination, which Shelley now calls the "Sun of life", contrasting it with the "cold and uncertain and borrowed light" of "reason".[51] Here is Shelley's Italian rethinking of his early simple utilitarianism, with Imagination as the God instead of Reason. The "Defence" amounts to a first attempt by Shelley to write his "great work" of moral and political science, using Imagination, or "poetry in a general sense", as the redeeming Power, the promoter of "true utility" as against the "limited utility" promoted by utilitarian "reason" and praised by Peacock and the earlier Shelley (pp. 480, 500–2).

Seen in this light, the "Defence" is an occasionally dazzling, but sometimes dangerously muddled, statement of the nineteenth-century idealist case against a narrow Enlightenment-utilitarian conception of the reasoning self. Coleridge, Thomas Carlyle, Matthew Arnold, F. H. Bradley, T. H. Green and others wrote in this tradition, as did Hegel and his successors on the Continent. "Imagination" is Shelley's word (as it was others') for a fuller creative functioning of the whole self, individual and social, working through its senses and passions, not just its intellect or "reason". "Poets" are therefore "not only the authors of language and of music, of the dance and architecture and statuary and painting: they are the institutors of laws, and the founders of civil society and the inventors of the arts of life and the teachers" (p. 482). Legislators are the unacknowledged poets of the world, so to speak; the "true Poetry of Rome lived in its institutions" (p. 494). Shelley refers to the "poetry in these systems of thought", and claims that we "have more moral, political and historical wisdom, than we know how to reduce into practice". We "want the creative faculty to imagine that which we know; we want the generous impulse to act that which we imagine; we want the poetry of life" (p. 502). This piece of social psychology is almost Burkean in temper: nor would Hazlitt have disagreed with it. Here Shelley does indeed approach a statement of the general social theory he believed it his life's task to articulate. But he does not sustain the thinking. Furthermore he betrays his *dirigiste* approach to this kind of theory, an approach which Burke and Hazlitt would not have approved, by going on to argue that the "poet", in this peculiar sense of the word, "not only beholds intensely the present as it is" but "discovers those laws according to which present things *ought to be ordered*" (pp. 482–3; my emphasis). On this account of society ordinary people would have to accept that the poet-as-legislator was really discovering the "laws" ordering it and not just making them. The difference between Shelley's claim for poetry here and Hazlitt's, that in showing us "things as they are" poetry "implicitly teaches us what they ought to be", is precisely the difference between implicit teaching and unacknowledged legislating, between "ought to be" and "ought to be ordered". The extra step is a dangerous one, as we shall see when considering the "Ode to the West Wind" in Chapter 4.

Those passages of the "Defence" in which Shelley's thought points in new directions occur in the section concerned with "poetry" in its normal or Peacockian sense (paragraphs 11–31 of the essay's 48; pp. 486–500), which in Shelley's terms is its "more restricted sense" (p. 483). This section of the essay is a grand synoptic overview of European literature and its function within its societies. Shelley is quite unable to make the crucial case concerning poetry's influence for "social good" (p. 492); Peacock-as-utilitarian wins this argument, as utilitarians always will, because its terms are their own. Shelley also lapses into some unsustainable claims about the lives of poets (they are the wisest and happiest of people), and makes some more disturbing suggestions about their prophetic role. There is an almost indiscernible line, in Shelley's account, between claiming a special vision of the age and exercising a right to change the age. Poets are the "ministers" of the "spirit of good" which they are "compelled to serve" (p. 508), but who knows it is the Good, apart from them? All this aside, however, there are occasions when Shelley separates his account of poetry from his conviction of its reforming capacity. He speaks of Shakespeare's "living impersonations of the truth of human passions" (p. 490), or of how in watching or reading Greek drama the "imagination is enlarged by a sympathy with pains and passions so mighty, that they distend in their conception the capacity of that by which they are conceived": in *this* way the drama "teaches . . . self-knowledge and self-respect" (pp. 490–1). Dante's *Vita Nuova* "is an inexhaustible fountain of purity of sentiment and language"; he and the other great poets of love since the Renaissance have planted "as it were trophies in the human mind of that sublimest victory over sensuality and force" (p. 497). Milton's "bold neglect of a direct moral purpose" in making Satan such a magnificent character "is the most decisive proof of the supremacy of [his] genius" (p. 498). A "great Poem is a fountain for ever overflowing with the waters of wisdom and delight" (p. 500). In all these places Shelley is noticing how literature seems to reflect the temper of its age, rather than proclaiming it as the saviour of its age. Social corruption "begins at the imagination and the intellect as at the core" (p. 493); this is a piece of cultural diagnosis which avoids the tone of social engineering that creeps into so much of the "Defence". In these places Shelley is developing that same new view of poetry which informed his final poems, as a distinctive mode of passional thought concerned with human lives independent of ideal or political externalities.

CONCLUSION

Shelley's two principal views of poetry converged. He began with a utilitarian view, that "metaphorical language ought to be a pleasing vehicle for momentous & useful instruction", and an expressionist view, that poetry was forced out from the frightening passional abysses of the self. He ended with a view of the Imagination as a redemptive power in touch with Power itself. Those abysses were not frightening if the passions they contained were really the Ideas ordering all human beings; poetry could by grasping those Ideas both understand humanity and reform it. Shelley showed some signs of developing a third view of poetry, as a manner of thinking metaphorically with the passions, not analytically about them, but when he died this view was still rudimentary. His developed view was thus very close to the Coleridgean-symbolist conception of poetry adumbrated in Chapter 1, but with a strongly moralist strain. His version of the Imagination both apprehended the Ideas beyond objects in the world and used its apprehension of them to justify its attempt to change the world. Shelley's detractors dislike the Coleridgean-symbolist conception of poetry; transcending the world may entail indifference to it. But Shelley's merging of the desire to transcend the world with the desire to change it has disturbed his opponents even more. Meanwhile, many of his defenders have adopted something very close to Shelley's symbolist-moralist view of poetry, although the best ones have played down the latter strain. What, then, is the reader to make of Shelley's thinking in poetry, as opposed to his thinking about it?

3

Shelley's Poetry, 1811–17

GENERAL INTRODUCTION: CHAPTERS 3–6

Each of the following chapters may be read in tandem with one section of Chapter 2: this chapter with the second section, Chapters 4 and 5 with the third section and Chapter 6 with the fourth section. The four chapters offer full readings of nine poems, three from each of the periods of Shelley's life outlined in Chapter 2, and briefer comments on other poems, some of them related dispositionally rather than chronologically to the major poems under consideration. The correspondences with Chapter 2, then, are by no means exact, even chronologically: nor should they be taken as gestures towards biographical or intellectual referentialism. One of this book's primary contentions is that Shelley's poems are too often read chiefly as the vehicles of extra-poetic "ideas", or the effects of life "experiences", existing before and outside the poems. As we have seen, Shelley himself regarded some of his poems in this way, giving the lead to his referential admirers. Our concern in these chapters, on the contrary, will be with the poems' own personalities, their various senses of and capacities for life, the degrees and kinds of passional and metaphoric pressure they put or conceive it their function to put on ideas and life experiences: in short, with the poems not as inert receptacles or decorative reconfigurations but as genuinely transformative responses to ideas and experiences.

Three varieties of thought can be identified in Shelley's poetry. The first variety begins with *Queen Mab* and continues through "Mont Blanc" and *The Revolt of Islam* to *Prometheus Unbound* and "Ode to the West Wind". Here Shelley's thought typically swerves aside from a natural or human object to a reformist politico-moral idea or subject connected with the object by external intellectual associations rather than internal metaphorical ones. The object may then become a symbol for the idea. The poem's thought evaluates human lives and passions principally in terms of their connections with the idea. The second variety of thought begins with *Alastor* and continues through "Julian and Maddalo" and *The Cenci* to *Epipsychidion*, *Adonais* and (in some respects) "The Triumph of Life". This response is initially critical of the first kind for its ignoring of human relationship and passion, but the criticism is so deeply imbued with the spirit of what is being criticised that the second response collapses into a version of the first, celebrating the kind of life it proposes to condemn. Furthermore even in succesfully symbolising the passions they advocate these poems objectify those passions, turning them into things thought about, new kinds of ideas, rather than things thought with. The third variety of poetic thought is so rare in Shelley's work that we shall only be able to notice it once or twice in passing; it appears chiefly in his verse letters and familiar poems for women. This is a kind of thought in which human relationship is paramount and in which the passions are modes of thought, not objects of thought. Symbol is less important than metaphor. Roughly speaking, these three responses correspond to Shelley's three views of poetry as summarised in the first and fifth sections of Chapter 2: the reformist-idealist poetry with the utilitarian view of poetry; the poetry of objectified passion collapsing back into reformist idealism with the expressionist view of poetry collapsing back into a view of it as a means of using the passions to see the Idea; the poetry of human relationship with the view of poetry as a manner of thinking with passion rather than about it. We shall not return to critical generalisation about Shelley's poetry, however, until the Conclusion of this book; its next four chapters, in nine sections, are resolutely specific.

QUEEN MAB

We should say no more, perhaps, about most of Shelley's earliest poetry, or about his novels *Zastrozzi* (1810) and *St. Irvyne* (1811), than that their Gothic machinery of death, charnel-houses and pale warriors would have aroused thè admiration of Jane Austen's Catherine Morland – or Peacock's Scythrop Glowry, a character based on Shelley. That schoolboy interest in death did come to look very much like a lack of interest in life when Shelley was an adult: in *Adonais*, that is, as well as in *Alastor*. And in

the poetry of those early years Shelley sometimes showed a conversational facility and a technical virtuosity which hinted as
much at an urbanity and satirical vividness to come as the Gothic
pieces did at later escapes from life; see, for example, the "Letter to Edward Fergus Graham" and *The Devil's Walk: A Ballad*.[1]
But none of these works is substantial enough to sustain serious
attention. Shelley's first undeniably important work, the poem
which together with *Alastor* most deeply influenced his future
practice as a poet, was *Queen Mab*. He turned twenty while writing
it; expelled from Oxford, estranged from his father, married to
Harriet, he was no longer a schoolboy. Its evident strengths of
organisation and purpose, its imaginative energy sustained over
2300 lines, distinguish the poem not only from Shelley's earlier
work but from a good deal of his later, as well as from the immature poetry of his contemporaries. Keats's *Endymion*, for example, looks aimless by contrast, while Byron's *Hours of Idleness*
precisely represents its eponymous subject.

   Queen Mab raises essential evaluative questions about Shelley's
poetic thought. Although the poem consolidated Shelley's nineteenth-century reputation, it was a canonical text chiefly for
Owenites, Chartists and other socialist groups. Although Cameron
calls it "a great poem in its own right",[2] the modern critics who
have spent most time thinking about it are those whose concerns are primarily with Shelley's politics, such as Cameron himself, Michael Scrivener and P. M. S. Dawson.[3] As Richard Holmes
says, "*Queen Mab* is essentially subversive in intent, vigorously
polemic in attack, and revolutionary in content and implication".[4]
Its chief targets are organised religion, especially Christianity;
tyranny, of which monarchy is represented as a prime example;
"commerce", or modern political economy; "custom", oppressive
habits and traditions; prostitution; and war. Shelley's radical
political and social reformism topically echoes Godwin and Thomas
Paine; his utopian perfectibilism, of great significance for his later
work, derives chiefly from Condorcet's *Esquisse d'un Tableau des
Progrès de L'esprit Humain* (1795), according to which mankind is
indefinitely perfectible; his materialist or atomist metaphysics is
ultimately Lucretian but immediately derived from Holbach's
Système de la Nature (1770); and his social anthropology combines Condorcet's progressivist ameliorism with the apocalyptics
of Constantin Volney's *Les Ruines d'Empire* (1791), a traveller's
vision of aeons of ruined empires instantaneously replaced by a

paradisal future. In short, *Queen Mab* is a referentialist's gold mine: a minor episode in the history of ideas, a slightly more important moment in the history of politics.

Another kind of scholarship, it is true, has investigated the poem's prosodic and imaginative antecedents, principally Robert Southey's narrative verse fantasy *Thalaba the Destroyer* (1801), Peacock's minatory orientalising poem on the decline of civilisations, *Palmyra* (1806),[5] and Volney's *Ruines*, which influenced both Peacock and Southey. Shelley's device of transporting the soul of a sleeping girl, Ianthe, in the chariot of Mab the Fairy Queen, to a magic temple from which she can see the past, present and future of mankind and the natural world, as exposed in radical social and political terms by the Queen in the poem's central cantos, belongs in this imaginative tradition. The division of the poem into two "measures", as Shelley called them, a "blank heroic" or blank verse measure occupying two-thirds of the poem, and a "blank lyrical" iambic measure with lines of various lengths for the remainder (i 352), is prosodically identical to the method of *Thalaba*; the "blank lyrical" stanzas resemble those of *Palmyra*. But this kind of scholarship merely subserves the referential kind. Shelley's imagination may be Gothic, but his purposes are political. The preponderant blank verse is "didactic", as even he said; only the lyrics are "narrative" (i 352). This bald division of its poetic thought into the referentially explicable and the imaginatively instrumental is precisely what makes Shelley's first major poem critically important. Nine years after writing it Shelley himself publicly denounced *Queen Mab*, just re-issued in a pirated edition. He called it "perfectly worthless in point of literary composition" and "crude and immature" in its "moral and political speculation" (ii 304). He said the poem was "better fitted to injure than to serve the cause of freedom" (ii 305): too bald and aggressive in its radicalism, too clumsy, perhaps, in its yoking of the fantastic and the polemical. Privately he said that his denunciation of the poem was for "the sake of a dignified appearance" and because he really wanted "to protest against all the bad poetry in it" (ii 301). Shelley never renounced the fundamental political positions taken in the poem: nor could he have meant to condemn its prosodic structure, since that, and indeed the poem's overall proportions, are almost exactly those of *Prometheus Unbound*. What Shelley's private reference to "bad poetry" really suggests is that he came to see *Queen Mab* not so much as different in kind from what came later as an embarrassing precursor, a gauche and premature revelation of that disabling bond between the political and the imaginative – a chaining together, not a fusion – which shaped so many of his poems. This poem stands at the beginning of his mature career, not at the end of his juvenilia, and it amply repays our attention not for its place in the history of ideas or of prosody, but for its formative role in the history of Shelley's poetic thought.

Queen Mab is organised into nine sections or "cantos". The lyrical, narrative third of the poem comprises the whole of Cantos I and II, and short passages in later cantos. This narrative is grounded in a characteristically Shelleyan movement of poetic thought, disclosing itself in various forms, but so deeply and consistently constitutive of his thinking, so habitual with him, that it might be called his foundational poetic manoeuvre; it is a kind of arbitrary transference of thought, an associative sidestep. Queen Mab had its genesis in late 1811 in the conjunction of Shelley's prolific reading and his exposure to the impressive mountain scenery around Keswick. His mind was teeming with "ideas millions of ideas", he beheld the "gigantic mountains", and his imagination was "resistlessly compelled to look back" to another age. Volney contemplated the ruins of Palmyra and reflected that "these places, now so desert, a living multitude formerly animated",[6] but Shelley looked at the Keswick mountains and thought of Volney's Palmyra, or Holbach's atoms, or Condorcet's perfectibilism. The lyrical narrative third of Queen Mab is the poetic outcome of that movement of thought.

Ianthe is first discovered "motionless"; "silent" are "those sweet lips,/ Once breathing eloquence,/ That might have soothed a tiger's rage,/ Or thawed the cold heart of a conqueror" (I 32–6[7]). "Hath then the gloomy Power/ Whose reign is in the tainted sepulchres/ Seized on her sinless soul?", asks the narrator (I 9–10). And yet, he reflects, "How wonderful is Death" (I 1), a "gate of dreariness and gloom" which nevertheless "leads to azure isles and beaming skies/ And happy regions of eternal hope" (IX 161–3). Ianthe, we find, is after all only asleep; she has been judged "alone worthy of the envied boon,/ That waits the good and the sincere; that waits/ Those who have struggled, and with resolute will/ Vanquished earth's pride and meanness, burst the chains,/ The icy chains of custom" (I 123–7). Her "spirit" is therefore to be shown humanity's past, present and future, before she returns to her lover Henry (IX 237) to continue their struggle against "tyranny and falsehood" (IX 191), in which they are encouraged to seek that death which is so indistinguishable from sleep, and in which they may inhabit for ever those "happy regions" first glimpsed by Ianthe in her dream. The Fairy Queen who transports Ianthe's "spirit" to those regions is "slight" as "yon fibrous cloud . . . which the straining eye can hardly seize"; but the morning star itself sheds "not a light so mild, so powerful". Her "clear silver tones" are "such/ As are unheard by all but the gifted ear" (I 94–113). Ianthe's spirit is the "perfect semblance of its bodily frame", yet "oh, how· different!" "One aspires to Heaven,/ Pants for its sempiternal heritage . . . [and] Wantons in endless being", while the other "like an useless and worn-out machine, Rots, perishes, and passes" (I 133–156). As for the magic temple where they go to look at the Earth and its history (II 1–29),

> If solitude hath ever led thy steps
> To the wild ocean's echoing shore. . . .
> . . . there is a moment
> When the sun's highest point
> Peeps like a star o'er ocean's western edge,
> When those far clouds of feathery gold,
> Shaded with deepest purple, gleam
> Like islands on a dark blue sea;
> Then has thy fancy soared above the earth,
> And furled its wearied wing
> Within the Fairy's fane.

None of these natural objects, however, affords so "fair, so wonderful a sight/ As Mab's ethereal palace": which in turn affords a still more wonderful Volneyan-Holbachian perspective on human history, as the Queen explains it to the spirit of Ianthe (II 162–243):

> "Where Athens, Rome, and Sparta stood,
> There is a moral desert now. . . .
>
> Spirit! ten thousand years
> Have scarcely past away,
> Since, in the waste where now the savage drinks

His enemy's blood, and aping Europe's sons,
Wakes the unholy song of war,
Arose a stately city,
Metropolis of the western continent. . . .

There's not one atom of yon earth
But once was living man . . .
Thou canst not find one spot
Whereon no city stood.

I tell thee that those viewless beings,
Whose mansion is the smallest particle
Of the impassive atmosphere,
Think, feel and live like man;
That their affections and antipathies,
Like his, produce the laws
Ruling their moral state;
And the minutest throb
That through their frame diffuses
The slightest, faintest motion,
Is fixed and indispensable
As the majestic laws
That rule yon rolling orbs."

This over-condensed summary of the poem's lyrical narrative
nevertheless reveals the persistent turning aside of Shelley's poetic
thought from a human or natural object to a moralised or intellectualised subject or idea. We are presented with the sleeping
Ianthe and her wakeful Henry, but told nothing more about them
than that she has "struggled" against "earth's pride and meanness". She is encouraged to seek death, not to explore life, because life is merely that struggle, while death is a place of "azure
isles". It is Ianthe's spirit which has "being", not her bodily self.
The Fairy and her temple are in some unexplained way *like* clouds,
stars and so on, but *better*. Real landscapes or objects are used
only to suggest ideal ones, which have no accidental qualities of
their own, but only the essential quality of being better; the connection between the two is otherwise undemonstrated. The account of man's "moral state", of the "moral desert" which has
succeeded Athens and Rome, does not extend to an exploration
of Ianthe's moral state, but only to a determinist consideration

of the "affections and antipathies" of plants and atoms in one direction, and to an enormously generalised account of human history in the other: "ten thousand years/ Have scarcely passed away". Shelley produced two important transformations of *Queen Mab*: *The Revolt of Islam* in 1817 and *Prometheus Unbound* in 1818-19. Both employed magic machinery, with revolutionary heroes and heroines (Laon and Cythna, Prometheus and Asia) instructed by wise gods (the Woman, Demogorgon) and transported to post-revolutionary paradises. The earlier poem more closely resembles *Queen Mab* in its characters; its plot is a kind of filling in and development of what is left unsaid in *Queen Mab*. The later one closely resembles *Queen Mab* in its proportions and prosody. Both operate within the terms set by Shelley's first major work; in both human terms are displaced by political ones. The turning aside from a human or natural object which characterises *Queen Mab* came, indeed, to be Shelley's signature in much of his later work. To his admirers, of course, this is precisely the symbolist or relational manoeuvre which they find attractive: the association of a discrete object with a complex structure of ideas. To others, however, to a Cora Diamond as well as a T. S. Eliot, this is not association but "dissociation".

The political argument of *Queen Mab*, meanwhile, takes place in the larger blank verse "didactic" portion of the poem, occupying most of Cantos III–IX. As we have seen, the basic structural feature of the poem, its division into the sketchiest of narrative passages and a manifesto-like didactic tome buttressed by copious prose notes, clearly exhibits that same dissociation of object from subject which is also present in the thought. Shelley later disliked the obviousness of the structural division, but it is still there in later work: only better hidden. He never really noticed the division as it operated in his thought. In Cantos III–VI we are told, in angry Enlightenment terms with some eccentric variations, that "Selfishness" and her twin-sister "Religion", sustained by "precedent and custom", have spawned all human and natural ills, including tyranny, war, commerce, prostitution and the eating of meat. In Canto VII the figure of Ahasuerus, the legendary Wandering Jew, is offered as the type of resistance to these ills, in terms closely anticipating Prometheus's resistance to Jupiter. In the last two cantos the paradise to come is described; again, there are anticipations of *Prometheus Unbound*. The whole intellectual structure of this argument is founded on two concepts, one metaphysical and the other psychological: Necessity and free will. These two ideas, and especially the former, are almost as important conceptually in Shelley's poetic thought as the dissociating transference or sidestep just mentioned is important figuratively.

Shelley's conception of what he calls "Necessity" is expounded by the Fairy Queen in two principal passages in the poem (IV 139–67, VI 197–219), and by Shelley in a long prose note. These are the key lines from the Fairy's exposition:

> "Throughout this varied and eternal world
> Soul is the only element; the block
> That for uncounted ages has remained
> The moveless pillar of a mountain's weight
> Is active, living spirit. Every grain
> Is sentient both in unity and part,
> And the minutest atom comprehends
> A world of loves and hatreds; these beget
> Evil and good: hence truth and falsehood spring;
> Hence will and thought and action, all the germs
> Of pain or pleasure, sympathy or hate,
> That variegate the eternal universe."

> "Spirit of Nature! all-sufficing Power,
> Necessity! thou mother of the world!
> Unlike the God of human error, thou
> Requirest no prayers or praises; the caprice
> Of man's weak will belongs no more to thee
> Than do the changeful passions of his breast
> To thy unvarying harmony . . .
> No love, no hate thou cherishest; revenge
> And favouritism, and worst desire of fame
> Thou knowest not: all that the wide world contains
> Are but thy passive instruments, and thou
> Regardst them all with an impartial eye,
> Whose joy or pain thy nature cannot feel,
> Because thou hast not human sense,
> Because thou art not human mind."

Shelley scholarship has traced the poet's debts to or differences from Godwin, Hume, Holbach, Drummond, Lucretius and Plato in his account of Necessity.[8] The first three of these philosophers are the most actively present in the verse and the note; the philosophical question to be raised is whether Shelley is more like Godwin and Holbach, dogmatically determinist in their account of necessity as a part of the structure of reality, or more like Hume, subtly sceptical in his account of it as a feature of the mind.[9] One might also speculate on whether something in Shelley was tugging him towards a Platonic–Kantian sense of some quasi-divine or noumenal enabler of experience which is nevertheless itself inaccessible to experience.[10] He is perhaps closest of all to Volney, who addresses the "Sovereign and mysterious Power of the Universe! secret Mover of Nature! universal Soul of everything that lives!"[11] But the significance of Shelley's account of Necessity in *Queen Mab* does not lie primarily in its contribution to the history of philosophy, which is negligible. It lies in what Shelley made of the concept in this poem, and subsequently in others. In the two passages quoted above he develops the image of the "viewless beings" from Canto II, such that Necessity becomes the "Soul of the Universe" (VI 190), a kind of world-soul (the phrase has a post-Kantian flavour, an air of Schelling or Schopenhauer), which permeates matter so that matter is not just physically but morally sentient. The moral world reaches right down into the atomic structure of matter; indeed the moral world is dissolved into materialism. Canto IV further argues that "soul" only falls into division, into separate atoms and their "loves and hatreds", when mixed with matter on earth. When free of matter soul again becomes one being, Necessity, the "mother of the world" who knows "No love, no hate", no "Evil and good". It is the goal of "soul" on earth, therefore, to regain this universal consciousness. Until then, however, Necessity cannot be an immediately available ally or guardian against Selfishness and Religion so much as an abstract principle of certainty that these ills are not eternal. Having dissolved the moral realm into the material one, human life into atoms, Shelley has nothing left to hold on to, short of an hypostasised principle.

Furthermore, he has nothing to hold on *with*, short of an equally hypostatic "will", the only link to that invisible divinity and to the "reality of Heaven" (IX 1, 11) to come. The "eternal world/ Contains at once the evil and the cure", the Queen tells Ianthe's soul, but the cure has to be administered by "Some eminent in virtue" such as Ianthe and Henry (VI 31-3). Their chief instrument is what Shelley called in a letter of this period the *"fixed and virtuous will"* (i 251). In *Queen Mab* "the outcast man" (III 199) is distinguished from all other "souls" by his larger capacity for good and evil, attributable to his "all-subduing will" (V 133). The "good and the sincere" are those like Ianthe, who "have struggled, and with resolute will/ Vanquished earth's pride and meanness" (I 124–6). Those of "resolute mind" (IX 200) know that "when the power of imparting joy/ Is equal to the will, the human soul/ Requires no other Heaven" (III 11–13). "The virtuous man" is the one who "leads/ Invincibly a life of resolute good"; before his "resolute and unchanging will" kings can only "tremble" (III 150–3, 166; V 171). His "life of resolute good,/ Unalterable will, quenchless desire/ Of universal happiness" is an "axe" to "Strike at the root" of selfishness (V 225–7, IV 82–3). The phantom of Ahasuerus wages "unweariable war" with his "almighty tyrant", mocking his "horrible curse/ With stubborn and unalterable will" (VII 198–9, 257–8); after this highly Promethean battle Religion the tyrant will be superseded by, and the human will subsumed in, "the will of strong necessity" (VI 234). "Will" appears in this poem not as a quality of character to be explored but as an empty psychological token, a desperate conceptual resolution of a metaphysical and moral dilemma. There is no real bridge in the poem between the evil present and the heavenly future, Selfishness and Necessity, a landscape and a vision of human history, Ianthe and the Revolution, human freedom and an inhuman divinity. Instead there is only "will", a naked and thin insistence, which is ultimately Shelley's own, that paradise be regained. This is a manoeuvre founded like the dissociation of thought we considered earlier, or like the parallel treatment of Necessity, not so much on a metaphorical connection between one event and another as on what Hume sceptically called "constant conjunction",[12] the mere adjacency of two ideas, or of an idea and a desire.

Queen Mab registers a radical discontinuity or arbitrariness in Shelley's poetic thought, especially about people or lives. This is not simply a matter of structure, of the poem's division into impassioned doctrinal polemic and indifferent human narrative. Nor is it principally a conceptual matter, a failure to show "Necessity" and "will" as any more than one-dimensional tokens, articles of faith without metaphysical or psychological plausibility or substance. The salient discontinuity is simultaneously metaphorical and moral. The poem juxtaposes human passions and intellectual ideas without finding those integrating metaphorical resemblances between them which would make their adjacencies appear causal rather than casual, and which might even initiate genuine life-discoveries involving both the passions and the ideas. *Queen Mab* is the first in a series of metaphysico-revolutionary works and passages of poetry by Shelley which constitute one of the principal voices or lines of thought in his poetry. All these works manifest the same radical discontinuity, notwithstanding their increasing panache in concealing it.

ALASTOR

The other chief line of thought in Shelley's poetry was inaugurated by *Alastor*, extending through "Julian and Maddalo" and *The Cenci* to *Epipsychidion* and *Adonais*. This line of thought is predominantly in heroic verse and concerns itself, as its rival does not, with self-exploration and with the passions. We should of course take care when speaking of two principal Shelleyan voices not to suppress others, above all that of the polished conversationalist and poet of human relationship, in a series of shorter lyrics starting with the "Letter to Edward Fergus Graham", and continuing through the poems for Claire Clairmont and Sophia Stacey to the "Letter to Maria Gisborne" and the poems for Jane Williams. The buffooning satirist of *The Devil's Walk*, and eventually of "Peter Bell the Third" and "Swellfoot the Tyrant", and the hallucinated seer, as demagogue in *The Mask of Anarchy* and as pilgrim in "The Triumph of Life", may or may not be assimilable to the two primary voices. But nearly all Shelley's major poetry was written with an eye either to the revolutionary intrusions of Necessity into the world, as in *Queen Mab*, or to the condition of the self within the world, as in *Alastor*.

The latter voice, notably, is critical of the former. Shelley's own preface reads the poem as an exploration of the consequences for the solitary self of a fanatical and vain search for Necessity. According to the preface (pp. 69-70) the poem "represents a youth" who is "joyous, and tranquil, and self-possessed" so long as his "desires . . . point towards objects . . . infinite and unmeasured". This is a state of "self-centred seclusion". When, however (or therefore), this "Poet" "images to himself the Being whom he loves" he does so in terms of an unattainable ideal, and "seeks in vain for a prototype of his conception. Blasted by his dis-appointment, he descends to an untimely grave". Even so, the preface concludes, how much better to be one of the few "pure and tender-hearted" seekers of perfection, albeit in their "vacancy of spirit", than to be one of the "selfish, blind, and torpid" mul-titude, the "morally dead" who "love not their fellow-beings". A closing quotation from *The Excursion* leaves the distinct im-pression that Wordsworth belongs to the second category, while the whole preface suggests that the younger Shelley belonged to the first. The preface is clearly being written by an older Shelley, of course, and – as criticism since Wasserman has repeatedly emphasised[13] – the poem proper is narrated by a speaker who is quite distinct from the Poet, the "youth" who is the poem's pro-tagonist. Clearly, then, *Alastor* is an essay in self-criticism, a re-flection on the self of *Queen Mab* and other earlier work. The few shorter poems Shelley had written since *Queen Mab* had perhaps disclosed to him the flimsiness of a self built on no more than the "moral sense", on moral indignation and political po-lemic, on belief in Necessity. The real passion in his relationship with Mary, or the realisation of its absence from his relationship with Harriet, collapsed this earlier self very easily. Poem after poem shows us nothing but dark moors, clouds veiling the moon, children "Sporting on graves", "changed and withered" poets, "Mutability" and "Misery, oh Misery".[14] Perhaps Shelley sensed that only a poetic revisiting of the passional self could heal the divisions of *Queen Mab*. In any case, where the foundations of *Queen Mab* are philosophical, those of *Alastor* are literary. Wordsworth, in particular, is everywhere. He is a possible model for the Poet; he is quoted in the preface; "Tintern Abbey", the "Immortality" ode and *The Excursion* are echoed within the poem. Coleridge is another possible model for the Poet, and there are echoes of "The Eolian Harp" and "Frost at Midnight". Godwin's novel *Fleetwood* (1805) attacks solitude in Alastorean terms.[15] The influential *Agathon*, by the German novelist C. M. Wieland, which Shelley read in translation in 1814,[16] also has a young poet-hero who pursues a vision of a woman. Although biographicalists have been interested in *Alastor* in relation to the Shelley-Mary-Harriet triangle,[17] the poem has far less to offer the referentialists than *Queen Mab*. This is poetry that at least wants to be poetry, wants to think about a life.

Alastor is in 720 lines of blank verse, and like *Queen Mab* it can be divided into two parts. The first contains the main narrative and a didactic framework. It comprises the two opening paragraphs (1–49), in which the narrator ritualistically asks a "Great Parent" to "favour [his] solemn song"; the central story of "the Poet" in seven paragraphs (50–271), from his birth *via* his education and his fateful imagining of a "veiled maid" to his disappearance from the human world; and a closing paragraph in which the narrator laments his death (672–720). The other part of the poem is a 13-paragraph, 400-line account (272–671) of the Poet's solitary boat and river journey, across a near-fantasy Caucasian landscape, in search of death. This is the more impressive part of the poem; it is symbolic rather than moralistic.

The opening invocation (1–49) is addressed to "Earth, ocean, air, beloved brotherhood", but immediately behind or beyond this natural trinity stands the single transcendent "Mother of this unfathomable world". She has no other name in *Alastor*, but she is almost indistinguishable from the "mother of the world" in *Queen Mab*: Necessity. The narrator tells her "I have loved thee ever and thee only", seeking her with "obstinate questionings" in "charnels and on coffins" like "an inspired and desperate alchymist"; like the Gothic Shelley of the early poems and novels, or the Frankenstein of Mary's novel. The narrator never found her "inmost sanctuary", but he glimpsed enough, he says,

> . . . that serenely now
> And moveless, as a long-forgotten lyre
> Suspended in the solitary dome
> Of some mysterious and deserted fane,
> I wait thy breath, Great Parent, that my strain
> May modulate with murmurs of the air,
> And motions of the forests and the sea,
> And voice of living beings, and woven hymns
> Of night and day, and the deep heart of man.

The reflection on Necessity carries far more experiential weight here than it did in *Queen Mab*. The passage from *Queen Mab* VI quoted earlier was an address to an utterly abstract concept, an ideal entity which was exciting for Shelley precisely because it did *not* have "human sense" or "human mind". Now, however, his attention is focussed not on Necessity but on the states of mind of her devotee, his earlier desperate searchings and his present serenity. This invocation carries the authority of the witness. Neither Shelley nor this narrator may ever see Necessity, but they know what it feels like to look for her. This means that the passage cannot be read as a successful ironical criticism of its own narrator, exposed as one of the "morally dead" of the preface, a Wordsworthian pensioner and apostate. Neither nature's "beloved brotherhood" in the first paragraph nor the search for the "Great Parent" in the second are presented by the narrator in anything like the terms of "Tintern Abbey" or the "Immortality" ode – quotations notwithstanding. Wordsworth obstinately questions "sense and outward things", but for him they are "beauteous forms", not forms of Beauty.[18] Even the Ode intimates something very different from a Shelleyan Necessity. Shelley may or may not have intended his narrator to be an ironically distanced Wordsworthian figure, but what he actually produced was a superficially Wordsworthian variant of his own current and recent poetic self, temporarily at rest after storms emotional and metaphysical; a variant whose serenity is asserted in terms neither ironical nor plausible. The narrator is represented as patiently awaiting, not anxiously seeking, the "breath" of Necessity, but there is little sign that the authenticity of this patience is being as closely questioned as it should be by a mind really thinking beyond the terms of *Queen Mab*. The narrator is still a believer, still alone, forgotten and motionless, but the poem's attitude to this continuing vulnerability is not one of ironical awareness or renunciation so much as of contented *un*awareness. The shape of the frame surrounding the Poet's story must fundamentally affect how we read the story, and the speaker of these introductory paragraphs is distinguished from the Poet only by persistence and luck; unlike the Poet, he happens to have seen enough of Necessity to content him. The outcome of the quest differs, but the quest itself is still the same. The standpoint of the narrator can thus hardly be distinguished from that of the poem as a whole.

The education of the Poet himself (67–128), meanwhile, is the first major appearance of a setpiece as important in Shelley's poetic thought as the address to Necessity in *Queen Mab*. Here, if anywhere, the thought's focus should shift from Necessity to the life of her devotee.

By solemn vision, and bright silver dream,
His infancy was nurtured. Every sight
And sound from the vast earth and ambient air,
Sent to his heart its choicest impulses.
The fountains of divine philosophy
Fled not his thirsting lips, and all of great
Or good, or lovely, which the sacred past
In truth or fable consecrates, he felt
And knew. When early youth had past, he left
His cold fireside and alienated home
To seek strange truths in undiscovered lands.
      . . . Nature's most secret steps
He like her shadow has pursued. . . .

            His wandering step
Obedient to high thoughts, has visited
The awful ruins of the days of old:
Athens, and Tyre, and Balbec, and the waste
Where stood Jerusalem. . . .
      . . . [on these he] ever gazed
And gazed, till meaning on his vacant mind
Flashed like strong inspiration, and he saw
The thrilling secrets of the birth of time.

The critical importance of this passage lies not in its account of
an education but in its final moment, when the "meaning" of
such an education must of course fail to flash upon the reader.
These "thrilling secrets" can only remain thrilling while they are
still secrets. Nor can we credit Shelley with a recognition of this
point. The Poet's wanderings, and those of his many fellows in
other versions of the passage elsewhere, are reflected upon sympathetically and appealingly in the poetry. No doubt the passage does constitute a comment of some kind on the links betweeen
such an education and its beneficiary's likely fate, but not an
evidently ironical or critical kind. So far, indeed, it is not clear
from the poem that anything at all is wrong with this Poet's life.
Still, it is true that from now on things do begin to go wrong.
We hear of "an Arab maiden" who "brought his food" and his
bedding every day, or rather gave him her own; though "Wildered,
and wan, and panting", she is too much in awe of him to "speak
her love", and he ignores her. This episode (129–39) does evoke

the Poet's self-centredness and vacancy of spirit, but one cannot help thinking that his inexperience and her silence between them amount to significant mitigating circumstances, at least in a first offence. The provoking little passage is the poem's only attempt to explore human relationship, but it does nothing to explore the deeper connections between such an offence, the Poet's only one against anyone other than himself, and its moral anteced- ents. *Alastor* may want to think about a life, but it seems uncer- tain how to.

What follows in the next two paragraphs (140–222) is never- theless the climax of the poem. An avenging "vision" is sent by the "spirit of sweet human love" to "him who spurned/ Her choicest gifts". Everything that now happens to the Poet, and in effect he is sentenced to death by a spirit of love, must depend heavily on that single word "spurned", just because of the thin- ness of the moral thought in what has gone before.

> . . . A vision on his sleep
> There came, a dream of hopes that never yet
> Had flushed his cheek. He dreamed a veiled maid
> Sate near him, talking in low solemn tones.
> Her voice was like the voice of his own soul
> Heard in the calm of thought. . . .
> Knowledge and truth and virtue were her theme,
> And lofty hopes of divine liberty,
> Thoughts the most dear to him, and poesy,
> Herself a poet.

She sings in "wild numbers" and plays "some strange harp"; he hears her heart beating in the "pauses of her music". Then she rises:

> . . . at the sound he turned,
> And saw by the warm light of their own life
> Her glowing limbs beneath the sinuous veil
> Of woven wind, her outspread arms now bare,
> Her dark locks floating in the breath of night,
> Her beamy bending eyes, her parted lips
> Outstretched, and pale, and quivering eagerly.
> His strong heart sunk and sickened with excess
> Of love. He reared his shuddering limbs and quelled

His gasping breath, and spread his arms to meet
Her panting bosom . . . she drew back a while,
Then, yielding to the irrestistible joy,
With frantic gesture and short breathless cry
Folded his frame in her dissolving arms.
Now blackness veiled his dizzy eyes. . . .

He wakes, to find the natural world empty of the meaning with which it had been charged for him before. "He eagerly pursues/ Beyond the realms of dream that fleeting shade;/ He overleaps the bounds"; he begins to wonder whether death may be the only way back to these "delightful realms" of sleep. Driven by "insatiate hope", goaded by a "passion" like "the fierce fiend of a distempered dream", he hastens in the next three paragraphs (222–307) across Europe and Asia until at "the lone Chorasmian shore" (probably the Aral Sea) he sets out in a "little shallop" to seek death. We must again distinguish here between the poem's evident moral purposes and its contrary emotional behaviour. The Poet suffers the fate of one who devotes himself to Necessity and ignores humanity, not least his own. His ardency in the pursuit of "thrilling secrets" is diverted into narcissistic passion in the shape of an alastor or evil demon by his spurning of the Arab maiden. But the pursuit of Necessity is so enthusiastically and the spurning of the maiden so cursorily represented that the poem's criticism of the Poet is not properly registered. And now the effect of his seduction by the alastor is far more erotic than cautionary. Glowing limbs, bare arms, outstretched and parted lips, shuddering limbs, gasping breath, panting bosom, irresistible joy, breathless cry: this is a discharging of feelings which Shelley has surrendered to but not thought with, feelings powerful enough to subvert his purposes. This alastor is no Keatsian lamia; this Poet is no Lycius. There are, to be sure, always critics who claim to see deeper ironies in Shelley's inconsistencies. William Keach, for example, argues that the

'short-circuited comparisons', 'self-inwoven similes', and other reflexive locutions in *Alastor* are intrinsic to Shelley's ambivalent exploration of solipsism, radical idealism and imaginative self-sufficiency. . . . Reflexive imagery functions . . . by enacting verbally the process through which the wandering poet's imagination projects the self as other. . . . The point of saying

that the wandering poet sees the dream-maiden's limbs 'by
the warm light of their own life' is, I think, that the very same
power is responsible for the life of those limbs and for the
fact of their being 'seen' – namely, the protagonist's imagination. . . . What might at first appear to be vague and gratuitous erotic intensification turns out to serve a distinct expressive
purpose. Even the words 'warm' and 'glowing' suggest the
way in which qualities of the dreamer's fervid imagination have
been transferred to the projected self-reflection.[19]

No short extract can do justice to Keach's subtle argument, but
this one is a fair representative of the case made out in his book
for *Alastor,* and indeed for all Shelley's poetry: that what look
like failures of thought are really purposeful successes. What we
are encountering in these lines is the Poet's surrender to emotional fantasy, not Shelley's. The reflexive imagery is not a failed
attempt to represent the dream-maiden's limbs but a successful
representation of the Poet's terminal narcissism. Shelley is a better dramatist and ironist than his detractors can understand.
Keach's argument combines theoretical ingenuity (that image isn't
meaningless, it's *reflexive*) with critical knowingness (he's doing
it *on purpose*), and confronted with it the Hazlittean's only recourse is to common sense. Will we make more sense or less of
the image of someone seeing a glowing object by the light of its
own life after we have been told that it is his fervid imagination
which has created and seen the object, its life and its light? Is
that a persuasive reading or a forensic *coup*? Which stays most
enduringly with us, the "vague and gratuitous erotic intensification" or the "distinct expressive purpose"? How compelling is
the pattern in the carpet when even after being pointed out it is
hard to find again among all the bold shapes and bright colours? Shouldn't we concede that the colours and shapes are the
carpet's compelling attributes, those which actually make it look
the way it does?

The colours and shapes of *Alastor* are still distracting the reader's
eye from its moral pattern as the poem's didactic framework is
completed, in the narrator's concluding lament for the Poet after
his eventual death (671–720). Here again the dramatic and ironic
separations between the poem and its narrator, the narrator and
the Poet and thus the poem and the Poet are hard to see.

> O, that the dream
> Of dark magician in his visioned cave,
> Raking the cinders of a crucible
> For life and power, even when his feeble hand
> Shakes in its last decay, were the true law
> Of this so lovely world! But thou art fled
> Like some frail exhalation; which the dawn
> Robes in its golden beams, – ah! thou hast fled!
> The brave, the gentle, and the beautiful,
> The child of grace and genius. . . .
> . . . Art and eloquence,
> And all the shews o' the world are frail and vain
> To weep a loss that turns their lights to shade.
> It is a woe too "deep for tears", when all
> Is reft at once, when some surpassing Spirit,
> Whose light adorned the world around it, leaves
> Those who remain behind, not sobs or groans,
> The passionate tumult of a clinging hope;
> But pale despair and cold tranquillity,
> Nature's vast frame, the web of human things,
> Birth and the grave, that are not as they were.

Despite the direct and indirect quotations from Wordsworth, this voice is no more Wordsworthian than it was at the poem's outset. The lines are elegiac, not critical or ironical; their distant precursor is Milton's *Lycidas*, their Shelleyan successor *Adonais*. The Poet may have suffered a "vacancy of spirit", as the preface put it, but here he is nevertheless a "surpassing Spirit"; this narrator will not allow us to remember his vacancy as vividly as his passion. And if the narrator is uncritical of the Poet, the poem is hardly more critical of the narrator. His initial serenity has become a "cold tranquillity" in the telling of this tale, but that earlier mood is not re-examined and re-evaluated in this conclusion: merely forgotten. We are left, as the poem closes, hearing not the admonitions of the preface but a passionate extenuation of the life just ended: the life of solitude and of the search for Necessity. Shelley's deeper fascination with that life has subverted his recent recognition and intended representation of its disadvantages.

The larger and more successful part of the poem (272–671) comprises an account of the Poet's journey in search of death:

from the "lone Chorasmian shore" where he launches his "little shallop", across a great sea, through a tempest and the collision of the "boiling torrent" with the foot of the Caucasus, up inside a mountain borne on a whirlpool, to an enchanted cove at the top surrounded by "yellow flowers" which (in rather better "reflexive imagery") "gaze on their own drooping eyes/ Reflected in the crystal calm". A "Spirit" seems to beckon him on, appearing in the end only as "two eyes,/ Two starry eyes, hung in the gloom of thought". He follows a "rivulet" through the "dell". "Thou imagest my life", he tells the stream; at first it seems "like childhood laughing", but later it flows through a barren landscape, rocky and treeless, indicative of old age, and finally falls, from beside a solitary pine tree, over a precipice and into "the universe". The Poet lies down to die in this last "green recess". Death, the "king of this frail world", has finally claimed him, and the closing lament follows. This prolonged symbolical evocation of the life of the solipsist intellectual is the poem's major success and the main reason to read it; the relatively brief treatment of it here is made possible only by the many fine accounts of it elsewhere.[20] The storm of passion, the boat which is the body, its navigator the self, the mountain which seems to be matter or physical energy, the cove and its narcissi representing the self-enclosed mind, the stream of life, the lone pine looking out over space as the lonely mind contemplates eternity: these images collectively have a force and resonance beyond anything Shelley had yet done, even beyond much of what he was still to do.

> Grey rocks did peep from the spare moss, and stemmed
> The struggling brook: tall spires of windlestrae
> Threw their thin shadows down the rugged slope,
> And nought but knarled roots of antient pines
> Branchless and blasted, clenched with grasping roots
> The unwilling soil. . . .
>   . . . A pine
> Rock-rooted, stretched athwart the vacancy
> Its swinging boughs, to each inconstant blast
> Yielding one only response, at each pause
> In most familiar cadence . . . whilst the broad river,
> Foaming and hurrying o'er its rugged path,
> Fell into that immeasurable void
> Scattering its waters to the passing winds.

Now Shelley really is rethinking Wordsworth for his own poetic purposes. His imagery achieves a mysterious reconstitution of physical objects as indications of something else, in this case the life-condition of the Poet, such that the images "take on a life of their own", as R. H. Fogle said.[21] This hallucinatory landscape-transformation informs Shelley's poetic thought at its most impressive as much as the landscape-avoidance we noticed in *Queen Mab* informs it at its least; indeed the former is the successful version of the latter, visible in much of Shelley's best work through to "The Triumph of Life", some of whose key opening passages are anticipated here. The admonitory doctrinal voice is absent; any underlying "moral sense" is absorbed in the physical details.

Still, even this haunting symbolical landscape has finally to be read within the poem's didactic framework. *Alastor* has a purpose or utility, an "inculcated moral"; the landscape is there to reflect the already-determined condition of the Poet, a solitary Necessity-seeking self. There is no chance of his stumbling across a difficult or contrary feature in this landscape, no prospect of that real rethinking of the self which would constitute genuine human discovery. The Arab maiden remains a token presence, for the Poet and also for the poem. Even this more successful episode is constrained by the very view of the human condition that the poem as a whole seeks to explode. The passions are still rendered as external to the experiencing self, even if an extended symbolical landscape is an experientially richer and more responsive instrument for thus rendering them than a narcissised incubus. The less impressive half of the poem leaves the desire for human relationship unexplored, representing it as either incomprehensibly remote or demonically self-destructive; the more impressive half all too effectively represents the self as hermetically sealed. *Alastor* may at its best be a profound statement of what can happen to a poetic self like the one of *Queen Mab*, but it presents no alternative; it only shows that self reflecting on itself. The passions are still only material to reflect upon, symbolically: not yet material to reflect with, metaphorically. This second Shelleyan line of thought is critical of the first without altering its fundamental terms.

"MONT BLANC" AND OTHER POEMS

We have already noticed how in the minor poetry between *Queen Mab* and *Alastor* misery and mutability appeared as the dark side of an earlier enthusiasm, as Necessity without faith, so to speak. Between *Alastor* and the highly Alastorean "Julian and Maddalo" three years later Shelley had little more success in breaking free from already established patterns of poetic thought. For example the seven-stanza 84-line "Hymn to Intellectual Beauty", written in Switzerland in the summer of 1816, was a re-dramatisation and renewal of the Poet's search for an hypostasised Necessity, without the Alastorean criticism. The "Hymn" is addressed to a "Spirit of Beauty" or "unseen power" which is compared in the first four stanzas to a long string of natural objects and events, and another of human emotions; but the objects and the emotions are completely unconnected except by the Spirit, whose sole attribute is thus their contiguity. This absence of metaphorical connection prevents us from learning any more about such a Spirit than that the speaker, whose voice is almost impossible to distinguish from Shelley's own, very much wants there to be one. The last three stanzas of the poem accordingly explore that desire; we see again the boyhood search for Necessity and a thrilling moment of discovery: "Sudden, thy shadow fell on me;/ I shrieked, and clasped my hands in extasy". Again, as in *Alastor*, all the reader can hear is the shriek; but this time the undiscoverable moment has important life consequences for the devotee and anyone connected with him: "I vowed that I would dedicate my powers/ To thee and thine" in "hope that thou wouldst free/ This world from its dark slavery". The "Hymn" has little to add to the thought of *Queen Mab* and *Alastor*, but the later poem suggests a disturbing political dimension to that thought: it may be no more capable of showing, other than by assertion, the connections between the political and metaphysical roles of Necessity, or between the political roles of Necessity and the speaker, than it is of showing the connection between Necessity and the natural world. We shall return to this point in Chapter 4 when considering the "Ode to the West Wind", the greater successor to the "Hymn".

Another poem unable, despite its size, to alter the patterns and styles of thought inherited from *Queen Mab* and *Alastor* was *The Revolt of Islam*, Shelley's major effort of 1817 and by far his longest work.[22] In this twelve-canto, 5000-line epic in Spenserian stanzas, another politico-metaphysical declaration in the voice of the "Hymn" introduces a story adapted from *Queen Mab*. The revolutionary Laon has the education of the Alastorean Poet. Cythna, his lover and, in the poem's earlier version, his sister, is also his comrade in their struggle against a tyrant. After their death at the stake the hero and heroine are translated to a magic paradise. Images of Necessity as a symbol of Truth and Liberty abound in the poem, but the relationship between the two revolutionaries is no more developed than those between Henry and Ianthe, or the Poet and the alastor. Passion is introduced into the story merely as decoration. The effect of the thought is that the best life is the one devoted to the search for Necessity, and that a satisfactory human relationship is only possible between two people for each of whom the relationship is secondary to the search. Few of the shorter and minor poems of the years 1817–19, to glance ahead into Shelley's Italian years for a moment, did any more than the "Hymn" or the *Revolt* to extend or challenge the styles of poetic thought established by *Queen Mab* and *Alastor*. Many of these pieces were "misery" or "mutability" poems resembling those of the years before *Alastor*, imbued with a curiously remote melancholic moralism ("Death", "Invocation to Misery", "Stanzas Written in Dejection", "Prince Athanase", *Rosalind and Helen*[23]). Some were political polemics, their anger provoked and their images informed by contemporary events, their politico-metaphysical assumptions foreshadowed in *Queen Mab*, the "Hymn" and the *Revolt*. Two outstanding examples from the autumn of 1819 are the sonnet "England in 1819", with its sulphurous catalogue of political and religious abuses, and the broadside ballad called *The Mask of Anarchy*, a more significant piece which we shall return to in Chapter 4.

The poems which did take Shelley's thought further were of two kinds. On the one hand were poems which invested their objects or landscapes with meaning in the symbolic, non-doctrinal manner of the more successful parts of *Alastor*. The best examples of these are "Marianne's Dream",[24] with its succession of haunting dream images dominated by a "great black Anchor" hanging over them all, and the sonnet "Ozymandias", the most compressed, pictorial and ironically suggestive of all Shelley's short poems. On the other hand were poems for the women other than Mary whom Shelley from time to time found himself drawn to, such as "To Constantia", written in 1817 for Mary's half-sister and Byron's lover Claire Clairmont, and the group of poems written in the winter of 1819–20 for Sophia Stacey, a young English tourist living in Italy ("To Sophia", "Love's Philosophy", "Good-Night"[25]). In their conversational poise, their clarity and brevity, and their wry sense of human relationship these otherwise slight and often sentimental pieces manifest a style of thinking about about lives quite outside the range of *Queen Mab* and *Alastor*.

But the most powerful poem of the period between *Alastor* and Shelley's final departure from England was within that range, not outside it. "Mont Blanc" had nothing to do with human relationship; it was another reflection on the relationship between the solitary self and Necessity. It was, however, Shelley's most compelling work of that kind, his most successful discovery of "power" in a present landscape rather than a prior idea. This made the poem quite unlike its precursors, and especially unlike the contemporary "Hymn", where the existence of the Spirit or "unseen power" was simply declared. The single real successor and rival to "Mont Blanc" was the "Ode to the West Wind", which was less effective because the balance of "power" between the landscape and the observer had shifted too far towards the latter. But as Harold Bloom and Michael O'Neill have insisted,[26] "Mont Blanc" should be read not only as a successful metaphysical meditation but also as a poem – notwithstanding its lapses into syntactical and imaginative obscurity, and into philosophical and political systematising. The work's major affiliations are not to works of philosophy but to other poems, chiefly Wordsworth's "Tintern Abbey" (1798), with its sense of "something far more deeply interfused", and Coleridge's "Hymn Before Sunrise, in the Vale of Chamouni" (1802), with its claim that no-one can look at such a scene and not have faith in God.[27] "Mont Blanc" participates in this conversation as a revelation of a "something" to have faith in, and as an assurance to the faithful onlooker of his own separate existence and value. Wordsworth's poem, however, is only incidentally concerned with that interfused "something"; it is everywhere interested in human being. Shelley's interest is above all in Being, in the "something". His thinking about the self is in its relation to Being, to unqualified existence, not in relation to its humanity, the quality of its own being. Where Wordsworth's poem is fundamentally ethical, Shelley's is fundamentally phenomenological. Next to Wordsworth's his poem will seem to many readers implacably speculative, abstract and indifferent to human relationship. Meanwhile his argument with Coleridge's effusive "Hymn", an insignificant affair beside either of the other poems, is merely about the name and nature of Being. Shelley replaces Coleridge's God with his own Necessity, Coleridge's Deist enthusiasm for a Universal Maker with a graver Enlightenment recognition of a Universal Principle, but a now uncapitalised "thou" is still at the centre of this universe.

"Mont Blanc" is 144 lines long, consisting of seven verse paragraphs of various lengths in what at first appears to be blank verse. On closer inspection random rhymes appear; a closer look still reveals that all the lines save two are rhymed, but in no discernible pattern. Milton's *Lycidas*, a poem of similar size which also uses this device, was evidently still in Shelley's thoughts: not the only respect in which "Mont Blanc" develops the thinking of *Alastor*. One might say that the underlying strength and consistency of the metre suggests the fundamental unity of the "universe of things", whilst from the rhymes gleam unexpected but persistent flashes of meaning and connection. The reality of that universe is one of the poem's two central subjects of meditation. "The everlasting universe of things/ Flows through the mind" just as "a vast river/ Over its rocks ceaselessly bursts and raves" (1–2, 9–10). This "clear universe of things" (40) is likened to the River Arve, above which the speaker stands; but the river is also the "likeness" of "Power", coming down from "his secret throne" (16–17) high on the mountain above. So the river represents both "things" and "Power", both the totality of beings in the universe and an hypostasised Being outside it. Shelley gives metaphorical credibility to this slightly insecure metaphysical position by following the river upwards, until "Far, far above, piercing the infinite sky,/ Mont Blanc appears" (60–1); and then by looking abroad, at the "fields, the lakes, the forests, and the streams,/ Ocean, and all the living things that dwell/ Within the dædal earth", including the "works and ways of man" (84–6, 92). The "universe of things" can seem chaotic and ruinous, indifferent to man; above it all, however, rises the mountain, and "Power dwells apart in its tranquillity,/ Remote, serene, and inaccessible" (96–7). In the poem's final paragraph (127–44) "Mont Blanc yet gleams on high: – the power is there,/ The still and solemn power of many sights,/ And many sounds, and much of life and death"; the power is always there, even when "none beholds" it.

> ... Its home
> The voiceless lightning in these solitudes
> Keeps innocently, and like vapour broods
> Over the snow. The secret strength of things
> Which governs thought, and to the infinite dome
> Of heaven is as a law, inhabits thee!

This metaphorical sequence is the poem's principal achievement. The river is both an image of the universe of things as descending from Power and an image of Power itself. The universe of things is threatening, but the things also signify a remote tranquillity and serenity. Shelley finds in the unobserved "innocence" of the "voiceless lightning" an image of the "secret strength of things" more deeply reposeful than any of the second-hand Wordsworthian objects at the beginning of *Alastor*. The secret strength of things intimates the Secret Strength beyond all things; this idea brings a sense of existential security much greater than any to be discovered by the declamatory and systematic *Queen Mab*. Shelley does not try here, as he does in the "Hymn", to abstract Necessity from a series of otherwise unrelated "things", such as moonbeams and a memory of music. The universe of things in "Mont Blanc" is actually given *in* the poem something like the unity and immanent presence which is claimed for it *by* the poem; the moments of transcendental deduction, as it were, are thereby also made more convincing.

The poem's other central subject of meditation is the perceiving mind. This subject is closely connected to the first, of course; the relation between the "universe of things" and the "human mind" had mesmerised European philosophy from Descartes to Kant, but one does not have to turn Shelley into a philosopher, or "Mont Blanc" into a verse essay on Drummond and Berkeley, on what Shelley elsewhere called "the intellectual system",[28] to see that this connection is vital to the poem. In *Queen Mab* Shelley was in the end unable to make sense of the relation between his idea of Necessity and the individual human consciousness, which appeared there as the "will", an abstract principle of insistence on the political immanence of Necessity. "Mont Blanc" avoids falling into this trap by attending not to the will but to perception (although in the process it falls into other traps, as we shall see shortly). The "everlasting universe of things/ Flows through the mind" as the Arve flows through its ravine. Looking at the river flowing through its ravine causes the speaker, he says (36–40),

> To muse on my own separate phantasy,
> My own, my human mind, which passively
> Now renders and receives fast influencings,
> Holding an unremitting interchange
> With the clear universe of things around . . .

The individual "human mind", then, is more than a passive receptacle-cum-processor (renderer and receiver) of impressions made on it by the universe of things. It has, and partly is, its "own separate phantasy". If the universe is a "vast river", "human thought" is a "feeble brook"; but it has its own "secret springs" (4–10). The mind, or ravine, contains both the river of "things" and the brook of original individual thought, that single "legion of wild thoughts" (41). So far so good; an impressive new apprehension of the universe of things is matched by a new sense of the self as a real and independent, if modest, participant in that universe. The poem's conclusion (142–4) is a fitting expression of this new understanding:

> And what were thou, and earth, and stars, and sea,
> If to the human mind's imaginings
> Silence and solitude were vacancy?

The poem's achievement lies in its affirmation that both "things" and "thou" (here the mountain, more generally Power) exist, and are even indistinguishable at times. The concealed syllogism in these last lines is: if to the imagination silence and solitude were vacancy, then there would be no "thou"; but there is a "thou"; so to the imagination silence and solitude are not vacancy. Thus the "secret strength of things . . . governs thought" without completely determining it. Belief in the existence of Necessity, a belief for which the poem has given some justification, provides the individual imagination with the strength to discover meaning even in silence and solitude: even in itself.

In other places, however, the poem's thought is less persuasive. Those "wild thoughts" also "rest" in "the still cave of the witch Poesy" (42–4), where they behold the universe in the form of shadows and ghosts: as if poetry, including this poetry, were a retreat from engagement with the universe. Further, they are represented as seeking "among" those shadows for "some shade of thee,/ Some phantom, some faint image" (45–7). Throughout the second paragraph of the poem the speaker is addressing the Ravine, which as we saw represents the mind through which the "universe of things" flows like a river. Clearly, however, the speaker cannot be addressing his own mind. The Ravine turns out to be something more like Mind. Human thought in general, individual human thought most especially, turns out to be a brook not just within the ravine of the mind, but within the ravine of Mind. This adds a confusing extra dimension to the thought. If the poem seeks to persuade us of the intimations of an essentially inhuman Necessity in the universe of things, and of the mind's need for such intimations, it should not seek in the same breath to turn Necessity into a giant projection of the mind, a World Mind; and then into the ultimate source, the "secret source", of all human thought. The "thou" of the Ravine is at loggerheads with the "thou" of the Mountain. We can think with the poem about the universe, a perceiver and Necessity beyond, but not at the same time about a Peceiver which is none of the above and yet all of them. This indecision in the poem is clearly indicated by the highly elliptical and confusing syntax in the first paragraph and at the end of the second, the points at which Shelley is attending most closely to Mind and mind, the points which have soaked up most of the critical and philosophical ink spilled on the poem. From "secret springs/ The source of human thought its tribute brings", but how does a source bring something from springs; surely springs *are* a source? Till "the breast/ From which they fled recalls them, thou art there" (47–8); who or what is doing the recalling, and what is being recalled? This kind of syntactical and imaginative uncertainty suggests that Shelley's mind was more at home with a large diagram, with a system to be sketched, than with the rich toils and self-critical rewards of exploratory poetic language.

   The achievement of "Mont Blanc", like that of *Alastor*, is in its suggestive sketching of a landscape of immanence and of transcendence, not in any detailed ethical exploration of the mind of the perceiver or of anyone else. The "infinite dome/ Of heaven", the "human mind's imaginings", the "everlasting universe of things": these phrases take concepts for granted in order to manipulate them as wholes. The concepts are not unpacked or questioned. There just *is* a dome, a mind or a universe, and the task is to make a picture of it, or use it as a symbol of something. Shelley falls into deeper and older habits elsewhere in the poem because of this tendency not to unpack an image, but always to let it do the same kind of job. "Some say that gleams of a remoter world/ Visit the soul in sleep", the third paragraph begins (49–50). Straight away we are returned to *Queen Mab*, with its reflection on whether the countries of sleep and death are the same. After such a start the paragraph ends (76–83) as one might expect:

The wilderness has a mysterious tongue
Which teaches awful doubt, or faith so mild,
So solemn, so serene, that man may be
But for [i.e. only through] such faith with nature reconciled,
Thou hast a voice, great Mountain, to repeal
Large codes of fraud and woe; not understood
By all, but which the wise, and great, and good
Interpret, or make felt, or deeply feel.

The four lines on the wilderness are entirely consistent with the poem's major claim, that the self may be reconciled with the natural world and with itself by the intimations of Necessity in the world. The concluding address to the Mountain, however, transforms this persuasive metaphysical and existential argument into a political harangue. The transformation itself is as deeply characteristic of Shelley's poetic thought as the harangue; it is that turning aside from a natural or human object to an intellectual or ideal subject which lay at the heart of *Queen Mab*. The speaker inserts the Necessity he has just so valuably removed from the sphere of human conflict back into that sphere, claiming wisdom, greatness and goodness for himself, discerning fraud and woe in others, above all claiming to be Necessity's interpreter and agent in the political sphere. "Mont Blanc" was not fundamentally damaged by this swerve of thought in the way that the "Ode to the West Wind" was to be. The poem was Shelley's most successful essay on Necessity and the self. But the argument of this chapter is that Shelley needed another way of thought more than he needed success in this one. Metaphysical meditation tended to turn into doctrinal assertion; in the terms of *Alastor*, this Poet tended to turn every human being into an Arab maiden. The way out of this trap, as *Alastor* itself had argued, was not to think more successfully about the relationship between Necessity and a life, but to start thinking about lives in their relations to each other.

4

Shelley's Poetry, 1818–20

Shelley's first two years in Italy offered artistic challenges both to his views of poetry and to the poetry itself. He became more receptive to a conception of poetry as the emanation of the passions; in "Julian and Maddalo" and other poems he renewed the Alastorean criticism of a poetry of idealist politico-moral reformism. Towards the end of 1819, however, new political stimuli impelled him back towards that poetry and that view, in the "Ode to the West Wind" and other poems. The composition of his most ambitious work of that kind, *Prometheus Unbound*, occupied him on and off for over a year during 1818 and 1819, and we shall consider the poem separately in the next chapter. Meanwhile Shelley also wrote during his Italian years some slighter poems about human relationship, familiar poems quite peripheral and insignificant from the poet's point of view, which nevertheless thought about the self in a completely different way. We shall glance at one or two of these at the end of the first section of this chapter.

"JULIAN AND MADDALO" AND OTHER POEMS

As a preamble to "Julian and Maddalo" it is worth dwelling briefly on a shorter poem, the "Lines Written Among the Euganean Hills", composed in the autumn of 1818. Reiman pointed out over thirty years ago[1] that the poem had been rather taken for granted; it still is. The essential significances of the poem are formal and tonal on one hand, metaphysical and moral on the other. Its thirteen paragraphs or 373 lines are in trochaic tetrameter couplets, most of the lines having only seven syllables. This form, as usual in Shelley, goes hand in hand with an easy, assured and familiar tone; compare the "Letter to Edward Fergus Graham", or the poems for Jane Williams, which we shall return to at the end of this section. This "urbane" Shelley, we recall,

has caught the fancy of many critics since the 1950s, and indeed
this is a voice of some charm, anticipatory of W. H. Auden, who
perhaps predisposed these critics with such lyrics as "Lay your
sleeping head my love". In Shelley's tetrameter poems the incantatory effect of the shorter rhymed lines compensates more
completely than his longer pentameter verses can for the kinds
of linguistic complacency noted towards the end of the previous
chapter; hence, perhaps, the effect of "urbanity". As with Auden,
in other words, the charm is often a triumph of tone over an
absence of any deeper explorativeness. Still, in the "Lines" we
can distinguish a kind of self-awareness or self-questioning quite
unlike what was to be heard in most of the earlier poetry; a
kind also discernible in "Julian and Maddalo" and, eventually,
"The Triumph of Life". On the metaphysical and moral plane
the poem extends the thought of "Mont Blanc". The first four
and last three paragraphs are concerned with the relation between a perceiver, who in this case is also a sufferer in the human world, and the landscape or "universe of things" around
him. The central six paragraphs are extensively and precisely
about political reform, as the central third paragraph of "Mont
Blanc" was briefly and abstractly about it. The earlier poem's
achievement amidst the wilderness of the Alps is refined within
the softened and civilised landscape of the Euganean Hills, in
that a transcendent Necessity is no longer needed as an explanatory
device. But the central political fault line has deepened. In the
first two paragraphs (1–65) the speaker tells us of a Poet-like
"mariner, worn and wan", drifting across "the deep wide sea of
Misery" towards "the haven of the grave", his final refuge from
unexplained "bitter words" and "distress". This is hardly an
improvement on a dozen earlier "misery" poems, but as the sun
rises in the next two paragraphs (66–114) the speaker derives
from the scene before him a serenity much deeper and more
plausible than any attained by the narrator of *Alastor*. The "wave-
less plain of Lombardy", spread beneath him "like a green sea",
is "Islanded by cities fair", and from Venice "Column, tower,
and dome, and spire,/ Shine like obelisks of fire". Here was what
Shelley called in his letters "the glory of nature & the arts", one
of the two emblems of Italy. The poem witnesses this glory in
these early paragraphs and in its last three, making of this "green
isle" a contingent but real refuge from the "deep wide sea of
Misery" (1–2). This is a salutary step back from the reliance on

intimations of Necessity in "Mont Blanc". In between the early and late paragraphs, however, we are forcibly reminded of what Shelley saw as the other emblem of Italy: "moral degradation", the miserable political and moral condition of "the Italians of the present day". Those buildings are really "Sepulchres, where human forms,/ Like pollution-nourished worms,/ To the corpse of greatness cling" (146–8). These are slaves, and their Austrian conquerors are tyrants. "Men must reap the things they sow,/ Force from force must ever flow" (231–2). The speaker dismisses Venice and the cities of the plain as "Clouds which stain truth's rising day" (161); he imagines that Byron, an emblem of "Poesy's unfailing River", whom Shelley had met again a few weeks before, and who was about to publish the fourth canto of *Childe Harold's Pilgrimage*, will redeem Venice by his mere presence. By the end of the poem the speaker's "green isle" has become a "healing Paradise" which will cleanse even the "polluting multitude" (355–6).

Shelley had inserted a utopian homily on Freedom into the middle of a hymn to landscape, as if *The Mask of Anarchy*, written a year later with the same metre and rhyme scheme, had been inserted into "Mont Blanc" – a possibility, indeed, which the third paragraph of "Mont Blanc" had anticipated. The "Lines" are significant because they show how tightly connected in Shelley's feelings, but how disconnected in the imagery of his poetry, were the excitements of political pronouncement and of beholding the "universe of things". His habit of moralising a landscape was as strong as it had been at the time of *Queen Mab*, but his capacity to metaphorise landscape and moral was no stronger. The "sun floats up the sky/ Like thought-winged Liberty" (206–7), and we know that Shelley thinks of Liberty when he sees the sun; but what other connection does the *verse* make? At its best it shows us how the perceiver's unexplained misery is temporarily dispelled by a scene of natural and artificial beauty, but it fails to show us how this effect is connected with political freedom or paradise by anything other than the fact that the poet's mind always turns to these ideas when he is elated. In the end what remains unexplored is precisely that turn: what it is a turn from and to, and why.

In "Julian and Maddalo", written during the first half of 1819, Shelley tried as he had in *Alastor* four years before to explore that turn, to discover those connections between passions and abstract ideas which remained unmade in poems such as *Queen Mab*, "Mont Blanc" and now the "Lines". The new poem had its immediate origin in a plan for a drama about the poet Tasso, about the situation of a mad poet imprisoned by a tyrant. This drama was never written, but its central conception of a personality assaulted simultaneously by political oppression and by its own passions appeared in both "Julian and Maddalo" and its successor, *The Cenci*, written in mid-1819. Shelley's aim in "Julian and Maddalo" was, furthermore, to write as far as possible in a "familiar style", to "express the actual way in which people talk with each other" (ii 108). He sub-titled the poem "A Conversation", and in this respect it belongs in the familiar tradition of the "Letter to Edward Fergus Graham", the "Letter to Maria Gisborne" and various other poems addressed to Shelley's friends, generally women. The story of the Madman in "Julian and Maddalo" is thus more politicised, and more sophisticated in its attitude to both language and the passions, than the story of the Poet in *Alastor*. The character of Julian is now generally taken to be Shelley's figure for his old Godwinian meliorist self. The Poet in *Alastor* was also an earlier Shelleyan self, but the narrator was unconvincing as a critic of that self. The dramatic monologue form of "Julian and Maddalo", in which Julian himself tells the story of his conversation with Count Maddalo (the Byron figure) and their visit to the cell of the Madman, is a much more subtle method of revisiting earlier Shelleyan selves; the Madman too has in him much of the Poet, and Maddalo has in him much of the more recent disillusioned Shelley. Finally, the structure of "Julian and Maddalo" is distinctly Alastorean: 618 lines to 720, rhyming couplets instead of blank verse, "truly lean and bare prosaic language" (as Davie put it)[2] to offset the greater polish of rhyme, a division into two parts, with a framing conversational narrative at beginning and end (1–299, 511–617) and the central drama of the Madman's tale (300–510) in the middle. In short, this is a new, more sophisticated and more political Alastorean reflection on passion, doctrine and the self. But the question must again be, as it was with *Alastor*, whether the poem is consciously mending or unconsciously reaffirming the disconnections it exposes. "Julian and Maddalo" is nowadays often praised[3] as an ironic depiction by Shelley of himself-as-Julian, or himself-as-Maddalo, or himself-as-Madman, or all three at once. Even if this is true, however, is the current Shelley, the self of

the poem, doing anything to deepen his thinking by transforming those earlier selves into more than just ironically distanced
aspects of some putative present self? How adequate *is* that present
poetic self?

The poem's long first paragraph (1–140) is its best; it would
have made a satisfactory poem by itself. Julian, the preface tells
us, is "an Englishman of good family, passionately attached to
those philosophical notions which assert the power of man over
his own mind". He is a social perfectibilian, an "infidel", and
"rather serious". Maddalo "is a person of the most consummate
genius", capable of redeeming his "degraded country", but he is
"proud", his "ambition preys upon itself", he has "an intense
apprehension of the nothingness of human life" (pp. 112–13).
Some readers may prefer to regard these as deeply ironised commentaries on Shelley and Byron; others will find them un-
remarkably compatible with Shelley's comments elsewhere on
himself and his friend. In any case Julian tells us in the first
paragraph of the poem itself of a ride he took with Count Maddalo
on the Lido opposite Venice. The landscape is an intrinsic part
of the ride and of the paragraph's mood. We see the "bare strand",
the "thistles and amphibious weeds", "one dwarf tree", the
"heaven-sustaining bulwark" of the Alps, "the Earth and Sea"
dissolved "into one lake of fire" at sunset, the "temples" and
"palaces" of the city like "fabrics of enchantment piled to Heaven",
the "living spray along the sunny air". The description is, as
Davie says, prosaic, but it is unpretentious and, unusually for
Shelley, unmoralised – like the best parts of "Mont Blanc" and
the "Lines Written Among the Euganean Hills". "If it has less
brilliancy, it has less extravagance and confusion", said Hazlitt;
it is "in Mr. Shelley's best and *least mannered* manner".[4] Necessity is forgotten, even when Julian tells us of his love for "all
waste/ And solitary places; where we taste/ The pleasure of
believing what we see/ Is boundless, as we wish our souls to
be". This pleasure is allowed to remain quotidian. Shelley is not
subordinating landscape to ideas even as he was in the "Lines",
let alone in *Queen Mab*. More importantly, however, is he subordinating character? The riders "descanted" on "God, freewill and
destiny", on "all that earth has been or yet may be,/ All that
vain men imagine or believe". Julian argues "against despondency", "for ever still/ Is it not wise to make the best of ill?": but
"pride/ Made my companion take the darker side". Maddalo

shows his friend the tower of the madhouse, and they hear the "hoarse and iron tongue" of its bell:

"And such," – he cried, "is our mortality
And this must be the emblem and the sign
Of what should be eternal and divine! –
And like that black and dreary bell, the soul,
Hung in a heaven-illumined tower, must toll
Our thoughts and our desires to meet below
Round the rent heart and pray – as madmen do
For what? they know not. . . ."

In Canto IV of *Childe Harold's Pilgrimage*, published a few months earlier, Byron himself had written: "We wither from our youth, we gasp away –/ Sick, sick; unfound the boon – unslaked the thirst"; "Who loves, raves – 'tis youth's frenzy – but the cure/ Is bitterer still"; "Love, fame, ambition, avarice – 'tis the same,/ Each idle – and all ill"; "Our life is a false nature".[5] Shelley wrote to his friend Peacock in December 1818 about this canto that the "spirit in which it is written is, if insane, the most wicked & mischievous insanity that ever was given forth. . . . I remonstrated with him in vain on the tone of mind from which such a view of things alone arises" (ii 58). (Shelley's belief, whether puritanical, misogynistic, naive or shrewd, was that "the true source of these expressions of contempt & desperation" lay in "the Italian women", in Byron's promiscuous but ineffectual attempts to escape his bitterness about his own marriage and past emotional life.) Peacock's own remonstration with this "tone of mind", including with these very stanzas, took the form of his sparkling novel *Nightmare Abbey*, published like *Childe Harold IV* in 1818.[6] But the novel was also a companionable tilt at Shelley's own "tone of mind"; Peacock's Scythrop Glowry bears much the same relation to Shelley's Julian as Peacock's Mr. Cypress does to Shelley's Maddalo. In other words the views of Julian and Maddalo about love and life appear to be very close to what Peacock and Shelley thought Shelley's and Byron's views were. Shelley is much harsher behind Byron's back than Julian is to Maddalo's face, but the voice of *Childe Harold* is hardly more bitter than Maddalo's or (as Shelley thought) Byron's own. With "Julian and Maddalo" Shelley found that it was possible and valuable to explore tones of mind, that there *were* other tones besides his own, and above all that a "view of things" may arise from a "tone of mind" rather than from a set of ideas. This dramatising of two characters Shelley knew very well, Byron's and his own, was an important first step in his thinking about lives or selves as distinct from their ideas about the world. *Alastor*, by comparison, was unconvincing in its criticisms of the effects of Shelleyan ideas on a life because it was so thoroughly and undramatically imbued with Shelley's own ideal tones of mind.

"Julian and Maddalo" is nevertheless a fledgling exploration of character at best, showing more the desire than the capacity to write dramatically. No less a dramatist than Robert Browning was impressed by "Julian and Maddalo",[7] but Browning's dramatic monologues are quite beyond the scope of Shelley's poem. Maddalo's words sound almost as much like the Shelley of the "misery" poems as the Byron of *Childe Harold*. The image of the soul as a bell tolling our "thoughts and our desires to meet below/ Round the rent heart" is one of Shelley's distinctive and most memorable symbolic moments, but the lines are also characteristic of his curiously monadic conception of such abstractions as "thought", "desire", "mortality" and the "eternal and divine". The terms sit lumpishly in their places, unexplored and uncriticised, taken for granted by the two civilised interlocutors, whose conversation looks from one angle like an eighteenth century commonplace, an abstract "Dialogue Between Reason and Desire". Still, let us at least read the poem as aspiring dramatic thought, not as a series of ironic self-displacements, as endless reflexive reflections on the poet's own mind. To ascribe profound ironical self-awareness to this poem is not only to exaggerate its qualities but to force Shelley back into precisely that introspectivity from which his poem was an attempt to escape.

The argument between the two friends continues the next morning, in the poem's even longer second paragraph (141–299). Julian calls on Maddalo, still Byronically in bed,

And whilst I waited with his child I played;
A lovelier toy sweet Nature never made,
A serious, subtle, wild, yet gentle being,
Graceful without design and unforeseeing,
With eyes – oh speak not of her eyes! – which seem
Twin mirrors of Italian Heaven, yet gleam
With such deep meaning, as we never see
But in the human countenance. . . .

Shelley now wanted to think about lives, not just ideas, and to think about the passions instead of evading them, but his thought still needed a predominantly intellectual setting, not a dramatic one. A dramatisation of one of Shelley's own philosophical conversations is one thing; this encounter with a child is quite another. It is infelicitous for Julian to say that he "played" with Maddalo's daughter as if she were a "toy", and unimpressive for him to describe her as "serious, subtle, wild, yet gentle", or remark that her eyes (although she is "unforeseeing") "gleam/ With such deep meaning". Nor should we try to save this passage by reading it as some kind of reflection by the poem on Julian's imperceptiveness. Shelley's ironist defenders sometimes gloss his more turgid or florid writing with the claim that he was writing this way on purpose, ironically. But the context offers no other standard of thought, no more perceptive exploration of character, against which to evaluate Julian's supposed inadequacies. He merely continues his intellectualised debate with Maddalo, and that debate's ethical terminology, though woolly enough itself, provides the only local contrast with his attempt to think about the child as a person:

> . . ."See
> This lovely child, blithe, innocent and free;
> She spends a happy time with little care
> While we to such sick thoughts subjected are
> As came on you last night – it is our will
> That thus enchains us to permitted ill –
> We might be otherwise – we might be all
> We dream of happy, high, majestical.
> Where is the love, beauty and truth we seek
> But in our mind? and if we were not weak
> Should we be less in deed than in desire?"

Is the child subtle and full of meaning or blithe and without care? Why or how are Maddalo's thoughts "sick", and the products of his will? Is this passage too intended to expose the shallowness of Julian's thinking, or is he shallow only in some kinds of thought? Maddalo's response is in any case too laconic to expose shallowness: "'Ay, if we were not weak. . . . You talk Utopia'". Unchastened, the utopian marches on:

"Much may be conquered, much may be endured
Of what degrades and crushes us. We know
That we have power over ourselves to do
And suffer – what, we know not till we try;
But something nobler than to live and die –
So taught those kings of old philosophy
Who reigned, before Religion made men blind. . . ."

This is the Shelley of the contemporary *Prometheus Unbound*, as much as of the superseded *Queen Mab*; if Julian's thought is being criticised here, we have yet to see how. So far, at least, his "view of things", in all its bareness, is being represented more sympathetically than Maddalo's. The Count does hit back; he has had enough of "such aspiring theories". He knew someone just like Julian, he says, who "was ever talking in such sort/ As you do", and who has "now gone mad". They will visit him in the madhouse on the lagoon, so that "his wild talk will show/ How vain" such theories are. But the irrepressible Julian still hopes "to prove the induction otherwise", or rather to assert that deduction is better than induction, by showing the lunatic's "want of that true theory" which looks for good even in "things ill". So far the paragraph prompts us to anticipate a madman who will prove both friends right and both wrong, and show each an aspect of himself as well as of the other. The poetry, however, is hardly searching enough of the terms of the debate or of its characters to frame or accommodate any truly complex human case. Such a case, if the poetry can rise to it, will certainly explode the debate, but could such moral thinking as we have so far seen be expected to rise to such a case? Julian's description of their journey to the island, of the madhouse, the cell and the "Maniac", and Maddalo's tale of the Maniac's past, are almost as economical and unmannered as Julian's account of their earlier ride on the Lido. "A Lady came with him from France", reports Maddalo, and when she "left him and returned" he "grew wild"; but he had also always seemed unusually "hurt" when he heard "of the oppression of the strong". Love and politics, drama and ideas, spare language and insistent doctrine, are never kept distinct for long in this poem. Maddalo himself had fitted up the Maniac's rooms; he explains this charity in terms of the golden rule of practical wisdom: act towards others as you would have others act towards you. This is an effective touch. Such

practical wisdom from the embittered Maddalo seems strange
to the theoretical Julian ("this was kind of you – he had no claim"),
who no doubt would merely have advised the Maniac to look
for what was good in his situation. The second paragraph thus
ends compellingly enough, with a taut introduction to the Maniac, an oblique criticism of Julian and a hint at an unexpected
side of Maddalo's character. But little more is made in the poem
of the last two suggestions, and a great deal of weight now rests
on the Maniac's narrative, which follows immediately.

The Maniac tells his story in 210 impassioned lines addressed
sometimes to no-one in particular, sometimes to the departed
Lady. The narrative's increasingly fractured syntax and paragraph-
ing are presumably intended to indicate the deep and progres-
sive disconnectedness of the narrator's thought as he works his
way closer to the centres of his pain. Those centres have to do
with political oppression and with love, as Maddalo intimated,
but in the end they are neither satisfactorily explained separately,
nor convincingly connected together. This must seriously weaken
a poem which rests so heavily on the credibility and depth of
this central character. To begin with, in the poem's third paragaph
(300–19) the Maniac simply cries out under his "load". He must
"drag life on" as if it were "a heavy chain" with "many a link of
pain": and yet he will not "give a human voice" to his "despair",
will not "speak [his] grief", because to do so would distress his
few friends, and he cannot "bear more altered faces . . . More
misery, disappointment and mistrust". In a brief aside (337–43)
to the Lady, the "spirit's mate" who is presumably the chief cause
of his pain, he refuses even to complain to her: "Thou wouldst
weep tears bitter as blood to know/ Thy lost friend's incommu-
nicable woe". Most of his other remarks to her are so violently
accusatory that the reader is inclined to wonder whether they
can be addressed to the same Lady as this one; still, this *is* a
madman. The aside to the Lady is part of a long elaboration
(320–37, 344–82) upon the material of the third paragraph. The
Maniac explains that he "met pale Pain", and that this was not
entirely his fault.

"I have not as some do, bought penitence
With pleasure, and a dark yet sweet offence,
For then, – if love and tenderness and truth
Had overlived hope's momentary youth,

My creed should have redeemed me from repenting;
But loathed scorn and outrage unrelenting
Met love excited by far other seeming
Until the end was gained. . . ."

Pain was not merely the follower of pleasure and consequence of sin; if it had been he would not have repented the pleasure, since his "creed", not unlike Julian's, is always to seek love and justice, no matter what rebuffs or criticisms he may incur. The pain stems from others' duplicity and hostile rejection of him; his love is "excited" by the appearance of reciprocal love, only to be ambushed by "loathed scorn and outrage unrelenting". This kind of rejection attacks not only hope – that much his creed would survive – but love and tenderness and truth (although the syntax is troublesome here: does "if" mean "that is, if" or "if in addition"?). But the Maniac will not tell his friends any more about his "secret load"; the "full Hell within" him will not "infect the untainted breast/ Of sacred nature with its own unrest"; he will not "find/ In scorn or hate a medicine for the mind/ Which scorn or hate have wounded".

"Believe that I am ever still the same
In creed as in resolve, and what may tame
My heart, must leave the understanding free
Or all would sink in this keen agony –
Nor dream that I will join the vulgar cry,
Or with my silence sanction tyranny. . . .
I am prepared: in truth with no proud joy
To do or suffer aught, as when a boy
I did devote to justice and to love
My nature, worthless now!"

No matter what his Pain, his "understanding" must remain separate from his "heart"; the Maniac insists ("Believe") that his "creed" and his "resolve" remain unaffected by his "secret load", and that he is therefore essentially "still the same". His self is more identifiable with his understanding, his creed and resolve, than with his heart and its load. "There is one road/ To peace and that is truth, which follow ye!/ Love sometimes leads astray to misery." Truth remains constant; love may be fickle. He will still "do or suffer" whatever is necessary to pursue his creed (presumably only as it regards justice now, however, not love), although pride and joy have gone, and his "nature" is "worthless".

We must remember that this is meant to be a disturbed mind, that the terms of its still incomplete self-disclosure will seem to Maddalo to show the futility of the Maniac's "creed", and hence of Julian's, and that Shelley must have meant here to dramatise and criticise an aspect not only of Julian's but of his own personality, not least as it was reflected in his earlier poetry. In "Julian and Maddalo" Shelley recognises even more fully than he had in Alastor his need to break free from his own "tone of mind", as well as his own "view of things". The Maniac is more effectively distinguished from Julian than the Poet was from the narrator. The poem registers as lunatic his determination "to do or suffer aught" despite the evident destruction of his nature, his desire to protect his friends and his Lady from a pain which derives largely from his own creed's vulnerability to assault, and even his morbid assumption that any communication of his pain must be by means of more "scorn and hate". But how perceptively does the poem think about the central disconnections in the Maniac's character: between creed and experience, free understanding and tame heart, resolve and tyranny, truth and love? These familiar Shelleyan concepts are not explored by the Maniac: are they by the poem? Are the effects of passion on principle, or the interdependence of the two, ever really considered? Or is this life story, like the earlier debate between Julian and Maddalo, a rather mechanical confrontation of categories? Has passion become just another idea?

Well, the story is not yet over. We must wait for more disclosure of the "pain", of the relationship between the Maniac and the Lady. So far there is nothing but a small abstract vocabulary ("scorn", "hate", "outrage") to explain the passion and the relationship. That disclosure now comes in the form of nine shorter, disjointed paragraphs, addressed to the Lady (382–510). "'I must remove/ A veil from my pent mind. 'Tis torn aside!'", exclaims the Maniac abruptly:

"O, pallid as death's dedicated bride,
Thou mockery which art sitting by my side,
Am I not wan like thee?. . . .

Nay, was it I who wooed thee to this breast
Which. like a serpent, thou envenomest . . .?
Didst thou not seek me for thine own content?
Did not thy love awaken mine?. . . .

That you had never seen me – never heard
My voice, and more than all had ne'er endured
The deep pollution of my loathed embrace –
That your eyes ne'er had lied love in my face –
That, like some maniac monk, I had torn out
The nerves of manhood by their bleeeding root
        . . . . they were ministered
One after one, those curses. . . .

                        It were
A cruel punishment for one most cruel,
If such can love, to make that love the fuel
Of the mind's hell; hate, scorn, remorse, despair:
But *me* – whose heart a stranger's tear might wear
As water-drops the sandy fountain-stone,
Who loved and pitied all things . . .
Me – who am as a nerve o'er which do creep
The else unfelt oppressions of this earth. . . ."

The first function of this passage is to give fuller expression to
an aspect of the Maniac's suffering which we already know about:
that the woman whose apparent love for him awakened his love
then cruelly vilified him, so that the intensity of his own love,
as well as of her scorn, fuelled the pain. The new information
here is that he was peculiarly vulnerable to this pain, because
he was exceptionally alive to oppression or imposition in general. There are some unsatisfactory features of this passage, no
matter what allowances we may make for any critical and dramatic distancing Shelley intended in his representation of the
Maniac. The imagery, particularly that drawn from Gothic melo-
drama, does not help to make this disclosure of madness arresting
or profound. Death's pallid bride, the serpent, the self-castrating
maniac monk, the curses: these bespeak violent feeling, but not
with eloquence or originality. The self-pity ("But *me* . . . *Me*") is
unattractive, and any biographicalist critic of Shelley who reminded us of the deep estrangement between him and Mary

following the death of their daughter Clara in 1818 would be doing the poet no favours in thus linking the Maniac's pain to the poet's. But what is more troubling is the passage's attitude to love and pity. What is essential to both, apparently, is an extraordinary vulnerability to others' feelings; this lies behind both the Maniac's love for the Lady (she loved him first, or he thought she did) and his pity for the politically oppressed. Neither the character nor the poem shows any sign of recognising that this conception of love and pity implies a complete *insensitivity* to the otherness of other people. To love the lady out of palpitating sympathy with her love for oneself, to think of oneself as worn down by strangers' tears or as pitying the oppressed more than anyone else does, to picture one's suffering from scorn as the exquisitely unfair pain of the benefactor wounded by the beneficiary: this is to place oneself forever at the centre of the stage, and all others, undifferentiated, around the edges. To conceive love and pity this way is to reduce both to an ideal sympathy, and thus to foreclose reflection on either passion. Nor may we dismiss this way of feeling, or not feeling, as merely the Maniac's. After all, his life-conception is so close to that of other Shelleyan figures, for example in the "Hymn", *Alastor*, *The Revolt of Islam* and *Prometheus Unbound*, and to that of Shelley himself in letters, prefaces, essays and poems, that it is a real critical challenge to read the Maniac's fate as Maddalo does, as an argument *against* such life-conceptions. This lack of dramatic definition hampered *Alastor* too, and as we shall see the "Ode to the West Wind" and *Adonais* make it harder still to think of this Christ-complex as the property of the Maniac, the Poet, Prometheus or Laon, and not as part of the "tone of mind" of the poet who created them.

After the Maniac's final turn back towards his Lady (492–510: "'Alas, love,/ Fear me not. . . . Do I not live/ That thou mayst have less bitter cause to grieve?'") and subsidence into apathy, Julian and Maddalo can debate no more (511–46: "our argument was quite forgot"). The poem gives no sign that this human case has prompted any re-consideration of their tones of mind or points of view. They agree, unsurprisingly, that "his was some dreadful ill/ Wrought on him boldly, yet unspeakable/ By a dear friend", but the unspeakability of the ill is the chief trouble with the poem. We already knew that this was "some deadly change in love" which "had fixed a blot of falshood on his mind which flourished not/ But in the light of all-beholding truth". In the poem's last two paragraphs (547–617) Julian entertains a daydream of remaining in Venice, befriending the Maniac and trying to "reclaim him from his dark estate", but recognises this as a dream of "baseless good". Returning to Venice years later he finds Maddalo's child grown like "one of Shakespeare's women" (Regan? Lady Macbeth?), and hears from her that the Lady had returned, only to leave again. There was more, it seems: "I urged and questioned still, she told me how/ All happened – but the cold world shall not know". These are the last two lines of the poem. The originating debate is simply forgotten, and so are the characters of the eponymous debaters, Shelley's first essays in dramatic character development. Julian remains unconvincing as self-criticism, Maddalo is hardly more than a sketch, and the Maniac's passion is never more than an idea of passion. His story shows not so much that the deepest feelings are inaccessible to language as that they are not yet congenial subjects for Shelley's poetic thinking. As in *Alastor*, Shelley had shown both his awareness that he needed to attempt a dramatic poetry of passionate self-exploration, and his awkwardness in making the attempt.

He tried again a few months later with *The Cenci*, a drama proper. Shelley's adaptation of the notorious sixteenth-century Roman family story, with its lurid themes of parricide and incestuous rape, is probably the only English Romantic drama still successfully staged. The Spanish seventeenth-century tragedian Calderón, whom Shelley had recently started to read, was an influential model; so was Schiller's *The Robbers*; so was Shakespeare's *Macbeth*, overwhelmingly so at times. Shelley's aims were much as in "Julian and Maddalo": to use familiar language, to explore human passion, and to reflect on the power of oppression to overcome the strongest and purest resistance. Correspondingly, the chief critical questions provoked by the play have been whether its language is fresh or melodramatically neo-Shakespearean; how successful the characterisation is; and whether the theme of "moral error" overshadows both language and characterisation. Recent criticism has principally found in the play, as in so much of Shelley's work (and in everyone else's, one sometimes feels), an explicit proto-modernist concern with the limits of language.[8] Mary Shelley confessed herself disappointed that Shelley did not write more in this vein. The "bent of his mind went the other way", she said in her note to the play. He repeatedly left

the delineations of human passion, which he could depict in
so able a manner, for fantastic creations of his fancy, or the
expression of those opinions and sentiments, with regard to
human nature and its destiny, a desire to diffuse which was
the master passion of his soul.[9]

But Shelley himself was genuinely uneasy about his capacity for
depicting passion, especially the passions of others. And with
reason: if we find his characterisations of "Julian" and "Maddalo"
less than satisfactory in the ways suggested above, then his exploration of the less familiar passions of Count Francesco Cenci
and his daughter Beatrice may well seem even more mechanical
and schematic. "I love/ The sight of agony, and the sense of
joy,/ When this shall be another's, and that mine", says the evil
Count in the first scene; "I have no remorse and little fear,/ Which
are, I think, the checks of other men" (I i 81–5). On his final
appearance the Count curses his daughter and her descendants
as if he were a sort of God: "He does His will, I mine" (IV i 139,
160–2):

> I do not feel as if I were a man,
> But like a fiend appointed to chastise
> The offences of some unremembered world.

The trouble with the characterisation is not so much motiveless
malignity as ideal malignity, the outward marks of passion without
the inward texture. Cenci says he feels like a fiend, not a man,
and that is what he is; he says he does not feel the checks of
other men, and we do not feel them in him. The play does not
have to think about remorse because Cenci declares himself to
have none; but neither does it, on close inspection of the feelings and language, think about avarice, or vengefulness, or per-
verted sexuality. The scheming prelate Orsino comments that "'tis
a trick of this same family/ To analyse their own and other minds",
and that this "self-anatomy" tempted Cenci until he "fell into
the pit", but all this is talking about the self, not exploring it:
making a virtue, indeed, of *not* exploring it. So with Beatrice
herself: Shelley comments in his preface that "the dramatic character of what she did and suffered" (not, be it noted, of what
she *was*) consists in "the restless and anatomising casuistry with
which men seek [her] justification . . . yet feel she has done what

needs justification" (her father rapes her, she murders him). What captures Shelley's imagination, as the etymology of his word "casuistry" suggests, is again an ethical *case*, a conflict of principles, rather than a person; the Tasso idea persists. His other prefatory comment, noted in Chapter 2, that the dramatic imagination here acts as a God, assuming flesh "for the redemption of mortal passion", similarly suggests that even in this supposedly most un-ideal of his works he is thinking of poetry as the instrument of a divine will, and of passion as an object of redemption rather than as an agent of thought. The outrage which Beatrice can "redeem" only by murdering its perpetrator, her own father, is as "unspeakable" as the Lady's treatment of the Maniac; Beatrice too feels the onset of madness. In Act III Scene i, the lynchpin of the play, her response to the incestuous rape she has just suffered is either in the Maniac's Gothic ("The beautiful blue heaven is flecked with blood!/ The sunshine on the floor is black!"; "These putrefying limbs/ Shut round and sepulchre the panting soul"), or in an impressively spare, intimate style in which nevertheless the central feelings are always gestured towards, never actually evoked: "Oh, what am I?/ What name, what place, what memory shall be mine?"; "If I try to speak/ I shall go mad. Aye, something must be done ... which shall make/ The thing that I have suffered but a shadow"; "I, whose thought/ Is like a ghost shrouded and folded up/ In its own formless horror"; "I have endured a wrong so great and strange,/ That neither life nor death can give me rest./ Ask me not what it is, for there are deeds/ Which have no form, sufferings which have no tongue" (compare the analogous passage, lines 764–1036, from Shakespeare's "The Rape of Lucrece"). The play's interest hereafter accordingly lies in the ideal casuistical framework, not the empty passional centre. Beatrice knows she is right, but she cannot show this to her father's world; she must take refuge in her conviction of innocence, and in silence. There is thus no real conflict of feeling either in her thinking or in the world's. To claim that the play is really about the limits of language in exploring passion is simply an ingenious way of redescribing its limitations of both language and passion.

To find Shelley's more familiar style employed to better advantage we must turn away from drama and back to the first person, to the language of lyric and verse letter. For example, in his 323-line "Letter to Maria Gisborne", written quickly in mid-1820, Shelley sent his friend in London a light-hearted description in rhyming couplets of the contents of her son's workshop, laughing at his own picture of the idealist poet using such a place as his study, and suggesting that friendship in exile is a greater good than worldly engagement. Even Hazlitt allowed that this self-deprecating verse letter was "pleasing and familiar", if "somewhat prosaic".[10] The much more interested poems of 1822 to Jane Williams (pp. 443–53) were better still; indeed these are Shelley's masterpieces of urbane conversational address. They are not "prosaic" at all;[11] Shelley's feelings were engaged. He and Mary shared their last house together at Lerici with Edward and Jane Williams, and Shelley's close friendship with Williams, to say nothing of his marriage to the long-suffering Mary, had to suffer his attraction to Jane. The poems he wrote for her are characterised by both intimacy and restraint, both simplicity of language and suggestiveness of tone, both joy in natural landscape and pleasure in human relationship. In thinking about his relationship with another person Shelley is deft and appealing, although he is not much concerned with the human particularity of that person, and the relationship is not one of any real depth. We must pass over most of these poems, however, and dwell for a moment on just one, "With a Guitar, to Jane", the most accomplished of them all, in 90 lines of the octosyllabic couplets which served and suited Shelley so well in the "Lines Written Among the Euganean Hills" and elsewhere.

The poem is founded on a delicate conceit in which Shelley, Williams and Jane are likened to Ariel, Ferdinand and Miranda in *The Tempest*. This is one of Shelley's felicitous Ozymandian discoveries, in which he finds exactly the right tableau for his emotional purposes. The myth is employed in serendipitous metaphorical counterpoint to the human reality. Just as Ariel now inhabits Shelley, the argument runs, so a Spirit inhabited first the tree which was felled to make the guitar being presented, with this poem, to Jane, and now the guitar itself (it still exists, in the Bodleian Library). Shelley's music is the poem; the guitar's music is Jane's song (she had a pleasant singing voice); both tell of the natural landscape surrounding the tree, up to the "seldom-heard myserious sound" of the earth moving in its sphere. The guitar, evoking all this, has become the tree's "happier form". "All who question skilfully", that is play it well, will be answered by the inhabitant Spirit. The instrument "talks according to the

wit/ Of its companions", and no-one will hear more in it than
he has "felt before":

But, sweetly as its answers will
Flatter hands of perfect skill,
It keeps its highest holiest tone
For our beloved Jane alone. –

Shelley's idealising imagination is perfectly at home when thus
domesticated by affection, by compliment and by music. One
looks not so much forward to Auden as back to the seventeenth
century for parallels; Richard Cronin justly invokes Robert
Herrick.[12] No obsession with "human nature and its destiny",
with Necessity, spoils this harmony, and its economy with passional self-exploration is its strength. We shall see in Chapter 6
how when Shelley attempted to raise the tone of this kind of
reflection in *Epipsychidion* he was less successful.

Other shorter poems of 1820, 1821 and 1822, for example "The
Boat on the Serchio" and "Evening: Ponte Al Mare, Pisa",[13] capture something of this ease and tone, but without the catalyst of
relationship. Still others fall more into the melancholic vein of
the introspective "misery" poems of 1814 and 1817–18. Such
lyrics as "When the Lamp is Shattered"[14] and "Music, when soft
voices die", notoriously savaged by Leavis and others, have been
rehabilitated on the grounds that they were songs intended to
appear within larger dramatic works; but this does not make
their own thinking any more impressive. In other poems again
Shelley's sheer lyrical inventiveness all but redeems his habitual
reduction of natural objects into ideas. In the energetic hurrying
voice of "The Cloud", for example, we can almost hear the silent laughter of Necessity herself ("I pass through the pores, of
the ocean and shores;/ I change, but I cannot die"). "To a Sky-
Lark" represents "unbodied Joy" so much more melodiously than
the "Hymn" did that we hardly hear the doctrinal bass ("Till the
world is wrought/ To sympathy"), and even discount that passionate rhetorical desire for an audience ("hear me", "The world
should listen") in which originates both the doctrine and the joy.
That desire is harder to discount in the "Ode to the West Wind".
On a much larger scale a kind of Necessity figure dominates
"The Witch of Atlas" (1820), a playful 672-line "visionary rhyme"
inspired by an eighteenth-century Italian verse romance,

Fortiguerra's *Ricciardetto*, and written in *ottava rima*, as *Adonais* was to be the next year. The Witch is a kind of capricious reincarnation of Queen Mab, forever playing tricks on mankind. The poem re-employs the boat journey of *Alastor*, the magic temple of *Queen Mab* and other Shelleyan *topoi*, but the Witch herself is hard to see, a Necessity so devoid of attributes as to be invisible. Bloom, her greatest admirer, wants us to read her domain as Shelley's equivalent of Spenser's Garden of Adonis, and hers as a "supreme offer of relationship",[15] but Bloom's "relationship" is Relationship, and the Witch's beauty is Beauty; it "made/ The bright world dim, and everything beside/ Seemed like the fleeting image of a shade" (137–9). The Skylark too could "deem/ Things more true and deep/ Than we mortals" can. Shelley's thought is turning back towards *Queen Mab*, away from *Alastor*.

"ODE TO THE WEST WIND" AND OTHER POEMS

As we turn from the "Witch of Atlas" to "Peter Bell the Third" (October 1819) we shift into the world of current events, but also remain briefly in that of playful fancy. "Peter Bell" has its roots in that early satirical ballad, *The Devil's Walk*. Although Shelley was solemn enough at times in his criticisms of Wordsworth the renegade and apostate, he is happy here to parody, to think of Hell as "a city much like London" (147), to paint a part-Hogarthian, part-Peacockian picture of its inhabitants and of Peter's (that is, Wordsworth's) career, ending in his incarnation as the new Devil of dullness. Shelley makes a shrewd point about Wordsworth's imagination ("he never could/ Fancy another situation/ From which to dart his contemplation,/ Than that wherein he stood": 299–302) without, perhaps, seeing its applicability, in a slightly different sense, to himself. Beyond "Peter Bell", but still in its parodic ambit, lies *Oedipus Tyrannus; or, Swellfoot the Tyrant* (1820),[16] a pamphleteering burlesque of the scandalous events surrounding the coronation of George IV and non-coronation of Queen Caroline. Some images recall *The Mask of Anarchy*, to which we shall shortly turn. This satirical buffoonery is more appealing than the serious political dramas which followed. *Hellas*, an 1100-line "lyrical drama" based on the *Persae* of Aeschylus and written in the cause of Greek liberty in late 1821, is an undramatic prophecy of freedom in which a despairing Turkish tyrant foresees his own overthrow, while Ahasuerus the Wandering Jew harangues him on "that which cannot change – the One,/ The unborn and the undying" (768–9). There is a disjunction between metaphysics and politics which even the resonant final lyric ("The world's great age begins anew,/ The golden years return. . . . A new Ulysses leaves once more/ Calypso for his native shore": 1060 ff.) cannot repair. Indeed the lyric actually exposes a certain poverty of political imagination, since the only terms in which Shelley can imagine the new age are old terms with the adjective "new" prefixed to them. The unfinished drama "Charles the First" (1821–2)[17] dispenses with the metaphysics but gets nowhere with the old themes. The shorter, more topical "Ode to Liberty" and "Ode to Naples"[18] of 1820 are prosodically virtuosic but imaginatively and emotionally lifeless.

In other words, the enormous political enthusiasm released in Shelley by the Peterloo affair in the autumn of 1819 had largely dissipated by 1821, and his creative energy was flowing in other channels. We know that his political-ideal style of thought, with its concentration on the linkages between Necessity and politics, had been subject since 1815 to an Alastorean passion-oriented criticism, which nevertheless repeatedly assimilated itself to the style it criticised. We have also seen that a third, familiar style, interested primarily in the relational self and speaking out of the passions rather than about them, was slowly gaining salience in Shelley's thought, sometimes by infiltrating the others. "Julian and Maddalo" shows the influence of both the second and third styles, the "Euganean Hills" of the first and third. But for the remainder of this chapter, and all the next, we must concern ourselves with that first voice, resurgent in Shelley in 1819. We can pass over the angry polemic of "England in 1819", "A New National Anthem", "Song to the Men of England" and other pieces of this kind.[19] They are an important part of the radical political literature of the period, but the imagery is off the peg: "Rulers who neither see nor feel nor know,/ But leechlike to their fainting country cling . . . A people starved and stabbed in th'untilled field".[20] The passions run high, but the thought does not run deep. As a prelude to consideration of the "Ode to the West Wind", however, we should pause briefly on *The Mask of Anarchy*, another mixture of the first and third of Shelley's styles of thought, but with a bitter polemical flavour. The *Mask* is only a line shorter than the "Euganean Hills", and with the same metre and rhyme scheme, but it is in ballad form. This one change turns incantatory meditation with political application into pure broadside, heightening the emphasis on single words and images, but at the expense of over-exposing the controversial and vulgar qualities of the language and the populist abstraction of the imagery. The *Mask* is thus handicapped as radical polemic by lingering traces and premises of metaphysicality, and hampered as metaphysics by its insistent angry topicality.

In the first stanza the speaker is "asleep in Italy" when "a voice from over the Sea" leads him to "walk in the visions of Poesy", and leads us to wonder whether this is going to be visionary Poesy or activist politics. In the next six stanzas (5–29) he sees the Mask, or masque: a series of allegorical figures, Murder, Fraud, Hypocrisy and others, each with a characteristic attribute, and each likened to a real political figure. Murder "had a mask like Castlereagh", for example; the British Foreign Secretary was hated by radicals for what they saw as his reactionary foreign policy, and especially for his suppression of Irish unrest. Murder *is like* Castlereagh; this lampooning image, reminiscent of and possibly influenced by contemporary political caricaturists like Thomas Rowlandson, the Cruickshanks and James Gillray, is a rhetorically effective reversal of Shelley's habitual leap of thought from a person or object to an abstraction or subject. In the next fourteen stanzas (30–85) Anarchy himself appears, likened to no-one but Death, God and Law, trampling the "adoring multitude" into "a mire of blood". This is anything but the philosophical anarchy, the utopian post-political human condition, espoused by Shelley's old mentor Godwin. Its imaginative antecedent is Petrarch's black-clad figure of Death in *The Triumph of Death*, which Shelley was reading;[21] a later consequence was the central figure in Shelley's own "Triumph of Life". But now the small figure of Hope, a "maniac maid", lies down in front of the horses of these great figures, and a huge "Shape arrayed in mail" rises up and destroys them (86–134), while a voice speaks to the multitudes of slavery and freedom, justice, wisdom, peace and so on, urging them to peaceful mass assembly, even in the face of slaughter, as the way to overthrow the tyrants: "'Ye are many, they are few'" (155, 346–7, 360–3, 372);

"Look upon them as they slay
Till their rage has died away. . . .

And that slaughter to the nation
Shall steam up like inspiration,
Eloquent, oracular;
A volcano heard afar."

This shows what happens when visionary metaphysical "Poesy" is carelessly sorted with violent political reality. The *Mask* is a poem of great rhetorical and visual power, but it also throws those it professes to help upon the mercy of those it abhors, offering to the former only the insulting consolation that their inevitable slaughter will be inspirational to someone else. Too many ordinary people have been killed or seen their loved ones killed during the past two centuries as a result of this kind of incitement for these lines to be allowed to pass uncensured.

The "Ode to the West Wind", written six weeks later, lacks the specific political *animus* of the *Mask*, but it gives cause for related moral and political concern. The poem does not, however, manifest the particular faults Leavis notoriously found in it;[22] his specific judgements of its "weak grasp upon the actual" have been repeatedly exposed as ill-founded. More careful vindicators of the poem[23] are hardly to be blamed if their "calm, patient, neutral" descriptions often sound slightly affronted or pedantic. Leavis sounded so hostile, and besides Shelley himself gave them the lead, as we shall see. Leavis's criticisms of this poem, indeed, disclose precisely that weakness of thought which their author claimed to find in the poem itself. That is, Leavis's hostility is divorced from his specific observations about the poem, so that the feeling, to use his own words, has the appearance of "a general emotion pumped in from the outside". But this critical dissociation is not by any means peculiar to Leavis, whose voice was only one in a long tradition of antipathy to Shelley. That tradition has never, perhaps, succeeded in making it plain enough to the poet's admirers, or indeed to itself, that its antipathy is not principally to the poet's intellectual positions, whether political, religious or ethical (although Leavis did try to point this out); nor principally to mere sensory "weakness", as if the antipathy might simply disappear if only every moment of alleged weakness could be shown on the one hand not to be a moment of weakness (the conservative position), or on the other to be not so much a failure to grasp the actual as a successful demonstration that the actual is ungraspable (the radical position).

The trouble lies with something like Shelley's whole texture or cast of mind. It seems that for some readers that texture is repugnant. Not surprisingly, most attempts to describe that repugnance have not merely failed, but have offended the poet's admirers, many of whom have nevertheless been equally unsuccessful in explaining what they find attractive, not about his ideas, but about his texture of mind.[24]

The conservative position, which in Chapter 1 we called the referential defence of Shelley, has contented itself with pointing out that the poem is sensorily and referentially sound and interesting at various levels. First, the syntax *does* make sense, the images *are* firmly "grasped". Secondly, the poem is technically virtuosic: an unparalleled interlocking of the Italian *terza rima* and the English sonnet, and of the odal and lyric traditions; full of internal rhymes, alliterations and assonances, so that we can "hear" the gusts of wind; visually compelling, so that we can "see" the coming storm. Thirdly, and by extension, this is a description of a travelling thunderstorm unrivalled in English literature for its meteorological accuracy; here the scholarship tends to be hilariously solemn.[25] Fourthly, and this is the biographicalist variant of the defence, the poem gives voice and shape to Shelley's feelings about his personal circumstances at the time of composition: he felt himself in Italy to be a political and social exile, just when events in England most demanded his presence; his longest work, *The Revolt of Islam*, had just been savaged by *The Quarterly Review*; his three-year-old son, William, had died four months earlier, only nine months after the death of Clara, and with all the added complications one may imagine for Shelley's marriage; nevertheless there were signs of a real and radical uprising in England, and Mary was about to give birth. If winter had come, in short, could spring be far behind? Fifthly, the poem manifests a typically Shelleyan breadth and depth of reading: not just in the Dantean–Petrarchan verse form, to be explored again in "The Triumph of Life", but in the Lucretian–Holbachian conception of the wind as materialist necessity; in Hindu mythology, where Shiva and Vishnu are respectively the "Destroyer and Preserver"; and in specific images, such as the Homeric–Virgilian–Dantean likening of the souls of men to dead leaves.

The radical position, which in Chapter 1 we called the symbolist–stylist defence, is felicitously stated by Angela Leighton in her account of the "Ode": those "'large gestures' which Leavis derides in fact beautifully describe a characteristic of the Shelleyan sublime: that its language generously reaches towards its object, but also fails to grasp it"; the gestures are "a measure of the poem's movingly inadequate reach".[26] That quality of reach exceeding grasp, of "straining away", as Bloom says, from "the minute particulars of experience",[27] seems to be just what Shelleyans have always been thrilled by; the Browning metaphor of reach and grasp is critically important for them and their opponents alike. (Indeed, Browning's own final abandonment of Shelley, his poetic working-out of what was and what was not valuable in his mentor, his journey from the Alastorean *Pauline* to the dramatic monologues, constitutes the profoundest of all criticisms of Shelley.) The quality Bloom notices is one of straining or reaching not just away from but towards something. This is a fundamentally religious perception. Bloom goes to the Psalms, the "Song of Deborah" and the Jewish theologian Martin Buber for help in articulating it, utterly rejecting the reliance of Leavis and Tate on experience, on the notion of "subject–experiencing–object". In the "Ode", says Bloom, there "is *no* consciousness of an inanimate world", of an "It" for the "I" of the poem to "experience". Shelley's sense is not of "experience of the world", which is what he strains away from, but of direct "relationship with the world" as a "Thou", which is what he reaches towards. Bloom accuses Tate of placing poetry within "the world of phenomenal objects of the scientists", rather than in "the world in which Nature wears a human face". If it is proper to do this, then "Tate is justified", but then also we shall all be the "poor loveless ever-anxious crowd" of Coleridge's "Dejection" ode.[28] Bloom is as scathing about some of the scientific referentialists as he is about Tate, or Leavis. For him Shelley's "Ode" is a hymn to and a prophecy of the Spirit which is not just in the Wind but everywhere, including in the poet. Even if it fails, this is what it fails in, this is where it is most "movingly inadequate". Bloom's is still, I believe, the definitive defence of the poem, and in so far as it is for him the definitive Shelleyan poem his account of it is one of the most important defences of Shelley's poetry. Still, an experiential criticism need not condemn all poetry to the fallen realm of Dejection, as Bloom claims; it may simply find some attempts to grasp the ungraspable less impressive than others. Not every failure to grasp is a moving inadequacy of reach. Nor need such a criticism doggedly persist in seeking out a "weak grasp on the actual" where there is none. Sometimes it may not have gone to the very root of the poetic thought which it has too hastily represented as just syntactically or metaphorically "weak". The worm at the root may be a matter of the poem's very disposition.

The "Ode to the West Wind" is in five stanzas, each one a kind of sonnet, a fourteen-line structure in iambic pentameter containing four *terza rima* verses with a concluding couplet. The five stanzas together comprise a seventy-line address to and invocation of the "wild West Wind", also called "Wild Spirit", referred to repeatedly as "thou". The first three stanzas enumerate the qualities of the Wind itself, while the last two, as foreshadowed by the ritualistic phrase "O hear!" at the end of each of the first three, concern themselves principally with the speaker or invoker and with his relation to the Wind. Thus there is a "turn" in the poem's focus three-fifths of the way through, from the hearer of the invocation to what that hearer is going to be asked to hear, roughly corresponding to the usual "turn" in a sonnet after eight of its fourteen lines. The sonnet form is thereby reduplicated on a larger scale. Broadly speaking, it is the treatment of the Wind's qualities in the first three stanzas which has given rise to most of the explicit disagreement about the poem, but it is the treatment in the last two of the invoker which must chiefly determine one's response to the attitude of the poem as a whole.

In the first three stanzas (readers will need the text before them) the poetry seems to concern itself less with a relationship than with a kind of entity. That entity is not so much what Wilson Knight called a "true object" which is "in some mysterious way more us than itself"[29] as an unseen power or presence external to us, a something which blows, drives, chariots, moves, destroys and preserves the visible things of the world whilst remaining invisible itself. It is not so much a Bloomean "thou" which is also an "I" as an object of the speaker's perception which is nevertheless more than an "It". We are not so much in a "world in which Nature wears a human face" as in a natural world of leaves, seeds, buds, clouds, waves and sea-blooms, all driven by an inhuman power. This entity, power or presence is a version of the Shelleyan Power we have become familiar with, the one he spent his life as a poet trying to represent in either its transcendent or its immanent aspect, the one whose "awful shadow ...

Floats though unseen amongst us" in the "Hymn to Intellectual Beauty", the one called Necessity in *Queen Mab* and *Alastor*, the one whose secret strength informed the universe of things in "Mont Blanc". There is reason to believe that Shelley himself thought the "Ode" to have been one of his most successful representations and discoveries of this Power. At the end of his notebook draft of the poem appears, in an excited scribble, a quotation in Greek from Euripides' *Hercules Furens*. The quotation translated reads: "By virtue I, a mortal, defeat you, a great god".[30] In this poem the god takes the form of the West Wind, and is perceptible primarily to hearing and touch, although its "shape" is discernible when visible things are attached to or driven by it, as a magnetic field can be "seen" in the movement and position of the iron filings within its influence. Clearly, however, the Wind, or the Spirit that for the moment is the Wind, is more than just an unseen physical presence; this is more than a description of a travelling thunderstorm. There is a crucial determining figure of thought beneath the surface of the poem: that just as the existence of an entity imperceptible to some of the senses may be induced from the evidence of the other senses, so the existence of an entity imperceptible to all the senses may be induced from the evidence of the senses alone. Claims that Shelley's imagination is directly in contact with an ideal object notwithstanding, he is using the sensory world as the enabling material of his thought, and imagining the object of his thought as an experiential object: as an idea, perhaps, but one held in a quasi-sensory way. Moreover, he is using ordinary language as the enabling medium of his thought, and ordinary language has its own resistance and momentum. This means that certain kinds of question about the poem cannot be suppressed *a priori*. In its first line, for example, the Wind is addressed as "thou breath of Autumn's being". In the first place if Shelley means by this that the Wind is the breath of the being of Autumn, and not that it is the being of the breath of Autumn (both are syntactically possible), why even so does he wish to address the Wind in this way, and not simply as "thou breath of Autumn"? If we are to take the poem as seriously as Shelley apparently wished us to take it, and took it himself, we must assume that there is an important difference between "Autumn" and "Autumn's being". He could address the Wind with complete metaphorical perspicuity as "breath of Autumn" ("breathe me till I pant no more", as the hymn might have said); that would be enough to suggest that Autumn has being. What might he mean, then, by addressing the Wind as the breath of *the being of* Autumn? Is this a meaningless reduplication, an assertion that Autumn's being has being? Shelley must have meant one of two things, it seems. Either "Autumn's being" is that metaphysical existence or reality, almost that Platonic Form, of which all the qualities or properties of Autumn (worsening weather, dead leaves, a sense of maturity tipping over into old age) partake, that abstracted and schematised Autumn from which they are deduced; or it is a kind of intensified and concentrated autumn-quality or autumn-ness, induced from all empirically known autumns. The difference between these mutually exclusive alternatives is that the first one looks to an Autumn which is different from the ones we have known, while the second implies an Autumn which is the same as, but as it were more itself than, the ones we have known. Now it is clear that both Shelley's admirers and his opponents will prefer the first alternative as an account of what he means by "Autumn's being". Keats's ode to Autumn gives us concentrated autumn-ness, perhaps; Shelley's directs our thoughts onwards and outwards, from the sensory world of seeds and leaves towards their invisible destroyer and preserver, and then towards all that that entity may mean or signify. The sensory world through which the Wind is to be apprehended is "always already determined", as the hermeneutic jargon would put it, by the meaning of the Wind.

We need not concern ourselves at this point in the poem with certain ways of reading Shelley which may be somewhat more relevant later in it, and are highly persuasive outside it, especially in the *Alastor* tradition. There is a subjective idealist reading which looks at first sight very like the objective idealist reading of Bloom and others: one in which, in Elton's phrase, "the reality is Shelley's own soul".[31] Setting aside the less plausible versions of this argument – one thinks in particular of the "expressionist" view of Shelley's poetry as simply the musical expression of ever-shifting moods and feelings – we can characterise this reading as one in which the poet is seen as thinking chiefly about the varying conditions of the self, with no reference at all to any metaphysical entity. This is not an "I-Thou" reading, but an "I-I". But whereas in "Julian and Maddalo", say, the self is perspectivised by reference to other selves, here there are only the realities of language, nature and the Wind to prevent a collapse into solipsism. Shelley clearly wanted to order his feelings in relation to an external "universe of things", and by means of ordinary language. There is nothing here to suggest that he had abandoned his belief in poetry as an instrument of "moral and political science". On the contrary: this poem is clearly intended to be an agent in the moral and political realm, not just a piece of self-expression. We shall see when considering the last two stanzas that the subjective idealist reading lands Shelley in some very deep waters indeed. The sophisticated ironist reading is no more satisfactory; indeed it is on the whole much less persuasive in Shelley's poetry than its recent popularity might suggest. The poet is deliberately presenting or projecting in the poem – so the argument goes – a *persona* or view of the world which is not his own, or which is only one of his *personae* or world-views. Far from committing himself to the self or position projected, he is ironically criticising or distancing himself from it, from "the speaker". This poet is the urbane dramatist posited as the author of "Julian and Maddalo", *The Cenci* and a number of late "misery" lyrics only partly redeemed by the claim that they belong to an unfinished play. The trouble with this argument is that one may posit an urbane, ironic and dramatic creator of any number of sentimentalities, without in any way diluting their sentimentality. Moreover the witty Shelleys of the "Letter to Maria Gisborne", say, or of "With a Guitar, to Jane", are heavily outnumbered by the humourless Shelleys of *Queen Mab*, *Alastor*, *The Revolt of Islam*, the "Hymn to Intellectual Beauty", "Mont Blanc", and so on. Why should we assume that the smaller group is in charge? As for the arguments that the sentimental angel has fought back, ambushing the urbane ironist, or, conversely, that the ironist has deconstructed the angel ("make me thy liar"): here again readers who perhaps want to save Shelley from some of the perceived excesses of the poem's second half are taking him less seriously than he clearly wished to be taken.[32]

The fundamental disagreement about the "Ode" must be between those who find in it an excited discovery of a fundamental metaphysical reality beyond as well as in the sensory world, beyond as well as in the poet himself (why otherwise would he be excited? what would be the point of the poem?); and those who are disturbed by the texture or tendency of the excitement, rather than by the plausibility of the discovery. The kinds of regressive question raised by "breath of Autumn's being" persist throughout the first three sections of the poem. Answering them on one level simply re-opens them on a deeper one, and to claim that this constant re-opening shows how multifarious or endless the poem's meanings are is to rely on an understanding of poetic meaning which is at least questionable. The dead leaves driven by the wind are described as "Yellow, and black, and pale, and hectic red,/ Pestilence-stricken multitudes". Why is this? Presumably, in the first place, because the dead leaves Shelley was looking at in the wood near Florence where the poem "was conceived and chiefly written" (as he tells us in a note) *were* these colours. But it is of the nature of Shelley's poetry to suggest that there is more to the appearance in it of physical objects than the fact that they are mentioned. The ravine of Arve "means" something. So what do these leaves "mean"? We know that Homer, Virgil and Dante all explicitly compared human souls to dead leaves, using the familiar sensory term, leaves, to convey something to us about the nature of the unfamiliar non-sensory term, souls. Shelley can exploit this fact of literary history, leaving it to us, who also know our poets, to make the connection between leaves and the races of man which will complement the meaning of the image. That is, whereas Dante and the others openly use the familiar to explain the unfamiliar, Shelley covertly uses the unfamiliar to explain the familiar. This is not a trifling detail, but, as his admirers readily acknowledge, an essential quality of Shelley's poetry. Something like a reference, an idea or an abstraction lies behind the familiar physical fact, and if we can share his awareness of its presence then the poetry will come to life. His detractors will say that this connection is often too tenuous or too ambiguous. For example, why are the coloured leaves, or souls (do souls have colours?), "Pestilence-stricken"? Well, these are the colours of disease: pale consumption, black plague, yellow jaundice, red flush. But still, why are the leaves represented as diseased, and as resembling people who have died of disease? Is death the same as disease? Does the wind blow away only diseased multitudes, and not healthy ones, or is the suggestion that we are all diseased, morally as well as physically? Some readers will believe that the poetry's capacity to invite an apparently endless series of such questions is a sign of its richness. Others will feel that the possible implications of the metaphors are just too various for coherence, and that this incoherence is not so much metaphysical ("do the metaphors persuade us of the existence of the Power?") as dispositional ("do they persuade us of the integrity of the poem?").

How are the leaves also "like ghosts from an enchanter fleeing"? How is the Wind like an enchanter? Again the nature of the simile, the likening of familiar to unfamilar, prods us into asking these questions; we are meant to ask them. If, as Bloom suggests,[33] this enchanter is "a necromancer who also exorcises" (does "enchanter" convey quite the same as "exorcist"?), and the dead leaves are therefore the unwanted ghosts of once living leaves, and if the dead leaves are "pestilence-stricken multitudes", then are these pestilence-stricken ghosts? Ghosts are not usually thought of as yellow, black and red, so is the leaves' resemblance to ghosts a separate and unconnected idea, or is that image meant to complement and reinforce the "pestilence" one? Are pestilence-stricken ghosts meant to be diseased dead souls, as opposed to just plain dead souls? Why must they be exorcised, or enchanted? Who are the living souls, distressed or frustrated by their presence? As for the Wind, it is both an enchanter and a charioteer (or chariot). It both exorcises the unwanted ghosts of the dead and ushers the new souls to their birthplaces. The fact that these two functions seem magically and mythically quite unrelated does not matter from a point of view such as Bloom's: "shifting abstract images can be condemned only if *on principle* one disapproves of images which shift or are abstract". But surely this is a matter not of principle, but of practice. One may find these shifting abstractions uncomfortable as a matter of intellectual experience. When Bloom tells us that an understanding of the word "Charioted" needs "a background of more of Shelley's poetry than this 'Ode' and of more poetry than Shelley's alone", so that the chariot is "the vehicular form of divinity when it is conveyed as man in many traditions", we can see how even for Shelley's least referentialist admirers a referred or deferred meaning may so often be necessary. If we always need so much more than the image we are experiencing in order to make sense of it, perhaps it is less surprising that so many readers experience particular images as unsatisfactory. If the Wind is a divinity taking the form of a chariot what does it mean to say that it is also "conveyed as man"? Are not the seeds images of man? If the seeds are "like" corpses, then what corresponds in a corpse to the shoots emerging from the seeds in spring: babies? They "are only 'like'", says Bloom, but in this kind of thinking, where the reader's imagination is constantly asked to follow several leads at once, how are we to know where to stop, or which are false leads? The very kinds of thinking which some readers of Shelley admire the verse for doing and provoking are the kinds which, when pressed, lead to those questions which the same readers find hostile or unimaginative. If the spring wind's clarion suggests the last trump, then this seasonal change is not seasonal. If winter comes spring cannot be far behind, but if *this* spring comes there will be no more winters. If the earth is not just asleep but dreaming, are we to wonder what its dreams are? How exactly are buds like flocks? Are they "sweet" because they taste sweet, or in some other way? What is evoked by the image of their "feeding in air"? How does it help to be told that Shiva and Vishnu are the "Destroyer" and "Preserver" of Hindu mythology? We know that this same Wind is an enchanter, or exorcist, a chariot, or charioteer, the breath of an idea of Autumn, a destroyer and a preserver; for many readers of Shelley these "varied but related abstractions" (Bloom again) are so varied that they are only related by that otherwise indescribable something which they are there to evoke. There is nothing to connect them if they are not connected to each other.

Readers who go on complaining in this manner about the next two stanzas as well will no doubt be accused of hostile prejudice or naive literal-mindedness; nevertheless questions of this kind will not go away, because the verse itself raises them. Bloom argues, *contra* Leavis, that in the second line of stanza two, "Loose clouds like Earth's decaying leaves are shed", that critical Shelleyan word "like" means "as", so that it is the process of shedding which is in question, rather than any particular similarity between clouds and leaves (although Bloom also wants to insist that there *is* a particular similarity).[34] But then why didn't Shelley write "as"? Now the leaves are decaying, not just dead, not like ghosts; are the clouds like the leaves in this respect too? Are they like rotting organic matter which will produce life? What is the seed in this case? We know that what will burst forth is "rain and fire and hail", but are these on the same level of the extended simile as the seeds and buds are? How can the Wind be both the stream onto which the clouds fall and the force which knocks them down? How can the clouds be both the seedbeds of the storm and its angels or harbingers? The Wind is now both the "Dirge/ Of the dying year" and the "breath of Autumn's being"; no doubt these metaphors can be unpacked to their mutual advantage, but in how many other directions would that explanation lead us? In the third stanza the word "coil", in "Lulled by the coil of his chrystalline streams", presumably has something of its secondary sense of "bustle" or "hubbub" ("mortal coil"), as well as its primary sense: or else why lulled *by*, and not lulled *in*? But then why not a word evoking murmuring or bubbling? If the other sense is primary, how does the sea lie in or by his own streams? How is the "intenser day" within the wave brighter or more vivid or more real than the one above it? When we come to the second half of the stanza Shelley himself tells us in a po-faced footnote that the "vegetation at the bottom of the sea, of rivers, and of lakes, sympathizes with that of the land in the change of seasons, and is consequently influenced by the winds which announce it"; this is a "phenomenon" apparently "well known to naturalists" (222). The tone of this note explains much about why meteorologists are fond of the poem, and about the kinds of defence it has attracted. Again, however, we know that there is meant to be more to the poem than botanical precision. This precision is intended to provide natural evidence supporting various non-natural hypotheses. Shelley keeps quiet in his note about the revolutionary and apocalyptic implications of the image, but in the poem even the remotest and most vegetative beings "grow grey with fear" at the coming of the Wind as revolution, or as the last judgment. History may have cycles like the seasons; a long winter may be about to end. There may be a controlling power behind historical phenomena as behind natural ones, and these powers may be the same power. The underlying figure of thought of these stanzas, as we saw earlier, is that a trans-sensory entity may be extrapolated from purely sensory evidence; but the poem believes in this entity from the start. The familiar sensory phenomena are presented both as confirmative of and as explained by a presupposed but indescribable entity; the movement of thought is deductive, not inductive. Again, some readers have trouble with this movement of thought, with the manner in which the metaphors are employed, not so much because it seems metaphysically unconvincing as because it seems to be in bad faith.

The poem's last two stanzas concern themselves more with the status of the person addressing the Wind than with the nature of the Wind itself, and there the question of metaphorical and intellectual disposition becomes vitally important. The Bloomean symbolist will find in these stanzas the *locus classicus* of the Shelleyan aspiration to Life (not life), soaring above alienation from the world of It. The experiential reader will find here the *locus classicus* of the Shelleyan struggle not just to discover Necessity but to assume her mantle. A kind of gestalt shift is involved: what looks to some like passionate self-abnegation looks to others like egotistical self-aggrandisement. In any case, there has been a crucial alteration in the poem's central figure of thought. Instead of seeming to extrapolate from natural evidence the existence of a trans-sensory "power" operating in the realm of nature, and just hinting at the power's human dimension, the poem suddenly assumes the existence of the power in the human world. This still isn't a matter of pure subjective idealism. Although that view of the poetry must have more weight here, Shelley does not appear to be talking "only" about his own desires, without reference to any external world. Nor is it quite a matter of dramatic irony; the attitudes of despair and exultation are somewhat stylised, perhaps, but not fully displaced or ironised. The passage has the air of a genuine first-person disclosure of relationship between their speaker and a natural power. At first there is nothing to take exception to in that. The conditional first ten lines of the fourth stanza ("If I were a dead leaf . . .", and so on) recreate an excitement at the power of a great gale which might be anyone's excitement, a regret at the loss of childhood capacity to be at one with nature which might be Wordsworth's regret. So far the ontological status of the Wind in relation to the natural world has not changed, and the speaker is a part of that world. One may still pause, of course, at some images: why wish to be a dead leaf, a pestilence-stricken ghost, and not a winged seed? why exactly is the cloud swift now, and not loose? why the sexual connotation of "pant beneath thy power"? what is intended by "skiey"? is to be "uncontrollable" the same as to be "free"? There is nothing really disturbing here, however, and much that is impressive. The change comes with "I would ne'er have striven/ As thus with thee in prayer in my sore need". Suddenly and for the first time the Wind and the speaker are principally in agonistic, and therefore moral, relation to one another. The speaker is not dead or swift or strong, but "tameless, and swift, and proud". Yes, we can see that a connection *might* have been made between a natural tempest and a moral one. Peterloo, for example, or more interestingly the poet's feelings about Peterloo, might have been likened to a thunderstorm. But the "power" hasn't been thought about explicitly in the poem as the sort of entity which affects moral, as opposed to natural, humanity. Only now, in discovering the speaker's desire to reform the world, do we find that the Wind has been a moral force all along; indeed its principal importance, the reason for the whole invocation and for the machinery of the first three stanzas, lies in that prior desire. The trouble is not with Shelley's excited apprehension of the power, nor even with the suggestion that it may be a moral power as well as a natural one; it is with the absence of any thinking about how that power could be a moral force outside the feelings of the thinker, which is also an absence of thinking about the feelings themselves. The only relation the power has, as a moral power, is with the speaker. The impression given, inevitably, is that he cannot distinguish, or does not want to, between his powerful desires and the power. Could he tell, even if he tried, where one stops and the other begins? The command is "Be thou me", not "Be thou in me"; not "may the force be with you", but "may you be the force".

Still, even all this might be no more than a matter of private morality, resolve or despair. The last eight lines, however, take the culminating step into the public realm. The speaker asks the Wind both to be him and to drive his dead thoughts, asks it to scatter his words "by the incantation of this verse". These assorted requests, provoking familiar questions about the many directions in which the imagery leads, are preambular to the crucial demand, which is that the Wind and speaker awaken the earth, mankind, the universe. The speaker may despair of his power, but what is essential to this demand is that he never doubts his rightness, his knowledge of what is true and good in human affairs, what is best for the "dead leaves" which are unenlightened humanity. This lack of genuine self-criticism has something of the odour of megalomania, the sheer desire for power without the limiting sense of moral fallibility. Those who attend to their own feelings in this way, who regard life as a bed – or crown – of thorns and themselves as saviours, who thus represent themselves to their readers or audiences or potential disciples, may come to look not so much like prophets, like a Job, as Bloom claims, but like something more sinister. Messianism has its dark side. Perhaps Shelley had no such inclinations, no such intentions, but the self of the poetry does look to some readers as if it has at least such a potential. Shelley has incurred the disapprobation of these readers not because he strains towards the ideal, not because he believes or wants to believe in a Necessity which is moral as well as natural, but because of the attitude of, or his manner of regarding, his poetic self and its represented feelings. To put the case another way: one of the "thorns of life" is the realisation that one cannot any longer be entirely as a child imagining oneself at the centre of the Wind's attention. Wordsworth and Coleridge knew this; their odes "Dejection" and "Immortality" are recognitions of what is lost with childhood, not attempts to *be* a child once more. If some readers find in the failure to grasp of Shelley's ode not a moving but a fortunate inadequacy of reach, they need not thereby be consigning themselves to perpetual alienation from either the natural or the spiritual realm. Perhaps they can just hear overtones of political authoritarianism and dispositional wilfulness in a poem springing from an unexamined passion for an *a priori* idea.

5

Shelley's Poetry, 1818–20 (continued)

PROMETHEUS UNBOUND

General remarks

C. S. Lewis called it "the greatest long poem in the nineteenth century";[1] John Todhunter had in 1880 already declared it "the supreme English poem of the nineteenth century".[2] Even those who are unwilling to accept these assertions in the light of *The Prelude*, *In Memoriam* or *Don Juan* would probably agree with Carlos Baker that *Prometheus Unbound* is Shelley's "masterpiece", and that it has been so regarded ever since its composition – "except by a few unreconstructed dissenters".[3] Baker was thinking of the kind of dissenter who prefers other things in Shelley: the political radical who finds the poem too ideal, the Peacock or Mary Shelley who prefers more "human passion". But even those who are so unreconstructed that they dissent from much of Shelley's work have still found *Prometheus Unbound* the epitome of all that they dissent from. *The London Magazine* in 1820 produced, says D. H. Reiman, a "triumph of Romantic critical theory" by finding in the poem "a symbol of the peaceful triumph of goodness over power", while in 1821 William Hazlitt concentrated his criticism of Shelley on the same work, calling it "all volatile intellectual salt of tartar".[4] Shelley's admirers this century have gone on regarding the poem as his central achievement, but twentieth-century dissenters have been less prepared than Hazlitt was to write about it at length. Why spend any longer than necessary with poetry one dislikes? But Hazlitt contributed so much to this debate just because he was prepared to build his case around the one poem Shelley's advocates regarded as central to his achievement. Shelley himself set more store by this than by any other of his poems, with the possible exception of *Adonais*. "It is the most perfect of my productions", he told his publisher, Charles Ollier, "my favourite poem": meaning, he added wryly, that it "cannot sell beyond twenty copies"; "it is written only for the elect", he told Leigh Hunt (ii 174, 200). His judgement was good. For all its reputation among the *cognoscenti*, the poem never had, in the last century, the popular appeal of its principal forerunner, *Queen Mab*. Similarly in this century: one or two lyrical excerpts aside, it has not had the anthologised visibility of the "Ode" and the shorter lyrics, *Adonais* or the familiar conversational poems.

Shelley was more explicit in his preface (pp. 132–6) than in those letters about what he thought would make the poem unpopular: its "moral interest". As we saw in Chapter 2, he intended Prometheus to be "the type of the highest perfection of moral and intellectual nature". While displaying "courage and majesty and firm and patient opposition to omnipotent force", the Titan was to be "exempt from the taints of ambition, envy, revenge". This made the character, Shelley thought, not less but "more poetical" than that of Milton's Satan, because all "pernicious casuistry" in the reader, all weighing of fault with wrong, would be rendered impossible. The characters would be homogeneous assemblages of idealised passions, questioning others but not themselves. Since questioning of character, "pernicious casuistry", is just what most readers want in a drama, this "poetical" one would not be popular. Readers were furthermore to be shown these "beautiful idealisms of moral excellence" in imagery "drawn from the operations of the human mind, or from those external actions by which they are expressed". Dante is the chief model Shelley cites here; he could be thinking of those damned souls in the *Inferno* whose punishments and conditions so aptly mirror their sins, their moral states. The "moral interest" of the *Prometheus*, then, was to lie in its quasi-pictorial representation of conceptualised mental and passional "operations", such as "courage". Shelley once said to Godwin that his peculiar power lay in his capacity "to apprehend minute & remote distinctions of feeling" (i 577); here he wanted to give shape to that apprehension. Shelley's strongest poetic habit, as we have seen, was to use a term "drawn from the operations of the human mind" as the *explicans*, rather than as the *explicandum*, in an image or simile. From *Queen Mab* onwards the intellectual subject, the concept or the abstraction, was for him more familiar and tangible than the sensory object linked with it. As William Keach says, "Shelley reverses the usual figurative function of imagery and makes a mental state or operation the vehicle in a figure whose tenor is sensory and physical".[5] For Keach, as we saw in Chapter 3, reversals of this kind in Shelley are intriguing and suggestive, not frustrating and elusive. Keach speculates that Shelley found the "amphibiousness" of the term "imagery" to be "philosophically valuable",[6] whereas other readers may have found a certain amphibiousness, a certain cold-bloodedness, in Shelley's imagery itself. Keach's comparison of Dante and Shelley, intended to reveal underlying resemblances in their imaginative practice, may leave many readers of poetry convinced that whether or not Dante makes us see more a scene "more *definitely*", as Eliot claimed and Keach denies,[7] he always makes us see it more feelingly. Shelley may have tried to emulate Dante, but whether he actually did so is another matter. In any case his practice, as he predicted, did not make his poem popular.

But Shelley had a more important objective than mere popularity, as he also made plain in his preface. The final goal of the whole enterprise was to prepare the minds "of the more select classes of poetical readers" for "reasoned principles of moral conduct". Shelley readily admits to his "'passion for reforming the world'",[8] to his belief that both he and the less "poetical" Milton were alike the "companions and forerunners" of social change. The entire imaginative undertaking, the representation of idealisms of moral excellence by intellectual imagery, is conceived in the light of a certain understanding of what moral excellence is: principally, "firm and patient opposition to omnipotent force". The poetry is never "didactic", Shelley affirms, but its imaginative practice is in keeping with its doctrinal purpose. Courage and excellence are assumed already to exist conceptually before they are imagined poetically. The poetry illustrates them, rather than exploring them. What distinguishes the "select" or the "elect" from the mass of unreconstructed dissenters, then, will be above all their receptiveness to a texture of thought which is both essentialist and moralistic, so that courage, majesty, and the will to oppose are conceived as isolable, picturable and desirable "operations" of mind. Thinking about these concepts will then be a matter of finding appropriate imagery with which to picture them, rather than testing the concepts themselves in richer human settings. To someone who holds the broadly

Hazlittean, experientialist view of literature and the self described in Chapter 1, a view which is also roughly Aristotelian, this manner of thinking poetically about courage, say, will look impoverished or "thin". To one who holds the symbolist view described in Chapter 1, which is roughly Kantian and Platonist, it looks perfectly acceptable, indeed highly desirable. Thinking poetically is part of the greater project of thinking philosophically, and politically, about the world. Shelley's "great work", as he said himself, would in the end have to be world-historical. *Prometheus* was Miltonic and Aeschylean, he conceded, not Platonic, but this was an Aeschylean and Miltonic machinery adapted to a greater Platonic and Hegelian purpose, discernible only to the elect.

Still, Shelley's imagination in 1818 was home to a much larger and richer tenancy than in 1812. Holbach, Godwin and Condorcet were still there, almost part of the furniture by now, but with Aeschylus, Milton, Dante, Spenser and perhaps Goethe had come an opulence and extension of pictorial metaphor, a range of vocabulary and rhythm, a congeniality of dramatic form (Lewis called this his "one perfect story"[9]), and a manner of thinking into the central Shelleyan concepts which showed that at least as much of the rent was being paid by the poets as by the philosophers. This is why in attending to the poetry Shelley's admirers do well to avoid giving too much room to referentialisms of various kinds. "The problem in interpretating [sic] *Prometheus Unbound*", wrote Cameron twenty years ago, "is to find the meaning of the symbols".[10] This is the language of the elect, whether "the symbols" are taken to operate in the political realm, as by Cameron, or the metaphysical, as by Wasserman. Know the "sources" of the symbolism and you will understand the poem. Demogorgon "is" or "stands for" Eternity, Necessity or Imagination; Prometheus is Will or the Mind of Man; Asia is Love; Panthea is Faith or Hope. Prometheus's condition confronted by the Furies is that of post-Revolutionary liberals. The two great visions of Act IV are poetic realisations of the science of Humphrey Davy. Panthea, Asia and Prometheus "are" Claire, Mary and Shelley. Even, or rather especially, the highly sophisticated version of this type of criticism of the poem practised by G. M. Matthews represents "meaning" as something endlessly deferred, forever unavailable to the ordinary reader. Matthews writes of Shelley's "over-determined" concepts, none of which is supposed to "stand for" any one abstraction in a systematic way, but each of which serves as a "collecting-point" for several of his "political, scientific, or philosophical perceptions of reality", so that to understand the meaning of a concept "one must reckon with the whole of Shelley – and not with his texts alone".[11] Bloom is right to insist that the poetry "resists philosophy and theology by being its own discipline", and that until this is acknowledged "criticism of Shelley will always be crippled by its tradition of intentionalism" (Bloom's term for what we have called referentialism). What "Shelley the man may have believed" has little to do with "what Shelley's poem believes and communicates",[12] which according to Bloom concerns the stifling of desire, the binding of energy and the abandoning of relationship. Bloom's account of this poem is, once more, *the* modern account with which a reconstructed dissent has to come to terms, by pointing out that there are those for whom desire, energy and relationship, no matter how "poetically" they are imagined or pictured, will always be only philosophical concepts unless they are tested in thinking about human lives and feelings. Their meaning can never be their meaning for our lives while they remain isolable intellectual constructions. What a Bloom may see as "apocalyptic humanism"[13] others will see as analytic idealism.

In Greek myth Prometheus the wise Titan, bringer of fire to mankind, refuses to tell the angry and fearful Olympian Zeus the secret of his downfall, which is that the nymph Thetis, of whom Zeus is enamoured, will have a child greater than its father. After long resistance and torture (inflicted in Hesiod's version of the myth for the giving of fire to mankind, in Aeschylus's version for the withholding of the secret from Zeus) Prometheus tells his story and is freed, while Thetis is married off to the mortal Peleus, father of Achilles. Shelley uses a variation on Aeschylus; his Prometheus knows the secret, but never reveals it, even under torture. In the first of the four acts of Shelley's "lyrical drama" Prometheus simply retracts his curse, earlier pronounced against his oppressor Jupiter (Shelley uses the Roman name); is tortured by Furies; and is consoled by spirits of the human mind. In the second act the nymph Asia, his beloved, a daughter of Ocean, travels with her sister Panthea to find the secret of Jupiter's downfall herself from Demogorgon, a kind of eternity- or Necessity-figure. The third act shows us Jupiter overthrown by Demogorgon, Prometheus unbound, and Asia and Prometheus reunited in a kind of earthly paradise. The fourth act is a series of lyrics celebrating this new world. At 2609 lines, roughly two-thirds of them in blank verse and the rest in assorted lyric measures, the poem bears a strong prosodic resemblance to *Queen Mab*, with the nine narrative cantos converted into four dramatic acts. But this is a "drama" in the sense in which its "desire" and "relationship" are desire and relationship. The first three acts are a kind of giant frieze depicting numerous images or moments of change, rather than being a dramatised process of change. The whole poem's central moment, Prometheus's recantation of his curse, which is also Jupiter's downfall, is in the poem's own terms a "deep truth" which is "imageless", a single, dimensionless, invisible and unrepresentable point in a million-year history. The poem's "moral interest" is static rather than dynamic, and conceptual rather than dramatic.

Act I

The one-scene first act, much the longest at 833 lines, is dominated by the figure and condition of Prometheus himself, and it carries so much of the "moral interest" that it very nearly preempts the entire poem. According to Bloom the act "is a complete visionary drama in miniature", a drama in which "Prometheus wills himself back into relationship" with the world and out of mere experience of it.[14] The protagonist's powerful opening speech (1–73) further intensifies that impression of frontloading. To paraphrase Bloom: in so far as the poem is a drama this speech is already its climax. Shelley's principal imaginative method in the first part of the speech, as his preface and his previous practice have led us to expect, is to conceive Prometheus's physical condition, "Nailed to this wall of eagle-baffling mountain", as emblematic of his already determined moral condition (20, 31–43):

> The crawling glaciers pierce me with the spears
> Of their moon-freezing chrystals; the bright chains
> Eat with their burning cold into my bones.
> ... and shapeless sights come wandering by,
> The ghastly people of the realm of dream,
> Mocking me: and the Earthquake-fiends are charged
> To wrench the rivets from my quivering wounds...
> While from their loud abysses howling throng

The genii of the storm, urging the rage
Of whirlwind, and afflict me with keen hail.

These natural objects – mountain wall, glaciers, earthquakes, whirl-winds – appear to give physical shape to but really derive their meaning from the subject "Prometheus". They do not have the ontological weight or depth of reality of the natural objects in "Mont Blanc", notwithstanding Bloom's claim that this, "like the icy ravine of Arve", is "an emblem of the supreme indifference of the natural world to man".[15] This ravine is ephemeral because it was conceived purely *as* an emblem, a quasi-physical analogue for the "operations of the mind". "Eagle-baffling" and "moon-freezing" add little to our conceptions of this mountain and these glaciers, or of their "indifference". That Prometheus is nailed or riveted to one and pierced by the other, that he is "afflicted" by "keen hail", is meant to tell us something about the sort of sub-ject he is, but it tells us so little about the sort of object they are that the intended effect is vitiated. Whether or not Prometheus is a kind of being who has at this point fallen out of relation-ship with nature and into mere experience of it, the poetry has certainly fallen out of the relationship with nature that it had in "Mont Blanc" and in the "Ode". "Burning" cold, "bright" chains, "shapeless" sights, "ghastly" people, "quivering" wounds: here there is still much of that old Shelleyan-Gothic adjectival obvi-ousness, that unmetaphorical attitude to individual words and feelings, which seem to matter so much less than the purpose they are serving.

As soon as drama and character are given precedence over landscape the poetry's moral and metaphysical suggestiveness increases. Prometheus asks Earth, Heaven and Sea if they have "heard" his "agony", and appeals to "Ye Mountains", "Ye Icy Springs", "Thou Serenest Air" and "Ye swift Whirlwinds" (59–73) to repeat the curse he spoke against Jupiter. They answer him in the poem's first lyric (74–106). The dramatic mechanism itself, the very conceit by which Earth or Mountains or Whirl-winds can "speak", does more to explain what kind of subject Prometheus is than all the set-piece objectifying imagery did. Part of his speech (1–24, 50–9) is addressed to Jupiter:

Monarch of Gods and Daemons, and all Spirits
But One, who throng those bright and rolling Worlds

Which Thou and I alone of living things
Behold with sleepless eyes! regard this Earth
Made multitudinous with thy slaves. . . .
Three thousand years of sleep-unsheltered hours
And moments – aye divided by keen pangs
Till they seemed years, torture and solitude,
Scorn and despair, – these are mine empire: –
More glorious far than that which thou surveyest
From thine unenvied throne, O mighty God!
Almighty, had I deigned to share the shame
Of thine ill tyranny. . . .
Ah me, alas, pain, pain ever, forever!

"No change, no pause, no hope", Prometheus continues, but he
can even welcome these "wingless, crawling Hours", because one
among them

Shall drag thee, cruel King, to kiss the blood
From these pale feet, which then might trample thee
If they disdained not such a prostrate slave.
Disdain? Ah no! I pity thee. – What Ruin
Will hunt thee undefended through wide Heaven!
How will thy soul, cloven to its depth with terror,
Gape like a Hell within! I speak in grief,
Not exultation, for I hate no more,
As then, ere misery made me wise. – The Curse
Once breathed on thee I would recall.

A "drama in miniature", or at least a complete dramatic monologue, is contained in these two addresses to Jupiter. The first
address discloses to us two empires. One, Jupiter's, contains all
"living things" except for that one thing which is the other empire, Prometheus. This second, inward empire-of-one, this single
plot of non-Jovian ground, has two principal attributes. First it
is a place of pain, "keen pangs", "torture", "pain, pain ever, forever". As Prometheus says later (477), "Pain is my element".
Secondly, it is a place of resistance, of pure determination or
will: "Yet I endure". Prometheus speaks later (114) of his "all-
enduring will". The second empire is "glorious" despite the pain,
just because it is so resolutely autonomous and self-sufficient.
But with the second address, and after only fifty lines of the

poem, these two empires fall. The state of resolute and pain-filled separation from Jupiter which has defined the Promethean empire and made it paradoxically so Jovian ("deigned", "dis-dained", "trample thee", "prostrate slave") dissolves. In that in-finitesimal moment between the two words "slave" and "Disdain!" Prometheus's condition becomes at a single stroke, and un-representedly, one of pity and sympathetic understanding. All at once, with no transition, he hates no more, he loses all "evil wish" (70), he passes from "misery" to being "wise". The oppressor is defeated at the moment when the oppressed stops seeing himself as oppressed and the other as an oppressor, himself as merely not-Jupiter and Jupiter as everything which is not himself, and begins to see both as equivalent beings. The very "Ruin" which Prometheus foresees for his adversary, and which prompts his sympathy, is initiated by his own impulse of recantation. How satisfactory is this exploration of the human conditions of moral oppression and oppressedness, of willed adherence to and self-liberation from an attitude of mind? For readers like Bloom, obviously, it is highly satisfactory. Unreconstructed dissenters, however, must point to that crucial absence of thought at the moment of reversal. The current suddenly flows the other way, but we do not see why. There is a moral discontinuity, one which the preface to the poem should have led us to expect. In this poem remorse and self-forgiveness are conceived as distinct and uncontiguous contraries, in fact precisely as concepts, and one may be preferred to the other just as a matter of will, like stepping from one side of a stream to the other. But are the self and its passions really like that? Is there a "will" which just chooses "self-forgiveness" as against "remorse" and, after an instantaneous struggle with itself, overcomes itself? Or do remorse and self-forgiveness subsist in permanent symbiosis, in a state in which neither term even begins to exhaust the moral possibilities and neither condition finally prevails? Even here on his abstract and idealising home ground, away from the dangers (for him) of false landscape-objectification, Shelley's thought will look to many readers too polarised, too intent on "minute & remote distinctions of feeling", insufficiently aware of the transformations worked in all feelings and states of mind by the constant adjacency and admixture of others.

In the next part of the act (74–221) the four elemental Voices mentioned earlier, and then their mother the Earth, who is also

Prometheus's mother, refuse in turn to repeat his curse upon Jupiter, remembering how none of the "Misery" inflicted upon the world by the tyrant and by their resistance to him was so awful as that consequent upon the curse. Prometheus reminds them unavailingly that only he, only his will and condition, have kept them in existence. The Earth speaks to her son in "the language of the dead", an "inorganic voice", so that Jupiter as ruler of the living, organic world cannot hear her. Prometheus is able to feel her thoughts, rather than hearing her words. She tells him that "there are two worlds of life and death", and that he must summon one of the "shadows of all forms that think and live" from the second world, the one "underneath the grave", where the dead also are. Only such a shadow may repeat the curse without repeating its effects on the living, since Jupiter will take revenge this time only upon the shadow world. While the two empires are "three thousand years old", these speakers take us back "Thrice three hundred thousand years". The two time-scales connect us both to pre-Aeschylean Greece, the life of humanity, and to the life of the earth. What we are to make of the Earth's "inorganic" language and the "two worlds of life and death" is not, perhaps, so clear, although commentators are always quick nowadays to emphasise Shelley's interest in the limitations of speech. The language of the Earth and her children is unremarkable in itself; it is the situation, the possible significances of these beings, which are clearly meant to engage our attention, for whatever reason. The ensuing speeches of the two Oceanids, Panthea and Ione (222–57), leading up to the utterance of the curse by the Phantasm of Jupiter (262–301), are simply poor poetry ("Cruel he looks but calm and strong/ Like one who does, not suffers wrong"). Commentators are nevertheless so interested in what all these characters "stand for" that they discount this. Even Bloom tells us to "wait upon an apprehension of the whole lyrical drama, of the entire poem simultaneously perceived" before deciding "what it is that we are given an anagoge of" here.[16] No wonder that understanding has been reserved for the elect. Understanding of *Paradise Lost* or *The Divine Comedy* is surely also completed in an apprehension of the whole poem, but we do not find ourselves needing to wait for that apprehension in order to make sense of, to find value in, an otherwise unremarkable component scene.

The curse and its retraction are central to the meaning of the act and the poem. The Phantasm speaks the words which were originally Prometheus's: "Fiend, I defy thee. . . . do thy worst. Thou art Omnipotent./ O'er all things but thyself I gave thee power,/ And my own will". But the curse calls down retribution on more than just the curser: "Let thy malignant spirit move/ Its darkness over those I love". The intention of all this is that the "sufferer's curse/ Clasp thee, his torturer, like remorse" in a "robe of envenomed agony", such that the more the curse causes Jupiter to multiply his "ill deeds", the more *he* will suffer ("then be thou damned, beholding good"), until in the end, says Prometheus, "thou must appear to be/ That which thou art internally" – this will be the "hour" of Jupiter's "fall". The moral logic of this curse is consistent with that of the poem's opening speech. Prometheus "is" pure resistance and will, Jupiter "is" power *over*. He has power over everything except himself, because power cannot have power over power, and Prometheus, because the Titan is *a priori* that over which power cannot be had. But resistance is also that which increases the ill effects of power over everything else, and thus resistance shares in the ill nature of power. Meanwhile power is likewise implicated with suffering and remorse. The passion of the victim of power, that victim over whom the power is had, is "like remorse" in the exerciser of the power; the keenest damnation or remorse of that "evil" exerciser lies in his beholding the suffering of the "good" victim, until that damnation or remorse becomes an outward as well as an inward "fall", and the very being of the exerciser of power disintegrates. This logic is not completed, however, until Prometheus rejects it, immediately after the curse is spoken: "It doth repent me. . . . I wish no living thing to suffer pain" (303–5). He renounces the fallen world of the curse in exorcising the Phantasm who *is* now the curse, and in eschewing the active resistance or power which *was* the curse. He remakes himself into a being in whom power and resistance do not subsist; he wishes no more pain even to Jupiter.

It is easy to imagine what a Christian apologist for the poem[17] might make of this curse and its recantation, although it seems unlikely, given his other remarks on the subject, that Shelley would have been as interested in any specifically Christian ethic of forgiveness as in the moral logic of renunciation and remorse which can also be found, or so he believed, in other ethics besides. He may perhaps even have intended these lines as a criticism of his

own earlier attitudes, such as in *The Mask of Anarchy* and the
"Ode to the West Wind", whose speakers' Prometheanism is more
that of the curse than that of its recantation. But does this poetry represent a remorse, a defiance or a suffering that we can
recognise? Can we sympathise with a poetry which has this sense
of these passions? Bloom says that no-one can accuse *this* Shelley
of being a "naive antinomian and childish rebel", of being insufficiently "complex, subtle, meaningful, coherent";[18] but this
Shelley asks us to accept that power and resistance, evil and
good, are as they are here, and that they do operate in these
ways. This is a posited human universe which is divided into
tyrannous omnipotence and pure wilful resistance and nothing
else, and then instantaneously dissolved into pity and recantation: a universe in which relinquishing of resistance instantly results
in the collapse of power, in which "evil" is something which is
itself tortured by beholding and torturing "good", in which the
"sufferer's curse" is "like remorse" in its effect on the torturer.
Shelley's poetry is certainly best understood as Bloom understands
it, as an attempt to engage with moral issues of this kind; it has
not been well served by those referential and even symbolist
admirers who have made too little of this engagement. But still:
is this an account of remorse, evil, power, politics or will which
most people will find persuasive; do those things really look like
this to many? Is the moral internality of Prometheus's recantation convincingly represented? Is that of Jupiter's fall? The poetry
no doubt seems complex, subtle and coherent to some, but will
it ever, in these terms, be completely credible? Does its moral
disclosure go deep enough for that? These are questions for
each reader to ask; the critical literature has not since Hazlitt
asked them with sufficient persistence. Obviously, this book's
answer to all of them is "no". If thinking in poetry about remorse, suffering, evil or the will, indeed about the self and its
world, is a matter of deepening our understanding of these concepts by dissolving them into a life or a life-situation in which
their human meaning is both interrogated and unfolded, then
Shelley seems to take their meanings for granted, to be interested
in representing them as the already-understood, clear and distinct
components of a self which looks, for that very reason, less than
fully human.

The remainder of Act I falls into two long sections or move-
ments. In the first one (316–657) Prometheus is questioned for

the last time by Jupiter's emissary Mercury and tortured by the Furies, thus expiating the re-spoken curse and asserting his new mode of being. Mercury still wants to know the "secret"; Prometheus, who has renounced power but not will, continues to withold it. To disclose it, to submit his will, to deal with Jupiter, would un-make him as the being the poem has posited. Mercury's "remorse" (436) is somewhat more credible than Jupiter's, if still thin enough, like his character in general. The poem's logic further requires, again questionably, that resistance brings with it the utter certainty of its own success and of tyranny's downfall, even if the exact details are obscure. "I know but this, that it must come", says Prometheus (413). The torture itself, however, repays much closer attention. Despite the reformed Prometheus's pre-emptive strike ("I weigh not what ye do, but what ye suffer/ Being evil", 480), the Furies exploit his own deepest self-recognitions in order to hurt him (539–631):

Chorus

... Dost thou boast the clear knowledge thou waken'dst for man?
Then was kindled within him a thirst which outran
Those perishing waters; a thirst of fierce fever,
Hope, love, doubt, desire – which consume him forever.
    One came forth, of gentle worth,
    Smiling on the sanguine earth;
    His words outlived him, like swift poison
    Withering up truth, peace and pity....

Semichorus I

... See! a disenchanted nation
Springs like day from desolation;
To truth its state, is dedicate,
And Freedom leads it forth, her mate ...

Semichorus II

... See how kindred murder kin!
'Tis the vintage-time for Death and Sin:
Blood, like new wine, bubbles within....

Fury

Behold, an emblem – those who do endure

Deep wrongs for man, and scorn and chains, but heap
Thousand-fold torment on themselves and him. . . .

The good want power, but to weep barren tears.
The powerful goodness want: worse need for them.
The wise want love, and those who love want wisdom;
And all best things are thus confused to ill.

"Thy name I will not speak", says the horrified Prometheus to
this "emblem", which is himself on his rock as well as Jesus on
the cross. Finally, however, he does manage to tell the Furies
that for all the pain their words have inflicted "I pity those they
torture not" – and the Furies vanish. His old refrain, "Ah woe!
Alas! pain, pain ever, forever", is now made redundant by the
renewed confidence which pity's understanding brings, and he
knows that "This is defeat, fierce King, not victory"; that the
"sights with which thou torturest gird my soul/ With new endurance, till the hour arrives". But although Prometheus is no
longer in active resistance, he is still prey to the thought (and so
should we all be, always, says the verse) that while he was, he
brought pain to man along with knowledge. The best-intentioned
and most self-abnegating moral actions and martyrdoms must
also have bad consequences for those they were supposed to
help, runs the thought, so that power and goodness, wisdom
and love, are everywhere dissociated. Prometheus's pity can
overcome the pain even of this thought, which he can finally
grasp as an evidence not a questioning of his virtue, and as a
harbinger of his victory; but the weight of the poetry comes down
on the Furies' side of the case. And the case is an impressive
one. Even though locally Shelley's language is metaphorically
frail in familiar ways ("fierce fever", "gentle worth", "swift poison",
"To truth its state, is dedicate", "Blood, like new wine") it
puts its case without the sluggishness and pedantry of his old
mentor Godwin: "actions in the highest degree injurious to the
public have often proceeded from motives uncommonly conscien-
tious".[19] Of course, at the level of general imaginative and emotional conception the Furies are entirely beyond Godwin's range;
as Bloom puts it, they "sum up something recalcitrant, something hardened, in the human spirit".[20] Nevertheless there will
always be readers who will find something abstract, doctrinal,
all too Godwinian, in this poetic manner of representing the human

spirit at odds with itself. Shelley is turning on himself, seeing the evils attendant on his own passion for reform; the French Revolution is as present to the verse as the Christian; but the turn is as single-minded, as simple-spirited, as the passion. Is this what it is, all it is, to "endure/ Deep wrongs for man", and then to see the consequent torment heaped on man? Is this the passion, let alone the Passion, it asks to be seen as? The words of the Furies "sum up" hardness and recalcitrance, but they do not, to use an unfashionable term, enact them. Michael O'Neill subtly suggests that the Furies embody the life of concepts in the mind,[21] and indeed even such a concept as "Freedom" has done much harm; but the very trouble, for dissenting readers, is that neither Prometheus nor the poem, despite the Furies, seems particularly aware of the harm done by concepts. On the contrary: the skeleton of a philosophical, conceptual argument, albeit a profound one, seems in this section of Act I to have been abstracted from the moral and poetic body, the whole poem, in which alone it might have had its full life and meaning.

In the final section or movement of Act I (657–833) the Spirits of the Human Mind foretell the victory of Prometheus. The Earth summons six Spirits from "the dim caves of human thought" to "cheer" Prometheus's "state". They know Prometheus will succeed, for (790, 796–800)

> In the atmosphere we breathe . . .
> Wisdom, Justice, Love and Peace,
> When they struggle to increase,
> Are to us as soft winds be
> To shepherd-boys – the prophecy
> Which begins and ends in thee.

For the most part the Spirits' language has "a slightness intrinsic in its very fluency". This is O'Neill again,[22] characteristically sympathetic; lines such as "I fled hither, fast, fast, fast" are certainly slight, and in many places the fluency seems a vice, not a saving grace. One can appreciate that this is meant to be a kind of being which feels abstract concepts as if they were soft winds; these are the atmosphere it breathes. Still, the dramatic sleight of hand, together with the "fluency", cleverly conceal a circularity of thought essential not just to Shelley but to Plato: that to grasp the Good is to instantiate it, to make it present. Justice

feels like a sweet breeze, but only to the Just: is this persuasive?
As in the "Ode" the wind is a prophecy of spring, and as in the
"Ode" Wisdom and Peace are "like" spring – inevitable, palpable.
But the most remarkable moment in this passage is the speech
of the Fourth Spirit (737–51):

> On a Poet's lips I slept
> Dreaming like a love-adept
> In the sound his breathing kept;
> Nor seeks nor finds he mortal blisses
> But feeds on the aerial kisses
> Of shapes that haunt thought's wildernesses.
> He will watch from dawn to gloom
> The lake-reflected sun illume
> The yellow bees i' the ivy-bloom
> Nor heed nor see, what things they be;
> But from these create he can
> Forms more real than living man,
> Nurslings of immortality! –
> One of these awakened me
> And I sped to succour thee.

It is probably an overstatement to call this, as Bloom does,"the
locus classicus . . . of the passionate defence of visionary poetry
in English".[23] Still, these are fifteen of Shelley's most important
lines, a vital key to his poetic method in this poem and elsewhere, and they are indeed singularly defensive, an essay on
visionary poetry as much as a vision in poetry. The insistent
rhymed octosyllabics, so successful already in the "Lines Written Among the Euganean Hills" and later in "With a Guitar, To
Jane", lend their characteristic emphasis to the simple, haunting
image of lake, sun, ivy, bees (little suns in the dark ivy), and
watching poet, all captured in a day-long moment. The scene
has the spiritual presence, the immanence, to be found only in
Shelley's best poetry. We could do without "mortal blisses" and
"aerial kisses", but the intenser reality of the "forms" and "shapes"
perceived by the poet in and through these ordinary "things" is
what Shelley perceives and tries to represent in *Prometheus* and
elsewhere. Perhaps to cavil at these lines is perverse: but is it
not also typical of Shelley that we are left in the end outside
this poet's vision; that we watch him, not the poem created "from"

these things? *How* will he "create" his "more real" forms? The bees and their surroundings are made outward tokens of thoughts, or inward associates of thoughts, not because of any deep affinity that we are aware of between bees and thoughts, but because the poet had certain nameless thoughts while looking at the bees. Is poetry a matter of contiguity or "constant conjunction", as Hume might have said, rather than of inner resemblance or metaphoric connection? Is Necessity just what a poet thinks about while he is looking at a landscape, any landscape? In this light "Mont Blanc" is more successful as visionary poetry than *Prometheus Unbound*; its "Forms", its Necessity, inhere more naturally, more congenially, in its particular landscape. But "Mont Blanc" is also less typical of Shelley's poetic thinking, which since *Queen Mab* had relied more on accidental intellectual contiguity than on essential metaphorical resemblance to connect subject and object.

Act II

As Act I ends Prometheus, for all his newfound pity and certainty, nevertheless says he feels most "vain all hope but love". Whereas Act I, his act, revolves around resistance, first active and then passive, Act II, Asia's act, concerns itself with love, first passive then active. The poem's task, however, will again be to represent the dimensionless moment of change, wrought this time by Asian love instead of Promethean will. The 687-line act has five scenes, but only the fourth has the power and suggestiveness of most of Act I. In the first half (lines 1-117) of Scene i we discover the Oceanid nymph Asia alone in a "lovely vale in the Indian Caucasus" instead of a "Ravine of Icy Rocks in the Indian Caucasus", but just as aware as Prometheus was in Act I both that "the wingless moments crawl" and that "This is the season, this the day, the hour". The spring breeze that the Spirits of the Human Mind have just promised Prometheus has already reached Asia ("O child of many winds!"). She sees that the "point of one white star is quivering still/ Deep in the orange light of widening morn/ Beyond the purple mountains", and then that the star is reflected in the "darker lake", where it turns magically into her sister Panthea's eyes, like "stars half quenched in mists of silver dew". Panthea has come from Prometheus; she is a go-between, but almost a message rather than a messenger:

"I am made the wind/ Which fails beneath the music that I bear/ Of thy most wordless converse". In her eyes Asia can "read" a "dream" in which "his pale, wound-worn limbs/ Fell from Prometheus", revealing "the glory of that form/ Which lives unchanged within". In the dream Panthea felt herself "dissolving" in the "atmosphere" of "love" which "Steam'd forth like vaporous fire" from the Titan; she "felt/ His presence flow and mingle through my blood/ Till it became his life and his grew mine/ And I was thus absorbed". The only "articulate" sound she heard was Asia'a name.

This is not some of Shelley's best poetry, however hard one works at its star-symbolism, the colours and visionary intensity of the landscape, or Asia's and Panthea's metaphysical significances. The attempt to make first mortal flesh, a pale Galilean, and then a divine form out of the idea of Prometheus which has already taken shape in Act I is ambitious but impracticable, and all the flowing, mingling and dissolving is unhappily reminiscent of the seduction scene in *Alastor*. Like the description of the Ravine at the beginning of Act I, this passage is a quasi-sensory representation of "operations of the human mind". But it is simultaneously an idealisation of the human body, as any admirer of Shelley will tell us. Some readers, in these amphibious circumstances, will feel that A is being used to explain or render B even as B is being used to explain or render A, and that the poetry is in either case not good at thinking about the more earthy of its two terms. As in Act I, an attempt to think about the metaphysical in apparently physical terms is less successful than the more purely metaphysical passage which follows, in this case in the scene's second half (118–208). Panthea had a second dream, of a "shape", a "thing of air" with "rude hair" and "grey robe", "its regard/ Wild and quick". This dream now actually appears as a character called "Dream", an embodiment, if that is the right term, of its only speech, "Follow, follow!" The word "follow" echoes through the remainder of the scene: spoken by characters called "Echoes", "stamped" on flowers, "written on the shadows of the morning clouds", "heard" as a "wind . . . among the pines", seen in Panthea's eyes, fading away in the "ebbing wind", always drawing Asia and Panthea irresistibly after it ("*O follow, follow, follow me!*"), but only once unpacked in a fuller articulation. "List! the strain floats nearer now", says Panthea (189), and the Echoes expand:

In the world unknown
Sleeps a voice unspoken;
By thy step alone
Can its rest be broken,
Child of Ocean!

This stanza discovered within the word "follow" turns an unspoken voice, an unknown world, into an active and audible
presence. The single performative word haunts the whole of the
act, not just this scene; Act II is Asia's pursuit of the "deep truth"
calling to her. This is a successful exploitation of language characteristic of Shelley at his best, when he is not trying to force sensory metaphors upon "minute and remote distinctions of feeling",
but is exploring the dramatic truth, the minute and remote feelings,
to be found in a single abstracted word.

In the second scene Asia and Panthea pass through a lush forest whose sights and sounds are celebrated by Spirits, themselves
the subjects of speculation by Fauns. The underlying metaphor
is of a volcanic natural energy sweeping everything towards the
"fatal mountain" where Demogorgon dwells. Scholarly commentary has successfully accounted for most of the cedars, pines,
yews, anemones, laurels, voluptuous nightingales, enchanted
eddies of sound, pink blossoms, folded violets and "wise and
lovely songs/ Of fate and chance and change" which fill the
scene: accounted for them, that is, as concepts and symbols which
have their meaning in a system of reference much wider than
the scene itself. This is a kind of thinking about the poetry, and
an attribution of a kind of thinking to it, which will not appeal
to readers who prefer poetic thought to be grounded in ordinary language rather than in an esoteric system, and who find
in this poetry an ordinary language which seems more self-in-
dulgent than symbolic ("Like many a lake-surrounded flute/
Sounds overflow the listener's brain"; "Or when some star of
many a one/ That climbs and wanders through steep night").

Nor does the more coherent thought of the third scene, when
Asia and Panthea finally reach "the realm/ Of Demogorgon",
work retroactively to underpin and integrate the dispersed imagery of its predecessor. Instead we find a more alarming kind
of élitism, political rather than symbolical. The "mighty portal"
of that realm, Panthea says, is

Like a volcano's meteor-breathing chasm,
Whence the oracular vapour is hurled up
Which lonely men drink wandering in their youth
And call truth, virtue, love, genius or joy –
That maddening wine of life, whose dregs they drain
To deep intoxication, and uplift
Like Mænads who cry loud, Evoe! Evoe!
The voice which is contagion to the world.

The lines should remind us that however much we may talk of "relationship" and "experience" this is a poem with certain not so deeply buried attitudes towards political and social life, attitudes which a great many of Shelley's admirers have found attractive, and which have done as much to recommend the poet to them as they have to discommend him to others. Poets here, as elsewhere in Shelley's writing, are seen as political oracles or prophets. They know what is true, virtuous and lovely, because what is true, virtuous and lovely is what they know. The "maddening wine of life" is what *they* drink; "life" is a wine or vapour which intoxicates and maddens *them* and which they then call "truth, virtue, love, genius or joy". There is little ironic or dramatic recognition here that these poets may be mad, intoxicated or just "lonely"; or that the world may not need their "contagion"; or that some "poets" may have quite different attributes or attitudes; or that political thought, attending to the life of collective humanity, may not be just a matter of oracular vision. Asia's next speech raises some related considerations:

.... – Hark! the rushing snow!
The sun-awakened avalanche! whose mass,
Thrice sifted by the storm, had gathered there
Flake after flake, in Heaven-defying minds
As thought by thought is piled, till some great truth
Is loosened, and the nations echo round
Shaken to their roots: as do the mountains now.

"This simile", according to Donald H. Reiman and Sharon Powers, "is one of the best examples of the reversal of imagery that Shelley mentions in ... the Preface" (p. 169). The lines explain an "external natural event", the avalanche, in terms of "the slow growth of new concepts" leading to "an intellectual revolution", rather than explaining the concepts in terms of the natural event. The "mental states or operations", as William Keach says, become the explanatory terms in Shelley's figures, while the sensory or physical terms become the underlying subjects to be explained.[24] For Reiman, Keach and many of Shelley's modern admirers this "reversal of imagery" is a bold and attractive poetic innovation. But the unreconstructed will recognise in it the lineaments of Shelley's oldest poetic manoeuvre, that turning aside from a human or natural object to a moralised or intellectualised subject which had informed his poetic thinking since *Queen Mab*. A poet who represents an intellectual revolution accumulating thought by thought as an avalanche accumulating flake by flake may well persuade us that nations can be shaken to their roots by "some great truth". But what if his imagination really is working in the opposite sense, seeing the avalanche as a revolution? Such an imagination does not search for an object to illustrate an idea; it sees all objects, including human ones, in terms of ideas. The dissenting few, or perhaps they are the many, may well believe that "Heaven-defying minds" of this kind quite literally see the world as conforming to their own dogmas, so that they feel obliged to tell the rest of us what avalanches are because we do not really understand them and need to be enlightened. What has disturbed the dissenting readers of Shelley is not the specific political standpoint of the poet but the neglectful and depreciatory attitude towards the natural and human world enacted in the poetry.

Scene iii closes with a "Song of Spirits" leading Asia and Panthea "Down, down" (an echo of "Follow, follow") to "the Deep", where in the darkness "there is One pervading, One alone", the "Eternal, the Immortal". "Resist not the weakness – / Such strength is in meekness", the Spirits tell Asia, recalling Prometheus's advocacy of wise passiveness in Act I. The complete blackness of Demogorgon's cave reflects Asia's un-Promethean resistlessness; here is no light, no picture, no will. Demogorgon himself appears in Scene iv as "a mighty darkness", "shapeless", with "neither limb/ Nor form – nor outline". He contributes a total of about twenty laconic lines to the scene's 174. Here are nine of his thirteen speeches: "Ask what thou wouldst know"; "All things thou dar'st demand"; "God"; "God, Almighty God"; "Merciful God"; "He reigns"; "He reigns"; "He reigns"; "Behold!". Demogorgon's function is to elicit from the understandably nervous

Asia, as answers to her own questions, statements of what she
already knows herself; the effect is almost comic. The bulk of
the scene consists of a long speech in which Asia redescribes the
universe and cosmology of the poem, already familiar to us from
Act I; little is added. What she really wants to know has to do
with Jupiter: "Who is his master? . . . Who is the master of the
slave?" In response Demogorgon intones by far his longest speech
of the scene:

>   – If the Abysm
> Could vomit forth its secrets: – but a voice
> Is wanting, the deep truth is imageless;
> For what would it avail to bid thee gaze
> On the revolving world? what to bid speak
> Fate, Time, Occasion, Chance and Change? To these
> All things are subject but eternal Love.

Demogorgon's point is that Asia herself is the answer to her own
questions, the embodiment of "eternal Love". "All things are
subject" to her: or rather to her reunion with Prometheus. "All
hope is vain but love", he said at the end of Act I; she is all he
hopes for, and he, all he represents, is what she represents Love
or Desire *for*. Her voice is here the only real voice, her image the
only real image. She knows this: "my heart gave/ The reponse
thou hast given; and of such truths/ Each to itself must be the
oracle". The answer to her final question, "When shall the destined hour arrive?", can only be what she must know by now it
will be: "Behold!" To ask is to have, for her in this place. The
hour itself appears as a character called, inevitably, "Spirit of
the Hour". Each of the other Hours is a "wild-eyed-charioteer";
some "with burning eyes lean forth, and drink/ With eager lips
the wind of their own speed", but the destined Hour has a "dreadful countenance", and a "dark chariot" to carry Demogorgon to
Jupiter. Scene iv is one of the poem's more powerful scenes, although it by no means matches the best passages of Act I. Whatever one feels about the "reflexive imagery" ("drink . . . the wind
of their own speed"), the Hours are convincing as images of the
mind's sense of the passing of time, although less powerful than
their counterparts in Act I, the Furies and the Spirits of the Human
Mind. The invisibility of Demogorgon, and the simultaneity of
Asia's wish and the event she wishes for, are both plausible and

explorative in terms of the poem's psycho-metaphysics, according to which Prometheus's recantation in Act I was also instantaneous (although there the moral thinking was much fuller). What is unsatisfying here in exactly the way in which Act I was unsatisfying is that very instantaneity, that unrepresentability of the crucial moment. The poem is telling us that if only Love or Desire for Knowledge or Wisdom, if only Will or Hope for Love or Desire, are strong enough, are most perfectly themselves, they will immediately realise their ideals. To think consistently about these concepts with this degree of abstraction is intellectually remarkable, but also humanly frustrating. Of its nature this kind of thought can never show us *how* the realisation of wisdom or love comes about, or fails to. The thought must jump over that process, collapsing it into a dimensionless point. Shelley wants us to see what Wisdom and Love would look like if they were perfect Beings. His interest is not in how wisdom and love might variously and unpredictably appear in human lives.

For those who are interested in such matters the first half of Scene v is frustrating in the same way. Asia is suddenly "changed". Panthea cannot look at the "radiance" of her "beauty"; she is again as at her Venusian birth, Panthea says, when "love, like the atmosphere/ Of the sun's fire . . . Burst from thee". She is the "Life of Life", the "Child of Light", the "Lamp of Earth", a "liquid splendour". Love, says Asia herself, is "common as light"; it "makes the reptile equal to the God"; those "who inspire it most are fortunate", but "those who feel it most are happier still". One accepts that this is meant to be a Dantean transfiguration scene, a vision (Bloom says) of "ultimate reality directly confronted". But in order to confront ultimate reality in poetry Shelley has to use the language that we have, as Dante does in the final cantos of the *Paradiso*. The second half of the scene, meanwhile, is one of Shelley's most famous lyrics, addressed by Asia to a spirit Voice:

My soul is an enchanted Boat
Which, like a sleeping swan, doth float
Upon the silver waves of thy sweet singing,
And thine doth like an Angel sit
Beside the helm conducting it
Whilst all the winds with melody are ringing. . . .
Till like one in slumber bound

Borne to the Ocean, I float down, around,
Into a Sea profound, of ever-spreading sound.

Meanwhile thy Spirit lifts its pinions
In Music's most serene dominions. . . .
And we sail on, away, afar,
Without a course – without a star – . . .
The boat of my desire is guided – [to]
Realms where the air we breathe is Love
Which in the winds and on the waves doth move,
Harmonizing this Earth with what we feel above.

. . . Beyond the glassy gulphs we flee
Of shadow-peopled Infancy,
Through Death and Birth to a diviner day,
A Paradise of vaulted bowers
Lit by downward-gazing flowers . . .
Peopled by shapes too bright to see . . .
Which walk upon the sea, and chaunt melodiously!

This lyric of three thirteen-line stanzas is in direct line of descent from "To Constantia Singing", but the imagery of music is
combined with a fuller development of the paradisal imagery
from *Queen Mab*, the "Lines Written Among the Euganean Hills"
and *The Revolt of Islam*. Bloom calls this a "voyage beyond the
comprehension of the senses",[25] but a notable feature of the lyric
is that its imagination of music and paradise is in sensory terms.
The images of boat, swan, waves, sea, voyage and sound, for
example, are not "reversed" but orthodox; the soul is like a swan.
Still, there are other questions to ask about the poetry. Asia calls
her soul a boat, says "I float", and speaks of the boat of her
desire; are these three utterances consistent? Is she identical with
her soul? Is her desire carried in her soul? Is she identical with
her desire? As in the "Ode", we feel uneasily that while answers
can be found to such questions, the poetry itself keeps raising
more of them. The music images have both cohesion and appre-
hensive purchase, as do some of the paradise images: the continuing voyage, the bright shapes, the flowers. But what about
"Realms where the air we breathe is Love", or "Harmonizing
this Earth with what we feel above"? Can "Love" be both Asia
and the air she breathes? Can even this spirit music "harmonize"

the earth, especially with "what we feel above", whatever that means? "Love" can readily be conceived as a metaphysical atmosphere or a kind of Person by symbolising readers, especially in a poem which they believe to be primarily about Relationship. But for other readers, to think about it in this way is actually a denial of human relationships, a two-dimensional abstraction from those multifarious cognitive feelings towards diverse objects which singly and collectively constitute what we recognise, too often sceptically now, as "love". The lyric, like the act, is about a passion and condition which is meant to transcend the human, but it cannot avoid working in the feelings and the language the human poet actually has. So long as Shelley can sustain the dramatic illusion that these are Beings in a metaphysical Reality, he succeeds, at least so long as he makes them intellectually interesting. As soon as he invokes more familiar feelings and situations, however, he is less successful. Act II is more vulnerable than Act I in this way because Shelley found thinking about "love" and "desire" less interesting and congenial than thinking about "will", "power" and "resistance".

Acts III and IV

"From the opening of Act III onwards the poem completely disintegrates", says Richard Holmes; its "great achievement . . . rests securely in the first two acts", while the "rest remains superfluous and second rate".[26] Perhaps "completely" overstates the case, but on the view of the poem taken in this chapter Holmes is right. Nearly all the poem's moral thought has taken place by the end of Act II. Much of what remains is a long-drawn-out attempt to represent Paradise, an attempt which merely elaborates upon without substantially adding to the earlier conceptions of Asia and Prometheus and their realms.

    Act III, at 511 lines, has four scenes. In the first scene (83 lines) we are told of the downfall of Jupiter, first encountered rejoicing in his omnipotence over all but "the soul of man", and expecting that his rape of Thetis will produce a "fatal Child" who will subdue even this resistance. Instead Demogorgon arives, calling himself "Eternity". The end is instantaneous; Jupiter cries "I trample thee! . . . Thou lingerest? Mercy! Mercy!" The fall is as unrepresented and unquestioned as its equivalent moments in Acts I and II; it is simply required by the poem's psycho-metaphysical logic. In Scene ii (50 lines) Apollo and Ocean speak of the fall (it "shook the solid stars", Jupiter "sunk to the abyss"), and look forward to the postlapsarian paradise. Then Ocean says he must depart:

> The loud Deep calls me home even now, to feed it
> With azure calm out of the emerald urns
> Which stand forever full beside my throne. . . .
> It is the unpastured Sea hung'ring for Calm.
> Peace, Monster – I come now! Farewell.

This passage escapes Holmes's strictures. Shelley does more in its last two lines to idealise the physical, to convey the desire for paradise which is so much more the poem's subject than paradise or desire themselves, than he does in the whole of the rest of the act. The "loud Deep calls", the "unpastured Sea" is "hung'ring for Calm"; no lines in Shelley better bespeak his peculiar genius for sensing being in a landscape. But why must he tell us that calm is "azure", and kept in "emerald urns"?

The third scene (175 lines) first shows us the unbinding of Prometheus by Hercules. Prometheus and the Earth then give long parallel accounts of a magic cave (a "simple dwelling, which shall be our own") from which Asia and Prometheus will observe the changed world; the Earth repeats her explanation of the language of the dead from Act I; Prometheus tells the Spirit of the Hour to carry a "mystic shell" across the world, full of a "mighty music" or a "voice to be accomplished", and to release that voice upon "the cities of mankind". This is Shelley's standard triumphalist account of paradise. The scene hardly improves on the final cantos of *Queen Mab*, and its triumphal tone is not, could not be, imaginatively connected with the unrepresented moments of earlier scenes and acts. It is a fantasy in which the poetic "voice that is contagion to the world" does after all contaminate it with perfection. In Scene iv (204 lines) a Spirit of the Earth describes one of the affected cities, in which suddenly "All things had put their evil nature off", as if evil nature were the kind of thing which could just be put off; in which ugly creatures ("toads and snakes and efts") become beautiful, their "foul disguise" falling off to reveal "mild and lovely forms". The Spirit of the Hour continues, in the act's concluding lines:

There was a change . . . the impalpable thin air
And the all-circling sunlight were transformed
As if the sense of love dissolved in them
Had folded itself round the sphered world. . . .
And behold! thrones were kingless, and men walked
One with the other even as spirits do . . .
None frowned, none trembled, none with eager fear
Gazed on another's eye of cold command. . . .
The loathsome mask has fallen, the man remains
Sceptreless, free, uncircumscribed – but man:
Equal, unclassed, tribeless and nationless,
Exempt from awe, worship, degree, – the King
Over himself; just, gentle, wise – but man:
Passionless? no – yet free from guilt or pain
Which were, for his will made, or suffered them,
Nor yet exempt, though ruling them like slaves,
From chance and death and mutability,
The clogs of that which else might oversoar
The loftiest star of unascended Heaven
Pinnacled dim in the intense inane.

We have already seen more than once how the poem is at its least convincing when it strays into the human. This sonorous culmination to Act III is one of the least convincing moments of the poem. An uncritically recycled post-Enlightenment and utopian conception of the self as potentially "free from guilt or pain", and yet still impassioned; as the ruler over chance and death, and yet not exempt from them; as the uncircumscribed ruler of itself in a kingdom of one: such a conception cannot be expected to attract general admiration. Can the passions be thus separated? Can justice, wisdom or gentleness retain any meaning or value without guilt or pain? The dream of ruling over chance or luck is an old one, but what sort of human being would it be who did so rule? What is "man" without tribe, class or nation? Such questions are necessary and even inevitable just because the poetry itself never dreams of asking them.

Act IV was written during Shelley's surge of political enthusiasm in the autumn of 1819, several months after he had finished what he then thought was the complete work. Apparently he was satisfied with his conception but not his depiction of Paradise, for the final act is prosodically virtuosic and doctrinally immobile. It comprises a single scene of 578 lines, in four definable sections: lyrical choruses of Spirits and Hours (1–179); a blank verse description by Panthea and Ione of the Spirits of the Earth and Moon in their chariots (180–318); a long lyrical dialogue between the Earth and the Moon (319–502); and a final triumphant chorus, led by Demogorgon (503–78). In the opening choral section the Hours "bear Time to his tomb in eternity", and the Spirits sing:

> We come from the mind
> Of human kind
> Which was late so dusk and obscene and blind;
> Now 'tis an Ocean
> Of clear emotion,
> A Heaven of serene and mighty motion.
>
> And our singing shall build,
> In the Void's loose field,
> A world for the Spirit of Wisdom to wield;
> We will take our plan
> From the new world of man
> And our work shall be called the Promethean.

These are two of the better stanzas from the Spirits' choruses, and yet they are mere jingle ("Ocean/ Of clear emotion", "the Void's loose field") by comparison with the songs of the Spirits of the Human Mind in Act I, which they devalue by association. Such a criticism cannot be made, however, of the next section of the act. In two "visions of strange radiance" later adapted by Shelley for "The Witch of Atlas" and "The Triumph of Life", Ione and Panthea see the Spirits of Moon and Earth piloting their respective vessels. Ione describes "a chariot like that thinnest boat/ In which the Mother of the Months is borne" carrying an intensely white and "winged Infant", its eyes "Heavens/ Of liquid darkness". The chariot's wheels are "solid clouds, azure and gold", which "as they roll/ Over the grass and flowers and waves, wake sounds/ Sweet as a singing rain of silver dew". Panthea, meanwhile, sees a "sphere, which is as many thousand spheres/ Solid as chrystal", and yet permeated by "music and light". "Ten thousand orbs ... Purple and azure, white and green and golden", the spaces between them "Peopled with unimaginable shapes", whirl

Over each other with a thousand motions
Upon a thousand sightless axles spinning
And with the force of self-destroying swiftness,
Intensely, slowly, solemnly roll on....
With mighty whirl the multitudinous Orb
Grinds the bright brook into an azure mist
Of elemental subtlety, like light....

The "odour", "music" and "light" of the wood are "kneaded into
one aerial mass/ Which drowns the sense". "Within the Orb itself" sleeps a child, the Spirit; "its little lips are moving", while
"Vast beams like spokes of some invisible wheel/ Which whirl
as the Orb whirls, swifter than thought" shoot from "a star upon
its forehead" and pierce to "the secrets of the Earth's deep heart",
to enormous "mines" and "wells", "melancholy ruins" of former
civilisations, huge extinct creatures. These two fantastic visions
have generated, as might be expected, a good deal of modern
scholarly commentary. Carl Grabo read them in scientific terms,
remarking on their prophetic grasp of atomic structure, the nature
of energy, the hypotheses of Herschel and Davy, and so on; this
"explanation" was one of the founding twentieth-century
referentialist accounts of Shelley's poetry.[27] Wilson Knight's was
the first important symbolist-humanist reading of the passage,
and an early benchmark for this kind of modern reading of Shelley
in general ("the earthy and heavily physical [is] being forced to
generate the conscious ... the child is the final fact").[28] Bloom
and Timothy Webb rightly remind us that the second vision, of
a divine child as "the secret principle of life", is better understood within "the great tradition of European religious literature", of Ezekiel, Dante and Milton, than as versified science.[29]
But within that specifically Shelleyan tradition originating in *Queen
Mab* this vision is an imagining of how "matter" would look
from the point of view of "soul". Necessity is no longer an
hypostasised "Soul of the universe" presiding over an abstract
"world of loves and hatreds", but a super-child seeing innocently
and quasi-scientifically into the whole of human and natural
history, represented in some detail. One can see why Shelley's
admirers would prefer this vision to its nebulous predecessor.
Still, the conception remains essentially Volneyan and Condorcean,
with premonitions of Lyell and Darwin: an amalgam of apocalyptic
fantasy and nineteenth-century scientism. The unreconstructed

reader may be less than impressed by yet more "azure", by the child's "little lips" and "wavy hair", even by the "Vast beams" shooting out of its forehead, and may be inclined to find the vision, while worthy of respect, in some ways less redolent of Ezekiel than of Spielberg.

In the third section of Act IV the Earth and Moon, rather than their Spirits, are suddenly joyous young adults ("Ha! Ha! the animation of delight"). The Earth sings a kind of hymn to man, a revisiting of Act III and of *Canto VIII* of Queen Mab: "Man, oh, not men! a chain of linked thought . . . Compelling the elements with adamantine stress"; "Man, one harmonious Soul of many a soul/ Whose nature is its own divine controul";

> His Will, with all mean passions, bad delights,
> And selfish cares, its trembling satellites,
> A spirit ill to guide, but mighty to obey,
> Is as a tempest-winged ship, whose helm
> Love rules. . . .

> Language is a perpetual Orphic song,
> Which rules with Dædal harmony a throng
> Of thoughts and forms, which else senseless and shapeless
> were.

The poetic thought here both rests on and promulgates a conception of the self as divided into a central controlling Will, which is divine, good and right, and unruly peripheral passions, which are bad, mean or selfish. "Love" is the near-meaningless exception to this pattern, the one passion which purportedly rules the Will. The conception can easily be extended into the physical world, since it is accessible to the senses which like the passions are subject to the rule of Will. Language can be understood on the same model, as the Orphic or Dædal ruler of senseless and shapeless "thoughts and forms". Shelley's notion of how the human self and its language will be in paradise is in fact a notion of how these things already are. No passage in Shelley's poetry better shows that in practice as well as in principle, and despite the discoveries he had made in "A Defence of Poetry" and in Italy in general, he still conceived both language and the self abstractedly and dissociatedly. One "has" a passion; one asserts one's will "over it". But are not the passions agents of thought, constituents of the self which "has" them? One has shapeless thoughts; one has language to rule them, express them, or even create them. But is not language a medium of thought, something thought works in? Shelley's Cartesian propensity to separate will from passion, mind from heart, Truth from symbol, transcendent from transcended, ruler from ruled, the elect from the ordinary, seems to his more unenlightened readers to be morally unconvincing and politically unattractive.

In the final section of the act Demogorgon reappears to deliver the poem's peroration. Addressing the assembled planets and spirits, and also "Man", he reminds them – and us, presumably – that "This is the day" on which "Love from its awful throne of patient power/ In the wise heart . . . springs,/ And folds over the world its healing wings": but that if ever "Destruction" again threatens "Gentleness, Virtue, Wisdom and Endurance", then the only recourse will be

> To suffer woes which Hope thinks infinite;
> To forgive wrongs darker than Death or Night;
> To defy Power which seems Omnipotent;
> To love, and bear; to hope, till Hope creates
> From its own wreck the thing it contemplates;
> Neither to change nor falter nor repent:
> This, like thy glory, Titan! is to be
> Good, great and joyous, beautiful and free;
> This is alone Life, Joy, Empire and Victory.

The poem's final lines remind us again of the abstractions and abstractness which are at its heart, and of the odd moral logic, also central to it, by which the greater the obstacle the greater the certainty of overcoming that obstacle. The degree of moral and political generality (Love, Power, Joy, Victory) and the idealisation of resolution (Hope, Will) have appealed to many readers, but not to all, or even to the silent majority, and on both sides one can see why. A "symbol of the peaceful triumph of goodness over power", or "volatile intellectual salt of tartar": readers must decide for themselves which phrase better describes the poem as it attends to those political and ethical concepts which are unquestionably its principal subjects.

6

Shelley's Poetry, 1821–2

During 1820 Shelley was already turning away again from that poetry of moral and political reformism which had been his trademark since *Queen Mab*, and to which he had returned with such excitement in the autumn of 1819. He had lost both confidence in that conception of poetry and enthusiasm for its practice, as we saw in Chapters 2 and 4, partly because of his own lack of popular success, especially compared with Byron's, and partly because of his disillusionment with the tendency of political events in England and Europe. As we saw in Chapter 3, however, Shelley had been aware since 1815, at least, of the dispositional shortcomings of this style of poetic thought. One all too marginal consequence of that dissatisfaction was a conversational poetry of human relationship, exemplified in 1820 by the "Letter to Maria Gisborne" and in 1822, more profoundly, by the poems for Jane Williams. But Shelley's other principal style of poetic thought, the one in which he explicitly criticised the disposition of *Queen Mab* and its successors, was a poetry in which the self is not the agent of the thought, as it is in the poems for Jane, but an object of the thought. Shelley's last two completed major poems, written in 1821, were both of this kind. *Epipsychidion* was a love poem in the vein of *Alastor*, and *Adonais* was a poem about a poet in the vein of "Julian and Maddalo". A third work, "The Triumph of Life", a bleak dream vision of humanity, a kind of *Mask of Anarchy* without Hope, was still being written when Shelley died in mid-1822. The fragment resists tidy categorising, but even as a fragment it constitutes the most mordant and graphic of all Shelley's Alastorean self-criticisms.

EPIPSYCHIDION

Epipsychidion stands in direct line of descent from *Alastor* and "Julian and Maddalo". It has 591 lines of pentameter couplets, where the latter had 618, and the former had 720 lines of blank verse. It has the conversational setting and tone of its two predecessors, although the tone rises to ecstatic exclamation in several places. It even has their framed structure, with reflective passages at beginning and end sandwiching a central life story that, in this case, is cryptically but obviously autobiographical. The distancing preface is there too, but this time the dramatic veil is a thin one. The two major themes remain the same. The primary theme is love, which on Shelley's account has to do with the nature of the self in its relationship to the loved one, not with thinking about the other self, or even with thinking about that mysterious third party, that unique combination of selves, which is the relationship. On this occasion love is not the feared passion of the two earlier poems, but a kind of transfiguring grace. The question, however, is whether Shelley has really overcome his reluctance to explore this passion, or has simply evaded the passion in a new way. The second theme is the nature or proper function of the poet, of poetic thought itself. This theme is important but secondary in *Epipsychidion*, while it dominates *Adonais*, the other Alastorean work of 1821. In *Alastor* and "Julian and Maddalo" the poet-hero in his search for love, truth and justice, finally had nowhere left to look but death. That is still his fate in *Adonais*, but not, or not so obviously, in *Epipsychidion*.

This is primarily a love poem, then, or at least what love poetry becomes when Shelley writes it. The poem has some of the urbane courtliness of the Jane Williams lyrics, but more of the rhapsodic and etherealised intensity of Asia's Love songs. In so far as there is a conception of the erotic, it is the generalising and narcissistic one of the Poet's vision in *Alastor* or Panthea's dream of Prometheus; there is little sense of the unique physical and moral presence of another person. Shelley scholarship has dealt in its usual two ways with *Epipsychidion* as a love poem. First of all there are the referentialists,[1] who in this case are of the biographical kind, as they were in "Julian and Maddalo". They have devoted much useful attention to the explicatory value of those events in Shelley's life which appear, thinly disguised, in the central part of the poem. They have been especially interested in the details of his relationship with Teresa Viviani, known to the Shelley circle as Emilia or Emily, who is one of the poem's objects, where Love is its subject. Meanwhile the symbolist and stylist critics,[2] including their deconstructionist cousins, have been more interested in that subject, in the poem's vision or critique of love and poetry in general, both in their idealising and in their politicising or heretical aspects. These critics have also considered the poem's debts to other poets; Webb calls it "bilingual in conception".[3] Shelley had been immersed in Dante (*Vita Nuova, Convivio, Purgatorio*), as the poem's "Advertisement" makes plain, but Petrarch and Boccaccio are here too, and Rousseau. One may in this light regard *Epipsychidion* as espousing a theory of ideal love deriving from the Middle Ages and the early Renaissance, from the integrations of Scholasticism, but modified by the Enlightenment and the disintegrations of Romanticism. (The word "epipsychidion", incidentally, means "upon the little soul", or "little soul within a soul".) The passage on love (160–73) arguing that "to divide is not to take away" is closely based on *Purgatorio* xv, the image of Emily as the sun on *Purgatorio* xxviii. Rousseau's reflections in the *Confessions* on "two souls in the same body" and on an "ideal world" peopled with "beings after my own heart" had long impressed Shelley, as we observed in Chapter 2.[4] Of these two approaches to *Epipsychidion* the biographicalist one is unlikely to persuade the sceptic of the poem's value. Information about the poet's life does not bear very heavily upon the quality of the poem's thought about love. But there is reason for dissent even from the symbolists' view, still too referential at its heart, that the poem thinks about love within a literary tradition of such thought. Dante's presence in the poem, for example, is doctrinal rather than experiential. What we have here is not so much a love poem as a theory of love, a theory, as Shelley said (ii 263, p. 373), for the elect, the "esoteric few", the *cognoscenti* "capable of judging and feeling", not for the "vulgar" who had no "common organ of perception for [its] ideas" (a remarkable phrase in which both the condescension and the intellectualisation are typical). Shelley was later to muse regretfully that he had been "in love with an Antigone", seeking "in a mortal image the likeness of what is perhaps eternal" (ii 434). This was exactly what *Alastor* had unsuccessfully attempted to warn Poets against; a biographicalist might conclude that poor Mary had become the "Arab maiden" of this new vision. The question to be asked about *Epipsychidion* (about a great deal of poetic thought since Rousseau, indeed) is whether the theorising determines the thought about the feeling, or precludes any other kind of exploration of the feeling as thought. Shelley had borrowed or adapted a theory of love which in Dante had rested and made sense in an enormously complex structure of faith and dogma, and had also been completed by real cognitive discovery about and in the feeling of love. If Shelley's poem "forfeits" Dante's "discursive underpinning", as O'Neill puts it,[5] abstracts the theory from its constitutive structure, and if it also avoids Dante's thought-in-feeling, then what is the nature of its own achievement?

The poem's short "Advertisement" (p. 373) employs the dramatic fiction of another "Writer", now dead, who had "fitted up the ruins of an old building" on a remote island, where he had hoped, impracticably, to live a "happier and better" life. Shadows of the Maniac from "Julian and Maddalo" and the Poet from *Alastor* invest this otherwise transparent figure. Shelley also maintains self-protectively that the poem may be understood "without a matter-of-fact history of the circumstances to which it relates". The biographicalist will not let him get away with that, of course, and will note that soon afterwards Shelley was wishing himself that he and Mary could retire to a similar unworldly island (ii 339). The advertisement concludes, and the poem begins, with a translation from Dante's *Convivio*: "My Song, I fear that thou wilt find but few/ Who fitly shall conceive thy reasoning/ Of such hard matter dost thou entertain". The "hard matter" was an alloy of a certain conception of love and certain reflections on Shelley's own experiences of love; the poem was an "idealized history of my life and feelings", as he said elsewhere (ii 434). In this poem, then, the fragile barriers which his ironist defenders elsewhere seek to put up between his poem and its speaker, the "Writer", seem all but non-existent. We may reasonably assume that the self which emerges in this piece of self-exploration, the self of this poem, is identical with that of its speaker. This is still not biographicalism, of course. Our business is with the thought, the self, of the poem.

The poem proper can be divided, like "Julian and Maddalo", into two framing sections and a central narrative. The first section (lines 1–189) is about the Writer's feelings for Emily and the nature of love in general; the second (190–383) is about his earlier experiences of love; the third (383–591) is an invitation to Emily to come away with him to their island. There is a short concluding address to the poem itself (592–604). The first section is the least impressive of the three, defined on the one hand by shoals of flickering but unsustaining metaphors, and on the other by a mass of stodgy doctrine. In the space of the first seventy lines Emily is addressed as all of the following: "Sweet Spirit!"; "Poor captive bird!"; "my adored Nightingale!"; "High, spirit-winged Heart!"; "Seraph of Heaven!";

Sweet Benediction in the eternal Curse!
Veiled Glory of this lampless Universe!
Thou Moon beyond the clouds! Thou living Form
Among the Dead! Thou Star above the Storm!
Thou Wonder, and thou Beauty, and thou Terror!
Thou Harmony of Nature's art! Thou Mirror

making "glorious" whatever it gazes on; "Youth's vision thus made perfect"; "Sweet Lamp!" to the poet's "moth-like Muse"; "lovely soul formed to be blest and bless"; "A well of sealed and secret happiness"; "A Star" which is fixed "in the moving Heavens"; "A smile amid dark frowns"; "a gentle tone/ Amid rude voices"; "A Solitude, a Refuge, a Delight"; "A lute" for "those whom love has taught to play" to "make music on"; "a buried treasure"; "A cradle of young thoughts"; "A violet-shrouded grave of Woe". In "To a Skylark", the "Ode" and the "Hymn", and before them in *Queen Mab*, Shelley had used the same technique of piling up similes and metaphors in order to suggest both endless directions for thought and the inadequacy of language to convey thought. "I measure/ The world of fancies, seeking one like thee", he regretfully concludes, "And find – alas! mine own infirmity". The infirmity is no less regrettable for being admitted. When so many metaphorical possibilities are evoked in so short a space ordinary readers simply do not know what to make of the result (would Emily?), and may resist being told by Shelley's defenders that this is because the result is inherently unattainable, and that this is a purposeful and successful representation of failure. Even the vulgar can understand that none of these "fancies" is "like" anyone at all, because Shelley is really trying to represent his own idea of "what is perhaps eternal". But in their multiplicity and their tenuousness ("Thou Wonder", "thou Beauty", "thou terror": compare Panthea on Asia, in *Prometheus Unbound* II v) the images are no better suited to convey that idea than they are to represent Emily. The old charge of "vacuity" or "insubstantiality" is not brought against Shelley's thought because some readers cannot appreciate intellectual subtlety, or have a prejudice about "concrete" and "developed" imagery. It is the response of those who think of language as a constituent of reality, and of another person as a substantial self, to a poetry which persistently and on principle thinks of language as an instrument and of another person as a Beauty, justifying itself on the grounds that it is written for the "elect", who alone will understand the nature of Reality and Beauty and the difficulty of finding the right language to represent them. This poetic "infirmity" looks to such readers like the symptom of a radical uncertainty (Shelley's, not the Writer's) in the use of language. "I never thought before my death to see/ Youth's vision thus made perfect. Emily/ I love thee"; the passage's central lines must struggle to escape bathos on the one hand and hyperbole on the other because the thought about the speaker's relation to the girl, about his own feelings, and about her, is palpably ill at ease with itself. "Would we two had been twins of the same mother", if only "the name my heart lent to another/ Could be a sister's bond for her and thee", "I am not thine: I am a part of thee": even if we put out of our minds the Shelley of those letters to Harriet, whose place is now taken by Mary (the kind of referentialist reading which sees the poem as socially radical, as advocating polygamy, incest, and so on, must recall the Shelley of those letters) – even then, we may well see the self of these lines as unstably founded on a combination of euphoria and polemic, with the central generating passion ("I love") and its object ("thee") almost completely unexplored.

The next paragraph (72–123) is hardly more successful. In "She met me, Stranger, upon life's rough way,/ And lured me towards sweet Death" the sudden self-consciousness of "Stranger" and the tired thinking of "rough way" and "sweet Death" are mere distractions. "An antelope,/ In the suspended impulse of its lightness" will sustain little pressure of thought, while "the brightness/ Of her divinest presence trembles through/ Her limbs" will sustain none at all; nor will the "liquid murmur" which "drops" from "her lips", or the "glory of her being", or "An image of some bright Eternity" (which one? why "bright"? can Emily be the image of something unimaginable?). The paragraph ends thus, however:

A Metaphor of Spring and Youth and Morning;
A Vision of incarnate April, warming

With smiles and tears, Frost the Anatomy
Into his summer grave.

The last three lines are one of Shelley's rare successes in the
transformation of an object, Emily, by a concept, April, although
the success does depend largely on those other objects, smiles
and tears. The fact of this success, however, should not lead readers
to applaud all the failures as well, as brave attempts to achieve
the impossible. The first line exposes the trouble with the whole
method, which as we have repeatedly seen is essential to much
of Shelley's poetic thought. Seeing Emily as a metaphor, not a
person, the poem casts about for a concept, all the concepts, of
which she could be seen as a metaphor. Instead of deepening
our thought within the concept "spring" or "youth" by exploring the person Emily or the speaker's feelings for her, the poetry blocks our thought in all three directions. She is still just a
metaphor; the concept is still just a word; the feelings are still
not achieved. The progression of the thought, in other words, is
as it was in the "Ode": towards an essentially and unattractively
complacent self whose impulses are primarily ideological. "What
have I dared? where am I lifted? how/ Shall I descend, and perish
not?", the poem continues in the last part of this first section
(123–89). The speaker is flung once more upon the thorns of life;
the "O lift me" of the "Ode" has become "where am I lifted?".
The thorns in his side now are his spouse (let us resist the
biographicalist temptation to identify her with Mary), and conventional conceptions of marriage, sexual relationship and love.
"Spouse! Sister! Angel!", "too late/ Beloved" and "too soon
adored": the two of them were "formed", the Writer says, "as
notes of music are,/ For one another, though dissimilar". The
new feeling about Emily somehow has to accommodate older
feelings about a "Spouse" once "adored" herself, but there is no
further thought about the latter. Instead there is this:

Thy wisdom speaks in me, and bids me dare
Beacon the rocks on which high hearts are wreckt.
I never was attached to that great sect,
Whose doctrine is, that each one should select
Out of the crowd a mistress or a friend,
And all the rest, though fair and wise, commend
To cold oblivion, though it is in the code

Of modern morals, and the beaten road
Which those poor slaves with weary footsteps tread,
Who travel to their home among the dead
By the broad highway of the world, and so
With one chained friend, perhaps a jealous foe,
The dreariest and the longest journey go.

True Love in this differs from gold and clay,
That to divide is not to take away.
Love is like understanding, that grows bright,
Gazing on many truths; 'tis like thy light,
Imagination! which ... fills
The Universe with glorious beams, and kills
Error, the worm, with many a sun-like arrow
Of its reverberated lightning. Narrow
The heart that loves, the brain that contemplates,
The life that wears, the spirit that creates
One object, and one form, and builds thereby
A sepulchre for its eternity.

... If you divide suffering and dross, you may
Diminish till it is consumed away;
If you divide pleasure and love and thought,
Each part exceeds the whole. ...

His spouse's "wisdom", apparently, supports this philosophy as
a replacement for the "code of modern morals", and prompts
the Writer to promulgate it as a warning or "Beacon" to "high
hearts" like his, so often "wrecked" on the "rocks" of conventional "doctrine". What we have here is a new doctrine, along
with something which new doctrines always need to justify themselves, namely a description of conventional practices as equally
doctrinal. The practice of marriage is described here as a matter
of selecting one person out of an undifferentiated crowd and
commending the rest to "cold oblivion". Such a description says
little for the describer's sense of human relational variety and
potential. To call the practitioners "poor slaves", their lives dreary,
their partners "chained" and perhaps "jealous", is the thinnest
of ideological cant, the most deliberate turning away from any
search for the meaning of the word "Spouse" used to introduce
the passage, or for the personality of the spouse whose "wisdom"

is claimed to encompass these views. The doctrine about the infinite divisibility of Love is from Dante's *Purgatorio* xv, where Virgil explains that "the more souls . . . there be,/ more are there to love well and more are loved", but Virgil is speaking of *carità*, that "love" which the King James Bible renders as "charity". What kind of love is Shelley thinking of? Did he see Beatrice as a "sepulchre" for Dante's "eternity"? The substitution of "monument" for "sepulchre" and of "Happy" for "Narrow" would entirely reverse the sense of the passage; how well sustained is the poetic thought of thirty words when twenty-eight of them are redundant? How impressive is a conception of suffering according to which it can be yoked to "dross" and consumed by division? What is the "True Love" of this doctrine? How is it to be distinguished from what the nineteenth century took it to be, in another senseless phrase: "free love"? Does the passage give us any reason to read "many truths" as the different forms that love may take: for friends, for children, for parents, for a spouse? If not, what does it take them to be? Does it give us any intimation of love as a way of knowledge of persons, including of oneself? Shelley is no longer thinking about the transcendent "eternal Love" represented by Asia; he has turned from the realm of Necessity to the human world. As in *Alastor*, however, the extent of his idealism, the degree of its evasion of the passions, is only fully revealed after he has begun to criticise it.

The second section of the poem (190–383) is an encoded autobiography, popular with the biographicalists. The Writer first describes a "Being" met everywhere by his youthful "spirit" in its "visioned wanderings". "Her Spirit was the harmony of truth"; this was a "soul out of my soul", he says, in an almost exact translation of the poem's title. He pursues this "loadstar of [his] one desire", but she escapes into "the dreary cone of our life's shade". He "would have followed, though the grave between/ Yawned", except that "a voice" tells him: "'The phantom is beside thee whom thou seekest'". He stumbles on in search of her, therefore, not in the realm of death but in "the wintry forest of our life". "In many mortal forms I rashly sought/ The shadow of that idol of my thought", until at last "into the obscure Forest came/ The Vision I had sought through grief and shame". Before this "Incarnation of the Sun", he says,

I stood, and felt the dawn of my long night
Was penetrating me with living light:

I knew it was the Vision veiled from me
So many years – that it was Emily.

This story may appear at first to be a successful rethinking of
Alastor. The "epipsyche", the soul out of the speaker's soul, is neither
a Necessity figure, a political and moral vision, nor an alastor, a
demon of neglected desire. Emily is an "Arab maiden", not just
a "mortal form" but the *right* one. Until his untimely death, re-
corded in the Advertisement, this Writer had apparently succeeded where the Poet and later the Maniac had failed, in finding
the human incarnation of True Love. On the other hand the poem
is no better at thinking about this incarnation than its predecessors were. For all we are shown to the contrary, including in the
Advertisement, the Writer's "Vision" may have been the same
one that the Poet and the Maniac were doomed never to find,
that being the very point of their lives. Does this epipsyche not
still remain in the end an epipsyche, not a woman? Even when
it turns out to be Emily, or Emily turns out to be It (or rather
Thou, *pace* Bloom), the tones of courtly hyperbole and visionary
excitement are both ill-assorted and indicative of continued Poetic idealism. That is the point, say Shelley's defenders; the Writer
attracts the poem's sympathetic criticism. But then Shelley's
thought has not moved an inch in six years. Indeed the poet is
more closely identifiable with the Poet than he was before.

The uneasiness in Shelley's poetry often increases with its prox-
imity to the human, and the more this autobiography concerns
itself with real people, rather than a Vision, the more disabling
its uncertainty of tone becomes. We now meet "One, whose voice
was venomed melody", whose "touch was as electric poison": a
prostitute, possibly. We meet some who were "fair", some who
were "wise" and "One" who was "true"; there are various hypotheses about who these women were. Next Mary appears, so
Shelley's biographers tell us, as a Moon which "warms not but
illumines", as "like the glorious shape which I had dreamed" as
the moon is like the sun. Under this Moon's influence the speaker
"lay, within a chaste cold bed". Two children also appear ("a
sister and a brother"), heralding an even deeper coldness in which
the "moving billows of my being fell/ Into a death of ice": Harriet's
suicide and Shelley's loss of his children by her? the deaths of
William and Clara? A "Tempest", a "Planet" and a "Comet" have
been variously interpreted,[6] including as Harriet, her sister Eliza
and Claire Clairmont. Emily then appears as the Sun, and the

last paragraph of this section is addressed to her and the Moon,
the "Twin Spheres of light who rule this passive Earth"; and to
the "Comet":

So ye, bright regents, with alternate sway
Govern my sphere of being, night and day!
Thou, not disdaining even a borrowed might;
Thou, not eclipsing a remoter light. . . .
Thou too, O Comet beautiful and fierce . . .
Oh, float into our azure heaven again!

The entire passage is a mixture of coterie knowingness and an
essentially complacent self-dramatisation. The astronomical scheme
is minimally constitutive of thought about the human relationships it purports to illustrate. In this moral climate the insensitivity displayed in the poetry towards the person who is the
Moon ("borrowed might", "remoter light") does not surprise. What
is most striking about this universe is its pre-Copernican
geocentricity, the speaker being at its very centre and all others
apparently revolving around him. The imagery is "developed"
and "concrete" enough (despite yet more "azure"), but as a way
of thinking about lives and feelings, including the speaker's own,
it is little more than a diagram, as evasive of real thinking about
these people as were those earlier images of Emily.

"The day is come, and thou wilt fly with me"; the third section (383–591) is tonally more assured, more at home in the human world of the "Letter to Maria Gisborne" and the poems for
Jane Williams. "Rise up, my love, my fair one, and come away",
says the *Song of Solomon* (II x), very much at home in that world,
and one possible model for *Epipsychidion*. Most of this section of
the poem consists of a long passage (407–564) describing the "isle
under Ionian skies" to which the Writer was planning to retire
with Emily. The isle is "peopled with sweet airs" (here is *The
Tempest* already, eighteen months before "With a Guitar, To Jane"),
"heavy with the scent of lemon-flowers", a "favoured place" of
"fountain, rivulet and pond", of "glades, caverns, and bowers,
and halls". The natural detail is of the kind which graced Shelley's
letters about Italian scenery and poems such as the "Letter" and
the "Euganean Hills": deers and doves, bats and owls, violets
and jonquils, fields and woods, winds and waterfalls. There is
also a hint of Asia and Prometheus in the "lone dwelling . . . as

it were Titanic" where the couple will live; here idealism is natu-
ralised. The whole passage has both charm and invention, main-
tained in the little *envoi* which concludes the poem, with its oblique
chat of "Marina, Vanna, Primus and the rest".

The real urgency and force in these closing paragraphs, however, is not to be found in their urbane account of· the isle, but
just before and after it (388–407, 560–91):

> To whatsoe'er of dull mortality
> Is mine, remain a vestal sister still;
> To the intense, the deep, the imperishable,
> Not mine but me, henceforth be thou united
> Even as a bride, delighting and delighted.
> The hour is come: – the destined Star has risen
> Which shall descend upon a vacant prison.
> The walls are high, the gates are strong, thick set
> The sentinels – but true love never yet
> Was thus constrained: it overleaps all fence. . . .
>
> Our breath shall intermix, our bosoms bound,
> And our veins beat together; and our lips
> With other eloquence than words, eclipse
> The soul that burns between them, and the wells
> Which boil under our being's inmost cells,
> The fountains of our deepest life, shall be
> Confused in passion's golden purity,
> As mountain-springs under the morning Sun,
> We shall become the same, we shall be one
> Spirit within two frames, oh! wherefore two?
> One passion in twin-hearts . . .
> One hope within two wills, one will beneath
> Two overshadowing minds, one life, one death,
> One Heaven, one Hell, one immortality,
> And one annihilation. Woe is me!
> The winged words on which my soul would pierce
> Into the height of love's rare Universe,
> Are chains of lead around its flight of fire. –
> I pant, I sink, I tremble, I expire!

The thought of Emily's remaining a "vestal sister" to whatever
is mortal in her lover is utterly lost in the passionate eroticism

of the remainder of his speech. He wants to say that "true love" is of soul for soul ("Not mine but me"), but he compares that sort of love to a bride's being "united" with her husband, which defeats his purpose. The second passage does not even want to keep these two kinds of love distinct. What is repugnant here is not the eroticism in itself but the deliberate blurring of this distinction, which produces a tone of euphemistic prurience. The poem's chief interest has been in the meaning of "True Love", and we know that where this is present "to divide is not to take away". Is this new "passion's golden purity" also to be regarded as divisible, shareable? No: that way lies insincerity of the deepest kind. Presumably this passion has at least the "purity" of exclusive sexual partnership (what is "golden" about that, however?). But then what of the "Spouse"? Can she be relied on show "wisdom" about such a partnership? So is this a "golden purity" of spiritual partnership only? Tell that to the spouse. Surely this thinking is at best naive, at worst disingenuous and self-deluding. That final cry of despair ("Woe is me! . . .") is another version of the earlier one: "And find – alas! mine own infirmity". Words can never represent "love's rare universe". This is because the kind of thinking Shelley wants to do about "love" has little to do with the kinds of knowledge it enables in most human beings, little to do with the kinds of passional knowledge language enables, particularly knowledge of oneself. The final line, his admirers will tell us, is a stylised cry of despair, a witty self-parody, emphasising the intended artificiality of the whole passage, which is about Shelley-as-Writer. The trouble is that the passage feels more serious and less ironical than it should in order to sustain such a reading. Shelley really is trying to write about erotic love, about love of man for woman: not about love of friend for friend, or of brother for sister, or love of the Good. But for doctrinal and domestic reasons he thinks and wants to think about erotic love as if it could leave out the body. His own language, his imagery, betrays this enterprise, and he blames the language, when language itself might have taught him that what he wants to write cannot be written, at least in the language that we have, and that what he wants to feel cannot be felt, at least by human beings who have bodies as well as thoughts, who could indeed be seen as bodies which think. *Epipsychidion* is more openly, autobiographically passionate than its predecessor *Alastor*, but the passion is not for the most part informed by intelligence, as it was to be in the poems for Jane. This body is not thinking. Bloom calls the poem "a unique attempt to extend and realize the limits of relationship and expression",[7] but Shelley refuses in it to recognise the limits of either. He wants Love to be an idea transcending the human, poetry to be a means of figuring that idea. He sees neither love nor poetry as a way of knowing the human condition precisely as *conditional*, as limited; and yet the most transcendent love poetry is informed by just that sense.

ADONAIS

Where *Epipsychidion* reflects on "love's rare Universe" and proposes poetry as a somewhat inadequate way into it (one Alastorean theme), *Adonais* reflects on death's rare universe and proposes poetry as a not so inadequate way into that (the other Alastorean theme). Notwithstanding its substantial human limitations, which Shelley himself half-recognised, the value of *Epipsychidion* lies in its assertion that the search for human relationship is a vital constituent of the self. *Alastor* too asserted this. What *Adonais* claims is that the pursuit of Necessity even unto death, indeed only unto death, is *the* constituent of the self, particularly the poetic self. *Alastor* made this assertion even more loudly than it made the other one. Both later poems, like their common forebear, attempt to reflect upon a self that is constituted in a certain way, instead of using that self unreflectingly as the model for a certain conception of the rest of the world. This makes all three of them preferable as moral thinking to *Prometheus Unbound*, the "Ode" and the rest of the *Queen Mab* tradition. But all three disclose, in this critical inward turn, an essential propensity to treat the self, the passions and language as ideas, as objects of thought rather than as agents of thought. They manifest the same idealism as the poems they seek to criticise; only the subject matter has changed. *Epipsychidion* takes refuge in a "creed" (Julian's word is worth adducing here) that allows its Writer, not to say its writer, to postpone emotional discovery. *Adonais*, meanwhile, is not so much a lament for the person or the poet John Keats as an attack on a hostile or uncaring readership of poetry, particularly Shelley's, and a consequent re-affirmation of his conception of poetry in the teeth of his own despair. Shelley was half aware of this too, of course. "I have dipped my pen in consuming fire for his destroyers", he said, adding that perhaps he had been "carried too far" by his "enthusiasm" (ii 300, 302, 308). On a friend's advice he suppressed passages from the preface "relating to [his] private wrongs" (ii 306). But the poem sprang from a doctrinalism necessarily too radical for Shelley himself to grasp. He wrote it a few months after "A Defence of Poetry" at a time of near-despair about his own poetic values and practices, a time when Byron's enormous success seemed further confirmation of his own marginality. He had *had* to see *Epipsychidion* as written only for an elect few. The silence which greeted *Adonais*, a poem Shelley had thought "better . . . than any thing that I have written", a "highly wrought *piece of art*" (ii 294), came as yet another proof of this marginal status. Shelley was "shaken to atoms & torpid"; he wished he had something other to do than write verse; if this poem "had no success and excited no interest what incentive can I have to write?" (ii 382). These remarks about the poem intimate what we shall find on looking at the poem itself: that it is polemical and self-justifying in ways that resist the efforts of some fine interpreters[8] to redescribe its salient passages as stylised, ironical and knowingly self-aware.

These interpreters have taken their lead, perfectly justly, from Shelley himself. The poem *is* "highly wrought" in its literary provenance and allusiveness, its appearance and style, its lapidary stanzaic brilliance: in short, in its aestheticism. The evoking of the pastoral-Christian elegiac tradition of Theocritus, Bion, Moschus, Virgil, Spenser and Milton, with its Romantic variants in Coleridge's "Monody on the Death of Chatterton" and Wordsworth's stanza on Chatterton in "Resolution and Independence";[9] the verse form from Spenser *via Childe Harold's Pilgrimage* and *The Revolt of Islam*: these antecedents certainly set the poem in the literary mould of *Alastor* rather than in the philosophical-radical mould of *Queen Mab*. This literariness, however, produces in combination with the poet's "enthusiasm" some inconsonance of feeling and tone. The aestheticism can stifle the "consuming fire". Some readers may find the style baroque, mannerist or "marmoreal", as Holmes puts it,[10] and indeed in its earlier stanzas the poem is hard to warm to. Still, it is as evident in this case as in the case of the "Ode" that the feeling, long moderated as it is by prosodic virtuosity and literary knowingness, does appear finally and rewardingly to burst through. The verse is in the end transfigured by the resonance, the sheer rhetorical force of those final stanzas, as they seem to soar upwards, transforming mere genre and technique into the true voice of poetry. This surge of feeling and verse is undeniable, and not in itself objectionable. Something about it is, however, disturbing. The feeling, both when and before it bursts through, is not what we expect. A kind of despair is converted into a kind of elation, which is the usual procedure in the elegiac tradition. But this is not despair at the death of a friend, or a poet, out of which somehow arises elation at his continuing life, or poetry's. This is a despair arising from the questioning of a certain kind of poetry followed by a defiant reassertion of *that* poetry's continuing value. The kind in question is the old Shelleyan kind: poetry as the principal means of finding Necessity. Despair does not, of course, have to be over one kind of loss rather than another; loss of belief in one's life-activity is reason enough for despair. What is disturbing here is the disguising of one kind of loss as another kind, the pretence of a kind of despair that is never really felt, the triumphal reaffirmation of a certainty that is never really questioned, and the conceiving of poetry, the vehicle and mode of that certainty, as an attitude of exultation over and a means of escape from ordinary human life. If all this is what constitutes the "consuming fire" of *Adonais*, small wonder if sheer artistry cannot redeem it. The poem on its surface celebrates art as a human end in itself, but more deeply regards it as a means to an end at which both the human and the art are disvalued.

The prose preface to the poem (pp. 390–2) evokes both the elegiac tradition, in its epigraph from Moschus's lament for Bion, and the contemporary literary-polemical context, in its blaming of Keats's death on his reading criticisms of *Endymion* in *The Quarterly Review* ("these wretched men know not what they do"). We are already dealing with the accommodation of a certain mode of thinking (the elegy) about certain human conditions and feelings (loss, grief) to contemporary politico-polemical purposes. Milton attempted the same accommodation, although less extensively and centrally, in *Lycidas*, one of Shelley's models. There is no reason in principle why such accommodations should not be attempted, but in reflecting on them we must attend to the adjacency in the self of the poem of these two quite distinct impulses, and see whether the result is a concordance or a discordance, an opening up or a foreclosure of the thought. The poem proper is 495 lines long, in 55 Spenserian stanzas. There is a clear and familiar division into three parts: stanzas 1–17, 18–38 and 39–55. These larger parts are further separable, as in the "Lines Written among the Euganean Hills", into briefer sections, here seven in number. The central subject upon which all these sections reflect is the redeeming power of poetry.

The first eight stanzas of *Adonais* repeatedly recall its elegiac models, but they also take us back to the equivocal ending of *Alastor*, where the Poet's fate is superficially lamented but more deeply celebrated. "I weep for Adonais – he is dead!/ O, weep for Adonais!"; "Wake, melancholy Mother, wake and weep!"; "Most musical of mourners, weep anew!"; "He will awake no more, oh, never more!": this is the conventional elegiac attitude of complaint and invocation. The deity invoked is Urania, a traditional name for Venus in her role as the goddess of heavenly or ideal love. In Greek myth Venus is also the lover, but in this poem she is the mother, of "Adonais", Shelley's conflation of the Greek "Adonis" with the Hebrew "Adonai", meaning "Lord". There is thus some suggestion of the Christian myth, too. "Urania" was the name Shelley gave to his own Muse ("my mistress Urania") when taking up Peacock's challenge and embarking on his "Defence of Poetry". Here, moreover, is yet another version of that prototypical Shelleyan "Mother of the world", the Necessity-goddess of *Queen Mab* and its successors. The speaker of *Alastor* referred to her at the beginning of the poem as "great Mother"; at the end of the poem he lamented the death of the Poet: "ah! thou hast fled! . . .thou art fled". *Adonais* is full of echoes from other poets, but their poems are not so helpful as Shelley's own earlier work in making sense of the characteristic feelings and attitudes, the modes of self-representation, displayed here. Another Poet, another devotee of Necessity (to be one is to be the other), dies and is celebrated in death. But the earlier Poet died doubly unknown, since *Alastor* was unread. Shelley now had a real and notorious dead poet to help him revive his idea of the Dead Poet, and the revival was even more emblematic than the original. Adonais was Urania's "youngest, dearest one", her "extreme hope, the loveliest and the last". In his beauty he was both frail ("broken lily", "pale flower") and potent (he "adorned and hid the coming bulk of death", "pity and awe/ Soothe her [corruption's] pale rage"). His only real significance, in other words, lies in his connections with poetry and death. Milton appears in the verse as the still-potent enemy of the "priest, the slave, and the liberticide"; "his clear Sprite/ Yet reigns o'er earth". Other poets, greater and lesser, are or are not still famous as poets. But this last and definitive Poet Adonais is to be famous only for dying. "He is dead . . . Died Adonais . . . bulk of death . . . he is dead . . . Death feeds . . . He died . . . the gulph of death . . . Died on the promise of the fruit . . . kingly Death . . . shadow of white Death"; death echoes and re-echoes through these opening stanzas, but the insistent word means very little, brings little feeling with it. The name "Adonais", conversely, has little meaning in the poem beyond "Poet", "dead", and of course "not-dead". From the start we are also told that "his fate and fame shall be/ An echo and a light unto eternity"; "he is gone, where all things wise and fair/ Descend"; he has a "grave among the eternal"; "he takes his fill/ Of deep and liquid rest". Instead of working through the elegiac progression from grief to recovery, Shelley anticipates both attitudes at the beginning. The mannerism and coldness that some have noticed is a function of the emptiness and formality of the feeling as well as of the prosodic and generic recognitions. Instead of an attempt to represent real feeling for the dead (there was more of that in *Alastor*, where nobody had died) there are "highly wrought" and highly conventional attitudes to death. Adonais himself is no more than a figure for the poem's central ideas.

After the first eight stanzas of ritualised mourning by the speaker come nine more in which many other mourners appear. "All he had loved, and moulded into thought . . . Lamented Adonais". Some of these mourners are the conventional nature-figures of pastoral elegy: "Morning . . . Dimmed the aerial eyes that kindle day"; "Pale Ocean in unquiet slumber lay"; "the wild winds flew round, sobbing in their dismay"; "Lost Echo . . . feeds her grief with his remembered lay"; "Grief made the young Spring wild". Others are unconventional creatures of Adonais's own mind: "quick Dreams", "passion-winged Ministers of thought", "Desires and Adorations,/ Winged Persuasions and veiled Destinies,/ Splendours, and Glooms, and glimmering Incarnations/ Of hopes and fears". The treatment of the first group of mourners exhibits the same generic mannerism as the first eight stanzas of the poem; the language and imagery are flaccid, and we have no sense of how the particular life of these natural figures, of nature itself, is evoked in the poetry of the deceased or in any other poetry. The treatment of the second group, for all the unconventionality of the mourners, likewise adds little to our sense of the dead poet or of poetry in general; it ritually reaffirms a Shelleyan conception and practice of poetry as disengagement from its own material, as an attending to desires and adorations, attitudes of desire and adoration, with no sense of what is desired or adored. The only fire in the passage is ignited at its end: "Albion wails for thee: the curse of Cain/ Light on his head who pierced thy innocent breast,/ And scared the angel soul that was its earthly guest!" An elegy is not usually a murder story; the significance of the death and the nature of the consequent feelings are altered if it is claimed that the Poet did not fall but was pushed. It doesn't matter here whether Keats was or was not "snuffed out by an Article", as Byron put it in *Don Juan* (XI lx); what does matter is the way in which the limpness and affectedness of the poetry when it is attending to his death and its own grief are exposed by that moment of high indignation at the supposed cause of his death. We suddenly see where the real feeling lies.

We see more of the poem's real feeling in its third section, stanzas 18–26, where the focus is once more on the speaker (18–22) and on Urania (23–26). Grief "returns with the revolving year"; the "airs and streams renew their joyous tone"; the "amorous birds now pair in every brake";

> Through wood and stream and field and hill and Ocean
> A quickening life from the Earth's heart has burst
> As it has ever done, with change and motion,
> From the great morning of the world . . .
> All baser things pant with life's sacred thirst. . . .
>
> . . . Nought we know, dies. Shall that alone which knows
> Be as a sword consumed before the sheath
> By sightless lightning? . . . .
>
> Alas! that all we loved of him should be,
> But for our grief, as if it had not been,
> And grief itself be mortal! Woe is me!
> Whence are we, and why are we? of what scene
> The actors or spectators? Great and mean
> Meet massed in death, who lends what life must borrow.

As long as skies are blue, and fields are green,
Evening must usher night, night urge the morrow,
Month follow month with woe, and year wake year to sorrow.

The renewal of spring, far from assuaging grief, exacerbates it; this is a pastoral-elegiac commonplace. Shelley's apprehension of the natural world as *natural*, however, is usually alienated; only when he is able to find in it evidences of the transcendent, of Necessity, does he feel at home in it. This mode of elegiac grief is thus particularly congenial for a poet who finds life thorny except when it is Life. For him the "quickening life" of "baser things" is always just an appearance; the "revolving year" is evidence of decay, not renewal. Revolution is apocalyptic, not cyclical. Life is a loan from death; blue and green, the colours of life, are signs of woe and sorrow. Shelley is giving expression here to a sense of life that goes much deeper for him than elegiac convention, although he finds in that convention the perfect correlative of his sense of life. The poet, the paradigm of "that alone which knows", as opposed to the "universe of things", that which is known, is by his knowing excluded from and "consumed" by "things", by Necessity in her impersonal aspect as "sightless lightning". He cannot be a part of life because he is always looking beyond it to that which cannot die and is therefore not life. It is true enough that only the speaker's "grief" keeps Adonais in existence, because that is all there is to Adonais; he is an emblem of that paradigmatic Shelleyan poetic grief at being locked out of the world. Poetry, on this model, *is* grief. So when Urania is woken by "Misery" to the reality of Adonais's death she feels a "wound more fierce than his". She is Necessity's earthly aspect, the poet's Vision of *Epipsychidion* and *Alastor*; she is Poetry, and therefore Grief. Adonais "will awake no more", or only to Eternity; she is "chained to Time, and cannot thence depart". "I would give/ All that I am to be as thou now art", she tells his corpse; she wants to be part of Eternity, not Time. "Out of her secret Paradise" she must endure "camps and cities rough with stone, and steel,/ And human hearts", which "wounded the invisible/ Palms of her tender feet", and "barbed tongues, and thoughts more sharp than they". Urania as Poetry in Time is alienated from both the natural and the human worlds. What has emerged in this third section of the poem is Shelley's conception and practice of poetry as a mode of thought which is always on the outside of life. Death and the grief of the not-yet-dead are the normal states of the Shelleyan poet.

The fourth section, stanzas 27–38, is full of "consuming fire" for Keats's "destroyers", who also happened to be Shelley's literary foes. Adonais is "Defenceless" before the "monsters of life's waste", the "herded wolves", the "obscene ravens", the "carrion kites", the "vultures", "reptiles" and "spoilers". One in particular is an "unpastured dragon", a "deaf and viperous murderer", a "nameless worm"; this was aimed at Robert Southey, whom Shelley wrongly thought to have attacked both Keats and himself in the *Quarterly*. Byron, on the other hand, "the Pythian of the age", "like Apollo, from his golden bow . . . one arrow sped" and put them all to flight. What one looks for in vain is any thought in the language about how these reviewers have offended other than in attacking a poet. Adonais is just the persecuted Poet, the Tasso figure, the Maniac. There is no sense in the poetry of what Keats, Byron or the reviewers said, or of why the reviews were misconceived, even politically motivated. Wolves, ravens and reptiles, arrows and golden bows: these are exhausted metaphors. They do nothing to explain the poetry's anger, which therefore seems artificially inflated. We next encounter two stanzas (30, 35) of oblique references to various other grieving fellow-poets, combining the political partisanship of the foregoing with the coterie knowingness of parts of *Epipsychidion*, together with four stanzas (31–4) referring to one of them in particular. "Midst others of less note, came one frail Form . . . companionless"; "he, as I guess,/ Had gazed on Nature's naked loveliness . . . and now he fled astray" pursued by "his own thoughts". He is a "pardlike Spirit beautiful and swift", a "Love in desolation masked", a "Power/ Girt round with weakness", "a dying lamp, a falling shower,/ A breaking billow"; his head is "bound with pansies overblown,/ And faded violets", his "light spear" vibrates "as the ever-beating heart/ Shook the weak hand that grasped it"; he is the last of the band of mourners, "neglected and apart", a "herd-abandoned deer struck by the hunter's dart".

> All stood aloof, and at his partial moan
> Smiled through their tears; well knew that gentle band
> Who in another's fate now wept his own;
> As in the accents of an unknown land,
> He sung new sorrow; sad Urania scanned

The Stranger's mien, and murmured: "who art thou?"
He answered not, but with a sudden hand
Made bare his branded and ensanguined brow,
Which was like Cain's or Christ's – Oh! that it should be so!

This passage has been defended on the grounds that it is a piece of ironical self-dramatising, "a dramatisation of an aesthetic process", the conscious assumption by the poet of a literary attitude as the elegist or bard.[11] Other readers must decide for themselves, but to this one it seems that the emperor has no clothes, and that there are few lengths to which his faithful subjects will not go in imagining clothes for him. Any poet may represent himself ironically in his poetry as a bard, even a misunderstood one, and in this case if we try hard enough (and we will need to try hard) we can separate the self of the poetry from that of the poet, and find metaphors of poetry's frailty and vulnerability. We may even (trying still harder) find the poet parodying his own role as exiled elegist. Nevertheless the principal experiential effect of the passage is to make the poem's dominant figure for the still-living poetic self (Adonais's essential attribute is that of being dead) one of frailty, abandonment, persecution and martyrdom. There is no need to accuse Shelley of self-pity and sentimentalism; our concern is simply with those metaphors for the poetic self that appear in the passage. What we find there is that everyone else is at best a herd; the reviewers, the unreconstructed, are hunters, wolves and reptiles. This is how the world looks to a self which appears to itself as a Cain or Christ *figure*; there is no attempt to suggest how it might feel to *be* Cain or Christ. A self, albeit a poetic one, to which the world looks like this, which looks like this to itself, just will be unattractive to many readers. The sophisticated defence of the passage as ironical or dramatic is overwhelmed, as it was in *Alastor* and elsewhere, by the sheer force of the poetry's own emotional conviction. No matter how stylised or conscious in conception, this passage actually *is* a thoroughly self-pitying and self-centred portrait of one who saw another's fate as an opportunity to weep his own.

The poem's third part comprises two exultant passages about Adonais (38–43, 52–5) and some intervening stanzas on the transience of worldly glory and on other poets who died young. This final part of the poem begins in that scorn for the dissenting many and despair for the elect few that dominated the middle part, but alongside these feelings now there is a completely different and unconnected one.

> Thou canst not soar where he is sitting now. –
> Dust to the dust! but the pure spirit shall flow
> Back to the burning fountain whence it came,
> A portion of the Eternal . . .
> Whilst thy cold embers choke the sordid hearth of shame.

> Peace, peace! he is not dead, he doth not sleep –
> He hath awakened from the dream of life –
> 'Tis we, who lost in stormy visions, keep
> With phantoms an unprofitable strife . . .
> . . . We decay
> Like corpses in a charnel. . . .

In well-worn imagery the speaker tells his audience that he and they are sordid, decaying, lost, mad, convulsed, cold, envious, calumnious, hating and in pain. Simultaneously Adonais is described as pure, glowing, eternally alive and freed from all illusion. All the evils associated with and inseparable from life are now absent from him; all the goods present for him are absent from life. The poem regards the moral world not as a globe but as a two-dimensional disc, black on one side, white on the other. To be able to say that "Envy and calumny and hate and pain . . . Can touch him not", even that "He has outsoared the shadow of our night", is surely an enduring human need in the face of death; here Shelley says finely what we all sometimes need to say, when in death someone has at least escaped affliction. The worse the affliction the greater that consolation may be. We may also want to say that human life at some times and in some places has been mostly affliction, and that death under such circumstances is generally welcome. But this poetry does not convey such a sense of life's affliction as the counterweight to its sense of death's desirability. Affliction is not felt here, although anger, scorn, resentment and frustration are; the joys of life are not felt, although an unbalanced triumph over death certainly is. "Death is dead, not he": what does that convey, except that Adonais is now a figure for not-dying, just as earlier he was a figure for dying?

This figure is developed in stanzas 42 and 43: "He is made one with Nature: there is heard/ His voice in all her music"; "He is a presence to be felt and known . . . Spreading itself where'er that Power may move/ Which has withdrawn his being to its own"; "He is a portion of the loveliness/ Which once he made more lovely" (*how* did he?). The language continues to be without metaphorical vitality; the feeling, which is certainly strong, is grounded neither in the language nor in a development from the earlier feelings but in a new figure of thought, familiar enough from Shelley's earlier poetry. The speaker is excited and consoled, and asks his listeners to be excited and consoled, by the idea of Adonais being absorbed into Necessity, a mote in the Eternal Mind. He does not set the joys of life against its pains as a way of modifying his own or our sense of life; he does not set the release of death against the loss of life as a way of extending his own or our despair into consolation; he leaps directly from depression at sordid life to exultation at glorious Life. Death "is a low mist which cannot blot/ The brightness it may veil" (44), but not having been given in the poem a real sense of death's pains, of loss and grief, we cannot easily adjust to this sudden dazzling brightness, which makes all life look dreary. Why live at all, then? Apparently this vision, this brightness, is reserved for poets of the right kind, for Adonais and those few others deemed by the speaker to be like him. For the rest of us, the ordinary herd, death will be as final as life has been unprofitable.

The next few stanzas (44–51) tell us that the only earthly glory which lasts is that of the "kings of thought", those "splendours of the firmament of time" who "waged contention with their time's decay,/ And of the past are all that cannot pass away". Anyone who still mourns for Adonais is invited to think of the immensity of the universe, and of the tiny dot which is the Earth; or of Rome, city of "ages, empires, and religions", and of the small cemetery within it where Keats was buried: and then from "the world's bitter wind" to seek "shelter in the shadow of the tomb". Confronted, in other words, by our own insignificance, and by the vanity of worldly success, most of us may take comfort in the thought of death. "What Adonais is, why fear we to become?" But who are "we"? Poets and thinkers such as Chatterton, Sidney, Lucan and "many more" welcome Adonais as "one of us". Only their glory "cannot pass away". We may all be portions of the eternal, it seems, but some portions will shine more brightly than others, and thus will remain famous on earth too. The passage both asserts the superiority of thinkers and poets over all other people and asserts the value of Life, a difficult concept accessible only to a privileged few, over life, the necessary condition of the many.

Here are the first two stanzas and the last stanza of the poem's famous *finale* (52–5):

> The One remains, the many change and pass;
> Heaven's light forever shines, Earth's shadows fly;
> Life, like a dome of many-coloured glass,
> Stains the white radiance of Eternity,
> Until Death tramples it to fragments. – Die,
> If thou wouldst be with that which thou dost seek!
> Follow where all is fled! – Rome's azure sky,
> Flowers, ruins, statues, music, words, are weak
> The glory they transfuse with fitting truth to speak.
>
> Why linger, why turn back, why shrink, my Heart?
> Thy hopes are gone before; from all things here
> They have departed; thou shouldst now depart!
> A light is past from the revolving year,
> And man, and woman; and what still is dear
> Attracts to crush, repels to make thee wither.
> The soft sky smiles, – the low wind whispers near:
> 'Tis Adonais calls! oh, hasten thither,
> No more let Life divide what Death can join together.
>
> The breath whose might I have invoked in song
> Descends on me; my spirit's bark is driven,
> Far from the shore, far from the trembling throng
> Whose sails were never to the tempest given;
> The massy earth and sphered skies are riven!
> I am borne darkly, fearfully, afar:
> Whilst burning through the inmost veil of Heaven,
> The soul of Adonais, like a star,
> Beacons from the abode where the Eternal are.

To believe in "the One", as this poem does and asks us to do, as it claims that all proper poetry does and asks us to do, is to see life as a stain and death as an urgent need. Why linger, indeed. This is poetry which claims that to be a poet, to have the poetic view of life, is to want to die. The smiling sky and whispering wind entice the speaker not towards Life but towards Death. Only his mortal, ordinary self gives him pause; if only he believed enough he would not hesitate. The poet tells himself to leave the "trembling throng", the herd; to "sail beyond the sunset", as it were (this passage presses hard on Tennyson's "Ulysses"). But what looks to some like an exultant triumph over Death seems to others to be an abject surrender to it, a headlong flight from the human. "Die", "Why linger", "hasten thither", "thou shouldst now depart": this is no longer elegy; it does not even pretend to follow its feelings from loss and grief to consolation and renewal. If Necessity cannot be seen as part of the unreconstructed world, as in the "Ode" or *Prometheus*, then the poet must leave that world. In *Epipsychidion* Shelley remained more or less still true to Urania, alienated from but still chained to nature, time and human relationship; now he will have no more of her or of them. If poetry cannot be his instrument for reforming the world it must become his passport out of it; Shelley's poetry, even in the Alastorean tradition, is so often like a coin, with only the two sides. He recognised the barrenness of an instrumental poetry, but that recognition was still enacted within an ideal view of the world, the self and the poem.

"THE TRIUMPH OF LIFE"

The despair and scorn concealed within *Adonais* are openly represented in Shelley's last major work, an unfinished poem in 547 lines of *terza rima*, called "The Triumph of Life". In what there is of the poem, at least, faith in a transcendent and immanent Necessity is nowhere to be seen, and life's vanity is more fully and vividly rendered than anywhere else in Shelley's poetry. He wrote the lines in May and June of 1822, while living in an isolated villa shared by the Shelleys and the Williamses, on the seashore near Lerici on the Gulf of Spezia. Here he also wrote the poems for Jane Williams mentioned in Chapter 4 and elsewhere.

Reading Shelley's life into his poetry is often hard to avoid, as we have seen, not so much because of the kind of life he had as because of the kind of poetry he wrote, in which a self defined

chiefly by its opinions and its feelings about those opinions is
the frequent burden of the images and metaphors, the persistent
object of the reader's attention. Poems which think in other ways,
which discover other ways of being a self, are exceptional. The
"Triumph" is the most important of these exceptions. The poems
for Jane and other works of that kind are exceptions too, but
that voice, attractive as it is, seems ancillary to the main thrust
of Shelley's poetic energies. The "Triumph" seems relatively congenial with those energies in its intensity, its scale and its imagery. It is a first-person witnessing, but the speaker's opinions
are invisible, and his feelings seem to be grounded in the visionary scenes he describes. The poem's opinions are indistinguishable from its feelings and likewise grounded in its images,
so that they do not seem to be imposed upon the poem from the
outside by Shelley the person. That person's life has less salience
here, too, than it did in *Epipsychidion* and *Adonais*; there is no
Teresa Viviani or Robert Southey to encourage biographicalism.
We have seen, of course, that during the previous eighteen months
or so Shelley had begun to question his own opinions, or at least
his way of thinking about them in poetry, more deeply than ever
before. He despaired of competing with Byron in popularity ("the
sun has extinguished the glowworm", ii 423), and he was deeply
discouraged by hostile or indifferent critical responses to his own
work, which was of a kind that demanded assent, not just appreciation. We can imagine how that refuge at Lerici must have
beckoned like the island retreat of the fictional Writer of *Epipsychidion*; how Shelley's mood must have improved there; how he
must have felt he could escape at last from politics and from
Byron, and share the contentment of Goethe's Faust with the
"passing moment" (ii 436). We observe the irony in Shelley's
quotation from Goethe; Faust promised Mephistopheles that when
he spoke these words he would be ready to die, and Shelley
drowned one month later. Paul de Man says that Shelley's "de-
faced body is present in the margin of the last manuscript page"
of the "Triumph", and that his death is "an event which shapes
the text".[12] Bloom remarks that the "Triumph" is "properly
Shelley's last work".[13] But all these reflections show how easy it
is to slide from an ancillary to a determinist biographicalism.
Fascination with fragmented lives and texts tempts us to see
Shelley's mood at Lerici not just as a dispositional orientation
evident in the poem too but as a kind of final renunciation, and

therefore to read the poem as a palinode. The irony in Shelley's quotation, however, is that he did *not* know he was going to drown. Certainly the poem, or what there is of it, has none of the usual consoling glimmerings of Shelleyan salvation above and behind its chilling vision of a phantasmagoric human inferno. But this vision, powerful as it may be, is by no means without precedent in Shelley's writing. In various forms it can be found in *Queen Mab, The Revolt of Islam, Prometheus Unbound* and the "Ode to the West Wind"; most recently in "the wintry forest of our life" from *Epipsychidion* and the "life's waste" of *Adonais;* perhaps above all in *The Mask of Anarchy* and "Lines Written Among the Euganean Hills". Always before there was the promise of salvation; here humanity is unredeemed (although this is a fragment). A less obvious but in some ways closer analogue in Shelley's earlier writing is to be found in his letters, in his many descriptions of the awful Irish, French, Swiss or Italians: those "pollution-nourished worms", those unrecalcitrant exemplars of the "degradation of the human species". In the "Triumph" as it stands the human species is entirely degraded and deformed. Shelley was content for the "passing moment" to give rein to an unqualified dismay at and scorn for "the human part of the experience"; this was not a Swiftian corporeal disgust but an intellectual condemnation. The poem that we have, then, is not *sui generis*, not a renunciatory *nonpareil*, but a haunting reimagining of the familiar Shelleyan vision of degraded humanity without (so far) the equally familiar Shelleyan vision of redemptive Necessity. Shelley's earlier poetic selves seem more helpful in making sense of this one than information about his life.[14]

The main difference between the "Triumph" and most of those predecessors is its success as a spectacle. Shelley was enjoying his copy of *Faust* as much for the etchings in it as for the poetry (ii 407), and in his own poem his visual images constitute an even greater proportion than usual of the overall effect. Dante and Petrarch are of course Shelley's principal prosodic models, but their facilitating presences are also clearly visible in his images, whereas in *Epipsychidion* they had been felt merely in the ideas. The enclosed valley, chariot, multitude and white-haired victim of Petrarch's "The Triumph of Love", the enervating sun of his "Triumph of Time", the central black-clad figure of his "Triumph of Death", Dante's meetings with Matilda and the chariot of the Church in *Purgatorio* xxviii: all these images and many more find responses in Shelley's "Triumph". Byron's near-contemporary *terza rima* poem *The Prophecy of Dante* sounds utterly un-Dantean by comparison.[15] Byron's Italian masters were Boiardo and Pulci, from whom he learned how best to project his poetic self in an attitude and a tone; the results were *Beppo* and *Don Juan*. Shelley meanwhile was learning from Dante and Petrarch how best to dissolve his poetic self into imagery, figures; hitherto he had only achieved this in "Ozymandias", "Mont Blanc", the poems for Jane Williams, and a few isolated passages in *Alastor*, the "Euganean Hills", the *Mask* and elsewhere. Where Byron turned to Renaissance romance the "Triumph" harks back to that familiar medieval poetic genre, the dream-vision. A "waking dream", a "trance of wondrous thought", a "Vision", appears to the speaker as he lies on an Apennine hillside early one morning (in an unfortunate echo of the ending of "Julian and Maddalo" he has been kept awake all night by "thoughts which must remain untold"). The chief constituents of this dream-vision are: a huge crowd of people, referred to as a "great stream" and the "million"; a smaller but still considerable chained group, the "captive multitude"; a Chariot, to which the captives are chained, with its sinister Charioteer; and a Dantean-Virgilian guide named "Rousseau", who tries like Virgil in the *Commedia* to explain this vision to the dreamer, but who is unlike Virgil and like the other characters in the *Inferno* in being himself a part of the infernal crowd, so that he also has to explain how he came to be there. These components of the dream-vision are not separated out like this in the poem, but we shall nevertheless consider them in this way, rather than following the narrative. The "Triumph" needs even more acutely than Shelley's other more successful poems to be approached through its dominant images.

The poem's opening description (1–40) of the speaker on his "green Apennine" is the last in a long line of Shelleyan considerations of landscape, going back to *Queen Mab* and *Alastor*. In 1811 Shelley contemplated the mountains at Keswick: but then, so suddenly and completely that the mountains and their admirer never even reached the poem, his mind turned aside to those "millions of ideas" which were *Queen Mab*. By 1822, however, the more Alastorean image of the watcher on the hillside, lying against the "hoary stem" of an "old chestnut" with the night fleeing before him and the day rising behind, with "the Deep" at his feet and "Heaven above [his] head", had become the originating image of the poem itself. This could also be said of the "Euganean Hills" in 1818, where he (the same "he"?) watched "the sun's uprise majestical" and the "unfathomable sky" above the "green sea" of Lombardy. There we saw with him the flowers "Glimmering" at his feet, the "line/ Of the olive-sandalled Apennine", the snowy Alps, the "altar of dark ocean"; in the "Triumph" we see the "green Apennine", the "smokeless altars of the mountain snows", the "Ocean's orison", the "orient incense" of the flowers burning "slow and inconsumably". Some of these images were in *Queen Mab* too, but there they were accidental to the poem's texture of thought. In the more Alastorean Italian poems the landscape and its observer have become cognitively essential. That old Shelleyan turning aside from the landscape still happens, of course; the watcher is only the starting-point. We are about to see a "Vision" which was also prefigured in 1812, when Shelley abandoned the mountain landscape for his "dazzling picture" of a "vast populous and licentious city". We are about to see another licentious multitude, even if the image of the watcher on his hillside remains in the background throughout. In the "Euganean Hills" the speaker turned from the glorious civilised and natural landscape to the "pollution-nourished worms" inhabiting the cities. Still, this habitual transference of thought from object to idea is accomplished in the "Triumph" only through an explicit transformation of the natural landscape itself, specifically of the sun:

> Swift as a spirit hastening to his task
> Of glory and of good, the Sun sprang forth
> Rejoicing in his splendour, and the mask
>
> Of darkness fell from the awakened Earth. . . .
>
> Isle, Ocean, and all things that in them wear
> The form and character of mortal mould
> Rise as the Sun their father rose, to bear
>
> Their portion of the toil which he of old
> Took as his own and then imposed on them. . . .

We recognise in this sun the creator and source of life from the opening of the "Euganean Hills", and from *Epipsychidion* and the

"Defence". On the other hand the sun as imposing or tyrannical "father" in a natural world of "toil", later hiding the stars and bringing the terrible Vision, is an idea from the world of *Adonais*, where the poet is alienated from "mortal mould", from life. We have yet to see how much imaginative substance this idea of nature as enervating and death-bearing is given by the rest of the poem, but at least this time the poem's dominant idea resides in its originating sensory image. The oldest Shelleyan *topos* has been profoundly rethought. Not in the individual words, of course: "faint limbs", "the kiss of day", "Swift as a spirit" and "hoary stem" indicate that the poetry is thinking in its images and its physico-symbolic situation, rather than in its language.

The vision of the "great stream of people", the larger multi-tude, is developed in three principal passages (41–73, 137–75, 469–543) and several brief references: in all, about a quarter of the whole poem. "This was the tenour of my waking dream", begins the speaker in the first passage:

Methought I sate beside a public way

Thick strewn with summer dust, and a great stream
Of people there was hurrying to and fro
Numerous as gnats upon the evening gleam,

All hastening onward, yet none seemed to know
Whither he went, or whence he came, or why
He made one of the multitude, yet so

Was borne amid the crowd, as through the sky
One of the million leaves of summer's bier. –
Old age and youth, manhood and infancy,

Mixed in one mighty torrent did appear. . . .

Here are the "ordinary" people of Italy, Ireland and Switzerland; the "mob" Shelley had always so disliked; the unreconstructed many for whom his poetry was not intended; the "Pestilence-stricken multitudes", the "leaves dead", of the "Ode"; the "adoring multitude" of the *Mask*, also run down by a Chariot; the "pollution-nourished worms" of the "Euganean Hills"; the "ugly human shapes and visages" of *Prometheus Unbound* III iv; the "vulgar" who have no "organ of perception" with which to appreciate *Epipsychidion*; the "human part of the experience" which Shelley feared he was unable to understand or describe. The way he saw this mass of other selves had disturbed and vitiated his conception of the political just as the way he saw the passions as an unruly mass had distorted his sense of the single self. But now his mind rests on the "multitude" in all its separated particularity, and rests not in distaste but in sympathy. Another old and unattractive imaginative habit is being rethought. Not quite completely, however: the multitude

   . . . weary with vain toil and faint for thirst
Heard not the fountains whose melodious dew

Out of their mossy cells forever burst
Nor felt the breeze which from the forest told
Of grassy paths, and wood lawns interspersed

With overarching elms and caverns cold,
And violet banks where sweet dreams brood, but they
Pursued their serious folly as of old. . . .

On the one hand "vain toil" and "serious folly", on the other "melodious dew", "mossy cells", "grassy paths", "caverns cold", "violet banks" and "sweet dreams": the rush of vacuous adjectives exposes a dogmatic underpinning to the thought. The thought is revealed as taking place somewhere other than in the language. When the multitude makes another brief appearance shortly afterwards (107–16) the same false note is struck. In "The million with fierce song and maniac dance/ Raging around" the adjectives extend the image's thought, but the likening of this "million" to a Roman imperial mob greeting "some conqueror's advance", when "Freedom left those who upon the free/ Had bound a yoke which soon they stooped to bear", spoils the dazzling image in the old Shelleyan way. The simile's classical experiential form ("As when") barely conceals its essentially dogmatic conception, its interest in "Freedom" rather than in lives.

    Fortunately the other two passages on the "million" are largely free of this characteristic swerve of thought. This is an extract from the first of the two:

            . . . . Swift, fierce and obscene
The wild dance maddens in the van, and those
Who lead it, fleet as shadows on the green,

Outspeed the chariot and without repose
Mix with each other in tempestuous measure
To savage music. . . . Wilder as it grows,

They, tortured by the agonizing pleasure,
Convulsed and on the rapid whirlwinds spun
Of that fierce spirit, whose unholy leisure

Was soothed by mischief since the world begun,
Throw back their heads and loose their streaming hair,
And in their dance round her who dims the Sun

Maidens and youths fling their wild arms in air
As their feet twinkle; now recede and now
Bending within each other's atmosphere

Kindle invisibly; and as they glow
Like moths by light attracted and repelled,
Oft to new bright destruction come and go. . . .

                  . . . – Behind,
Old men, and women foully disarrayed
Shake their grey hair in the insulting wind,

Limp in the dance and strain with limbs decayed
To reach the car of light which leaves them still
Farther behind and deeper in the shade.

But not the less with impotence of will
They wheel, though ghastly shadows interpose
Round them and round each other, and fulfill

Their work and to the dust whence they arose
Sink and corruption veils them as they lie –
And frost in these performs what fire in those.

Together with its companion passage on the "million" this

constitutes Shelley's greatest vision of doomed and fallen humanity, one "full of morbid genius and vivifying soul", in Hazlitt's words.[16] The enjambed lines, the vivid picturing, the preponderance of active verbs and the subtle mingling of physical and psychological states owe a good deal to Dante, but this is unquestionably Shelley's own dance to the music of Life. That "fierce spirit" in her "car of light" who "dims the sun" is a kind of Venus Pandemos or life-sapping mortal passion, nature seen as ruin; the promise of the poem's opening is kept. The moral thinking is done in the imagery, as it was in "Ozymandias", without the tendentious adjectivalism and the intrusive doctrine of the "Ode" ("obscene", "unholy" and "mischief" perhaps apart). Life is seen as a fruitless, monotonous and addictive expending of energy and passion unto death; old and young alike are helpless before Life, possessed by her fierce spirit. The strength of this oddly puritanical imagining of humanity as a carnal inferno lies above all in its panoramic visuality; the lives are seen collectively and as caricatures, as by Hieronymus Bosch, not individually and as persons, as by Dante.

The third and last description of the "million" is offered at the end of the poem by Rousseau, the guide, who is explaining to his companion how the crowd first appeared in his own life. The sight, says Rousseau, was "a wonder worthy of the rhyme" of Dante, who "returned to tell/ In words of hate and awe the wondrous story/ How all things are transfigured, except Love". Here is the poem's not-so-secret imaginative source, Dante; here too, perhaps, is a hint at its doctrinal source, "Love", and at the possible completion of this compelling Shelleyan *Inferno* in a less impressive *Paradiso*, as foreshadowed in *Prometheus Unbound* III and IV. Be that as it may, here is part of Rousseau's description:

"The earth was grey with phantoms, and the air
Was peopled with dim forms, as when there hovers

A flock of vampire-bats before the glare
Of the tropic sun, bringing ere evening
Strange night upon some Indian isle, – thus were

Phantoms diffused around, and some did fling
Shadows of shadows, yet unlike themselves,
Behind them. . . ."

These "phantoms" assume various shapes: flying "eaglets ... lost in the white blaze"; dancing elves; chattering apes mimicking kings and popes, those "worms" who "monarchize/ And make this earth their charnel"; "small gnats and flies" which "thronged about the brow/ Of lawyer, statesman, priest and theorist"; "discoloured flakes of snow" which fall on the youngest and most beautiful of the crowd like a kind of spiritual acid rain, extinguishing their "youthful glow". The phantoms all emanate, as it turns out, from the multitude.

> "From every firmest limb and fairest face
> The strength and freshness fell like dust, and left
> The action and the shape without the grace
>
> Of life; the marble brow of youth was cleft
> With care, and in the eyes where once hope shone
> Desire like a lioness bereft
>
> Of its last cub, glared ere it died; each one
> Of that great crowd sent forth incessantly
> These shadows, numerous as the dead leaves blown
>
> In Autumn evening from a poplar tree ...
>
> ... Mask after mask fell from the countenance
> And form of all, and long before the day
>
> Was old, the joy which waked like Heaven's glance
> The sleepers in the oblivious valley, died,
> And some grew weary of the ghastly dance
>
> And fell, as I have fallen by the way side,
> Those soonest from whose forms most shadows past
> And least of strength and beauty did abide."

The idea that objects throw off shadows is used by Lucretius to explain how we see,[17] and Lucretius had loomed large in Shelley's imagination ever since *Queen Mab*. Here, though, Shelley turns an epistemological idea into an image as visually powerful and morally suggestive as the earlier one of the dance of Life. The dancing crowd shed their "strength", "freshness" and "beauty" like "shadows" or "dead leaves", "Mask after mask", until what is left is the "action and the shape without the grace/ Of life" (an echo of Burke's "unbought grace of life"?). Beauty, strength, freshness and grace are seen here as accidental to life, while mechanical action and crooked shape are essential; conversely in *Prometheus Unbound* III iv their ugliness was shed by the "lovely forms" of men and women. Shelley's pandemotic Desire is "like a lioness bereft"; the imagery is for once unreversed, to great advantage. Out of his Lucretian figure Shelley had made a visual correlative for his sense of the human condition as consumed by Desire, not redeemed by Love. The underlying thought is still as doctrinal as in *Prometheus* or *Adonais*; all those apes, worms and gnats do little more than reinforce the idea that the condition, the conditionality, of ordinary humanity should incur our scorn and contempt. Redemption is for those who evade life, not for those who endure it. But Shelley's great achievement in these two passages is to think with, to think forth, his distaste for the multitude, rather than let it influence his poetry as an unexamined and frightening power shaping his utopian ideas.

We turn now to the smaller "captive multitude", the one "chained to the car". This part of the dream-vision is described twice, the first time briefly by the dreamer (118–36) and the second at greater length by Rousseau (208–95). The captives, says the dreamer, are

... all those who had grown old in power
Or misery, – all who have their age subdued,

By action or by suffering, and whose hour
Was drained to its last sand in weal or woe,
So that the trunk survived both fruit and flower...

All but the sacred few who could not tame
Their spirits to the Conqueror, but as soon
As they had touched the world with living flame

Fled back like eagles to their native noon,
Or those who put aside the diadem
Of earthly thrones or gems, till the last one

Were there; for they of Athens and Jerusalem
Were neither mid the mighty captives seen
Nor mid the ribald crowd that followed them. . . .

Here are the "mighty" rather than the many: all except for "the sacred few", represented by Jesus and Socrates ("they of Athens and Jerusalem"). Apart from these few the mighty are even more completely subjugated than the many, who were not captives, not actually "chained to the car". Their degree of subjugation is thus in proportion to their former "power or misery". The wielder of power, whether by "action or by suffering", always seemed to Shelley to be even more of a slave than its victim. One feels the force of this claim, but one looks in vain in Shelley's poetry, in the characters of Jupiter and Cenci, for example, for the claim to be given substance in the representation of a powerful self. Life is "the Conqueror", so those who conquer most are those who are most conquered. The thought relies on a prior idea and an ingenious and half-plausible conceptual inversion, not on self-discovery, or on the visual compulsion of the descriptions of the "million". Is this really what power is like? or misery? How much help does the poetry give us in weighing the truth of this difficult thought? The lines on "the sacred few" raise these questions even more acutely. We are told that those who "put aside the diadem" of rule or wealth are not conquered by Life: but why not? How do these particular forms of renunciation take effect? We know that Jesus and Socrates are "eagles", and "sacred", but what does this tell us? Are they both sacred in the same way, both eagles of the same kind? What way, and what kind? What is their "living flame", their "native noon"? What does it mean to suggest that fleeing from Life (back to the Sun?) is the only way to live? Is this what either Jesus or Socrates actually taught? Is some prior conceptual understanding, available only to those with the proper "organ of perception", required to make sense of this thought?

The main description of the mighty captives is provided by Rousseau (208–95). Those "chained to the car" are "The Wise,/ The great, the unforgotten", the guide says;

". . . they who wore
Mitres and helms and crowns, or wreathes of light,
Signs of thought's empire over thought; their lore

Taught them not this – to know themselves; their might
Could not repress the mutiny within,
And for the morn of truth they feigned, deep night

Caught them ere evening."

Here Rousseau divides the captives into two groups: the mitred
and crowned, or the leaders of Church and State, and those described in *Adonais* as "the kings of thought". In the first category Rousseau mentions Napoleon, who "sought to win/ The
world, and lost all it did contain"; Frederick the Great and
Catherine the Great, "Chained hoary anarchs"; Leopold II;
Alexander the Great, singled out by Fame "from the flock of
conquerors" as "her thunderbearing minion"; the Roman emperors,
"heirs/ Of Caesars crime" whose "force and murderous snares . . .
spread the plague of blood and gold abroad"; and Gregory the
Great and the other popes, who "rose like shadows between man
and God" like an "eclipse" which was "worshipped by the world"
in place of "the true Sun it quenched". This account of the secular and spiritual leaders of mankind adds little to the earlier description of them by the dreamer. The poetry's understanding of
greatness and power, of their internal weaknesses and external
influences, is just as preconceived as it was in *Prometheus Unbound*,
even *Queen Mab*. Attaching tendentious predicates to the names
of the great is substituted for thinking about their lives, or about
the concepts "power" or "greatness", a certain attitude to which
is simply assumed. Moments of real discovery only underscore
the superficiality and dogmatism of the passage as a whole.
Rousseau is watching Napoleon:

– I felt my cheek
Alter to see the great form pass away
Whose grasp had left the giant world so weak

That every pigmy kicked it as it lay –
And much I grieved to think how power and will
In opposition rule our mortal day –

And why God made irreconcilable
Good and the means of good. . . .

The watcher's cheek is altered by Napoleon's shadowy form almost as the faces of the "million" are deformed by the phantoms emitted by other figures. The image of Napoleon as a giant stronger than the world, and of later leaders as pygmies, is worthy of Goya, or at least Gillray. But in that bald "opposition" between "power and will" (Shelleyan terms for tyranny and resistance) and the speaker's unreflective attitude to it the poetry suddenly stops thinking and falls back on preconceptions. The irreconcileability of "Good and the means of good" is more old coin, cashing in existing ideas rather than minting new images.

The "kings of thought", the other group of captives, are represented here principally by Plato and "the great bards of old" ("Homer & his brethren" in a cancelled manuscript reading), but also by Voltaire, Kant, Aristotle and Bacon. They failed "to know themselves", we have been told; they could not "repress the mutiny within". In Plato "Life . . . Conquered the heart by love which gold or pain/ Or age or sloth or slavery could subdue not", and so he "Expiates the joy and woe his master [Socrates] knew not". Homer and the "great bards of old . . . inly quelled/ The passions which they sung"; their "living melody/ Tempers its own contagion to the vein/ Of those who are infected with it". This is not the surrender to mere carnality of the "million". The captives are those whom Life conquers by virtue of their own strength, over themselves and over the world. The stronger they are the more completely they are subjugated by means of that part of themselves they have not overcome or known. This failure to "know themselves" provokes "the mutiny within", in which the unknown passional self becomes a Promethean state within a state, a centre of resistance to omnipotent Jovian thought. Rousseau admires the "great bards" because they "quelled" their passions before and in writing their poetry, so that it appeals to its readers only up to the limits of their own passional capacities or weaknesses, without inflaming them, pushing them beyond these limits. His own writing, Rousseau later admits, did have these inflammatory consequences. But even these bards are still Life's captives, because that suppression of their passions provoked an inward mutiny against their own suppressing selves. These lines are difficult, partly because Shelley was still working on them;[18] interpretation must be speculative, evaluation provisional. There is a moment when the poetry seems to be on the verge of real insight into the "tempering" of passion. On balance, however, the thought here seems all too reminiscent of the old Shelley. The passions are conceived as revolutionary mobs or resistant heroes, as admirable or frightening, but never as intrinsic constituents of the self. We quell, surrender to or admire them, but in each case we idealise or hypostasise them, instead of seeing them as ceaselessly variable enabling conditions of selfhood. And yet who are "we" if not partly "them"; and are "they" all alike? The poem's dazzling central figure of thought is itself an outcome of this two-dimensional moral psychology. Life captures or tramples us all, chains us by our own power or wastes us by our own impotence. Our "passions" betray into slavery all of "us" but "the sacred few", of whom we hear no more in the poem, but whose nature and fate seem likelier to confirm than discompose its thought. For all its visionary brilliance, this figure cannot fully satisfy those with a less binary, puritanical and autocratic way of thinking about the self and the passions.

Still, we have not yet considered the third part of the dream-vision, the account of his own life offered by "Rousseau" himself. He is both the guide to and the most important representative of the multitudes because we hear about his life in detail, as it were from the inside. The moment of his appearance, following the dreamer's first vision of the two multitudes, is another of the poem's pictorial triumphs (177–96). "And what is this?", says the dreamer of the "sad pageantry". "Whose shape is that within the car?"

... a voice answered ... "Life" ... I turned and knew
(O Heaven have mercy on such wretchedness!)

That what I thought was an old root which grew
To strange distortion out of the hill side
Was indeed one of that deluded crew,

And that the grass which methought hung so wide
And white, was but his thin discoloured hair,
And that the holes it vainly sought to hide

Were or had been eyes.

"'If thou canst forbear/ To join the dance, which I had well forborne'", says this "grim Feature", "'I will tell all that which to this deep scorn/ Led me and my companions'". The figure grows out of the verse like the root out of the hillside, where we are suddenly reminded that the narrator is still sitting. Landscape here is as fruitfully and precisely transformed, as fully realised and as completely idealised, as in the earlier dance to the music of Life (the closest Shelley had previously come to achieving this figural effect was in his description of the landscape surrounding the dying Poet in *Alastor*). The promise of the poem's opening to show nature as enervating and life as decline is once more fulfilled. To this point the "grim Feature" has no name, but during the passage (200-95) in which he describes the great captives he tells us who he is, and sets himself apart from them:

> "I feared, loved, hated, suffered, did, and died,
> And if the spark with which Heaven lit my spirit
> Earth had with purer nutriment supplied
>
> Corruption would not now thus much inherit
> Of what was once Rousseau – nor this disguise
> Stain that within which still disdains to wear it. –
>
> If I have been extinguished, yet there rise
> A thousand beacons from the spark I bore. . . .
>
> For in the battle Life and they did wage
> She remained conqueror – I was overcome
> By my own heart alone, which neither age
>
> Nor tears nor infamy nor now the tomb
> Could temper to its object. . . .
>
> . . . their living melody
> Tempers its own contagion to the vein
>
> Of those who are infected with it – I
> Have suffered what I wrote, or viler pain! –
>
> And so my words were seeds of misery –
> Even as the deeds of others."

Ten years before, under the influence of Godwin and Mary Wollstonecraft, Shelley had accused Rousseau of "giving licence by his writings, to passions that only incapacitate and contract the human heart".[19] Four years later, in Switzerland, he had come under Rousseau's spell, thinking of him as the semi-divine creator of an ideal world of love which overshadowed the real one. He showed signs of still being under that spell as recently as one year before, during the composition of *Epipsychidion*. So in the character of "Rousseau" Shelley had made an inspired choice of vehicle for his late self-questioning. Rousseau is not one of the great captives, because his ideal conception of the passions prevented his ever being a powerful agent, and therefore a slave, of Life. On the other hand he is part of the dance, one of the corrupt "million", because he did not "quell" his passions. He suffered what he wrote, was "overcome" by his own heart, could not "temper" it to its "object", was ruled by his passions instead of ruling them. His heavenly "spark" or spirit, the source of his ideal conception of Love, was trapped in corrupt impure "nutriment", forced to wear an earthly disguise or stain (the language of *Adonais*), but it still remained a spark and a seed, the cause of both inspiration and misery in others (the language of the "Ode"). Shelley's thinking here is unusually self-searching. The voice is Alastorean; the poem both admires and condemns the Poet's idealist conception of love and the passions, recognising both its transcendent truth and its everyday destructiveness. But this is no Poet, no Maniac, not even a Tasso; "Rousseau" was the name of Shelley's own former mentor and guide to Love. This is one of Shelley's most morally penetrating passages; might he this time have broken the binary framework, sprung the Alastorean trap, avoided the idealist criticism of idealism?

Rousseau now gives a long account (300–468), amounting to nearly a third of the poem, of how he came to "this dread pass". He tells the story of his life as if it were a single day. He knows, he says, where he came from, and how he came here, but not where he is going, or why all this has happened to him. This could be anyone's life, in other words; it could be his companion's, or even the reader's. Rousseau tells the dreamer to "follow" him, "and from spectator turn/ Actor or victim in this wretchedness". There are no mere spectators of Life; even watchers on hillsides and readers of poems are Her agents or victims, captives or dancers. The life story itself is heavily symbolised. Rousseau wakes

up one April day in a "valley of perpetual dream", an Alastorean
dell of forgetting, full of "soft grass" and "sweet flowers", and
traversed by a "gentle rivulet" whose sounds make those who
hear them forget "All pleasure and all pain, all hate and love,/
Which they had known before that hour of rest". Such was the
"oblivious spell" of the place that Rousseau cannot remember
his life before waking; "a gentle trace/ Of light diviner than the
common Sun" lingered there. Then out of "the Sun's image radi-
antly intense" reflected in the well, the source of the rivulet, there
emerges a "shape all light" carrying "a chrystal glass" full of
"bright Nepenthe" (the classical drug of forgetting). She walks
on the surface of the water, and her feet

> "... seemed as they moved, to blot
> The thoughts of him who gazed on them, and soon
>
> All that was seemed as if it had been not,
> As if the gazer's mind was strewn beneath
> Her feet like embers, and she, thought by thought,
>
> Trampled its fires into the dust of death,
> As Day upon the threshold of the east
> Treads out the lamps of night...."

Rousseau dares to ask her "whence I came, and where I am, and
why"; in answer she tells him to drink from her glass,

> "And suddenly my brain became as sand
>
> Where the first wave had more than half erased
> The track of deer on desert Labrador,
> Whilst the fierce wolf from which they fled amazed
>
> Leaves his stamp visibly upon the shore
> Until the second bursts – so on my sight
> Burst a new Vision never seen before. – "

This is the coming of the Chariot and the multitude into the
valley. Just as "all like bubbles on an eddying flood/ Fell into
the same track at last and were/ Borne onward", so Rousseau
too "among the multitude/ Was swept", plunging into the "thickest

billows of the living storm". Although the "shape all light" is rendered invisible by the new fierce light of the Chariot, her "unseen . . . presence" remains with him like Venus's during the day; he is as "one who hopes/ That his day's path may end as he began it/ In that star's smile". She keeps her "obscure tenour" beside his "path, as silent as a ghost", and throughout the "sick day" he senses her like a "light from Heaven" which "Glimmers, forever sought, forever lost". The unresolved double-mindedness that we noticed in the earlier part of the characterisation of Rousseau is carried through into this story, which is also Shelley's and any Poet's. Rousseau wakes up in a moment and place of Shelleyan awakening, not unlike those moments and places in the "Hymn", *The Revolt of Islam* and *Alastor*, when the Poet first recognises his own identity and purposes, sensing in them their "diviner" affiliations and sources. A figure not unlike Intellectual Beauty or Necessity is in attendance, and forever after, during his fallen life, he continues to feel and draw hope from her "unseen presence". And yet she is at best an unreliable ally, at worst a treacherous foe. She tramples on her admirer's mind and thoughts, rather than scattering them among mankind; she plays sun to their stars, just as the Chariot plays Sun to her Venus. Her Nepenthean drink completes the damage, even if she is the deer to the Chariot's wolf. She is both that which destroys Rousseau, or initiates his destruction, and that which saves him from captivity and gives him hope (false hope?). Because of her, and his memory and pursuit of her, he cannot be a conqueror, utterly conquered by Life; but also because of her he becomes part of Life's vain dance, of morbid nature, of that "sick day" which is the poem's central concern. Shelley's story of "Rousseau" is his finest piece of self-criticism; his depiction of the condition of the idealist achieves here an unprecedented clarity and visual presence. This poetic realisation of the condition of a self is of an entirely different order of plenitude from the hasty dogmatisms about the great captives. The "sacred few" might still have turned out to be Necessity's devotees, the doctrinal preconceptions may be unaltered, passions may still be objects rather than agents of thought, this may still be essentially the old Alastorean intellectual recognition of idealism's frailties. But never had Shelley represented those frailties more compellingly.

We come, finally, to the last constituent of the dream-vision, the image which most obviously offers itself as the focal point of the poem: the Chariot of Life, with its charioteer, its dark occupant and its team. All are described in one short early passage (77–106), part of the dreamer's first account of the larger multitude; later brief references add very little. A "cold glare, intenser than the noon/ But icy cold, obscured... The Sun as he the stars", the dreamer begins. "Like the young Moon" bearing "the ghost of her dead Mother",

So came a chariot on the silent storm
Of its own rushing splendour, and a Shape
So sate within as one whom years deform

Beneath a dusky hood and double cape
Crouching within the shadow of a tomb,
And o'er what seemed the head a cloud like crape

Was bent, a dun and faint etherial gloom
Tempering the light; upon the chariot's beam
A Janus-visaged Shadow did assume

The guidance of that wonder-winged team.
The Shapes which drew it in thick lightnings
Were lost: I heard alone on the air's soft stream

The music of their ever moving wings.
All the four faces of that charioteer
Had their eyes banded... little profit brings

Speed in the van and blindness in the rear,
Nor then avail the beams that quench the Sun
Or that these banded eyes could pierce the sphere

Of all that is, has been, or will be done. –
So ill was the car guided, but it past
With solemn speed majestically on...

Shelley's chariot may, as Bloom suggests, be a savage revision of the Christian chariot of Ezekiel, Dante and Milton; Blake too made such a revision.[20] The chariot of the soul in Plato's *Phaedrus*, which Shelley had read enthusiastically in 1818, may also have influenced him. But the Shape, as the poem repeatedly tells us, is "Life the Conqueror", and this was an aspect of Life Shelley had feared all *his* life. This was not the "Sun of life" celebrated by the "poetry of life" in the "Defence" the year before, not the transcendent Life of Necessity to which the Alastorean Poet aspires and dies, but the "wintry forest", the life of custom and commerce in *Queen Mab*, the life of the "cold . . . light of reason", the condition of ordinary people, of material fact, of earthly passion, of misery, mortality and mutability; the life of morbid nature. This Life's chariot is driven by enormous natural energy and yet unguided by that Promethean reason and science which could be all-seeing and all-directing were it not absurdly blindfolded by Life. This is indeed the focal image of the poem, Shelley's most powerful representation of his deepest fear: that Life is uncontrollable decay, blind passion, malign natural Necessity. This fear was the counterpart of his deepest desire: that Life be unchanging Truth, pure Idea, beneficent transcendent Necessity. This is the dilemma or polarity which informs so much of Shelley's poetry and which so often makes it unpalatable to his more unreconstructed readers. In its violent oscillation between these two polar conceptions of Life the poetry so often neglects or devalues the human, and more particularly the feelings. So in leaving the last word to Shelley, here confronting his dilemma for the last time, such readers must hope that his poem's answer to its own most famous question was not to be just another variant of: "a dome of many-coloured glass". Here are Shelley's own last words as a poet:

"Then, what is Life?" I said . . . the cripple cast
His eye upon the car which now had rolled
Onward, as if that look must be the last,

And answered. . . . "Happy those for whom the fold
Of

Conclusion:
The Divided Self

This book's assumptions and arguments are summarised in the first and fourth sections of Chapter 1, the first and fifth Sections of Chapter 2, the first section of Chapter 3, and the opening paragraphs of Chapters 4 and 6. What follows is not a summary but a general statement of what the book claims.

Poetry is a kind of moral thinking or perception in which the passions and the language are constitutive. They are respectively the agents and the medium of the thought, rather than its objects and its instrument. But to say that there is no poetic thinking which is not affective and not linguistic is far from saying that there can be no thinking in poetry. A view of poetic thought as affective and linguistic "all the way down" is not anti-rational: only anti-rationalist. On such a view poetic thought cannot be divided into a reasoning part and a passional part, or into "ideas" and the language which expresses or fails to express those ideas. The language of poetry, furthermore, cannot on this view be divided into "fact" and "value". Like other kinds of moral thinking, poetry is always evaluative in its perceptions; its statements of fact are value-soaked. Poetry which struggles to separate fact from value, passion from reason and language from idea is poetry which is trying to be something else. One might almost say that poems are like persons, or that passages of poetry are like passages of a life or lives. They have dispositions, characters, selves. People's beliefs, principles or ideas, and the facts about them, their circumstances, are vital parts of their characters, but in attending to them as persons we cannot attend to their ideas and facts in isolation from their characters. We may disagree with their ideas, or envy their circumstances, but still like them as people: or conversely. So with a poem: is its thought pleasing? simple-minded? wise? afflicted? The primary questions one might wish to ask of a poem have to do not with its ideas, not with the facts it may represent or emanate from, but with its manner of being, its cast or tone of mind. To regard a person or a poem like this, to regard the moral realm like this, is to assume that the most effective manner of attending to poems and persons, and the best way to persuade others to do the same (regardless of whether or not one actually likes the poems or persons in question), is to do so without recourse to normative abstractions, to general principles and theories of ethics or poetics. One should behave towards a poem as if one were a person oneself. We are all no doubt the bearers of theory-laden beliefs, but we have lives which are not just the sums of our beliefs. Reading poetry untheoretically does not mean reading it carelessly or irrationally or in an unprincipled way. It means reading in such a way that any theories one may have about poetry, reading or anything else are so thoroughly assimilated that they do not function in the reading as theories at all, but as constituents of practice.

Those who have disliked Shelley's poetry, including several of the greatest critics of the last two centuries, have taken more or less this "experiential" view of poetry and criticism. They belong therefore to a larger tradition in moral thought, which includes Johnson and Hume in the eighteenth century and the later Wittgenstein in the twentieth, and which has its roots in the moral philosophy of Aristotle. They have seen Shelley's poetry as divided within itself: passion from reason, fact from value, language from idea. Instead of thinking with its passions and its language, they say, his poetry treats them as its objects and its instrument. The classic statements of this view of Shelley were made by William Hazlitt in the 1820s; the later criticisms by Matthew Arnold, T. S. Eliot, F. R. Leavis and others are essentially restatements. Shelley's detractors find that the division in the self of his poetry leads to political and moral tendentiousness, symbolical arbitrariness and linguistic and metaphorical obscurity. The self of the poetry is disturbingly authoritarian, élitist and childish, and its political dogmatism and apparent indifference to human feeling and even human life make it hard to insulate the poet himself from criticism on humanitarian grounds. There is a whole library of Shelley appreciation, however, as against one volume or so of detraction. Nearly all of this library consists of "referential" criticism, of works which argue or assume that the value of the poems lies in the biographical and historical facts, or the philosophical, moral and political ideas, to which the poems refer. The biographical referentialists seek an overall order or unity in Shelley's work deriving from the facts of his life; the philosophical referentialists seek one deriving from his

ideas. Much of this scholarship has been indispensable in producing incorrupt texts and eliminating misunderstanding. But
very little of it addresses its own central assumption: that the
poetry is worth all that scholarly effort. For the referentialists its
value resides in its systems of reference, its facts and ideas, not
in its disposition or personality. A few critics (one shelf in the
library) have tried to explain their liking for the poems in non-
referential terms. These may be termed "symbolist" and "stylist"
critics, and they include Coleridge, Yeats, C. S. Lewis and Harold
Bloom. As with the experientialists, these critics have affiliations
outside literary criticism. They assume that poetry can be, and
they argue that Shelley's poetry admirably is, a way of signifying
or symbolising a transcendent, non-linguistic reality, in language
which is characterised by a sense of its own necessary alienation
from that reality. Human lives and feelings, like language, have
value only in so far as they approach or at least aspire to that
reality, which is seen as an ultimate and quintessential Idea. This
is a Coleridgean, Kantian and ultimately Platonic view of the
self, of reality, of language and of value. It is an idealist and a
rationalist view; it sees in that numinous Idea the fundamental
and certain explanation of all phenomena. Its adherents include
most philosophers since Descartes and most modern literary
theorists. This idealist-rationalist conception of the world and
of the human is fundamentally opposed to the experientialist
conception.

Shelley's own views of poetry were idealist and rationalist.
He had two principal views. On the one hand he held all his life
a strongly utilitarian (one might as well call it a rationalist) view
of poetry as the instrument of moral and political reform and
the container of political and moral, or more generally philosophical, ideas. Poetry is decorative; it embellishes the ideas it
contains; it tames or improves the masses. (Shelley in his prose
everywhere scorns and despairs of the masses.) On the other
hand he held an expressionist view of poetry as the all but uncontrollable outlet of the passions, which he saw as, like the masses,
fearsome in their potential for destruction of the self, whether
individual or collective. Shelley later attempted to rationalise and
idealise this expressionist view, to bring it more into line with
its rival, by seeing the passions as intimations of Truth or the
Idea, to which poetry must remain subordinate. But he remained
uncomfortable with the incompatibility between the two views.

He did have a fledgling third view, detectable in one or two passages in the "Defence of Poetry" and elsewhere, according to which poetry might be a distinctive manner of thinking with the passions, from inside a whole self; but he never developed this. First in England in 1811–17, then in Italy in two distinct phases, 1818–19 and 1820–2, he oscillated between his two principal views of poetry, trying to reconcile them but increasingly sensing, especially under the influence of Italian art, that the first view exposed poetry to a purely political judgement while the second did not yet fully capture poetry's depths and energies; and that perhaps both together arose out of a disabling conception of the self and of poetry.

The poetry itself falls into two principal categories, each corresponding to one of the two views of poetry just described. The first category contains poetry of politico-moral idealist reformism. Its central line of thought runs from *Queen Mab*, in many ways the *fons et origo* of Shelley's poetic thinking, through *The Revolt of Islam* to *Prometheus Unbound*; but it also includes the "Ode to the West Wind", the "Hymn to Intellectual Beauty", "Mont Blanc" and aspects of "Lines Written Among the Euganean Hills" and *Adonais*. This category is distinguished by its persistent reference to and search for a kind of goddess figure, known sometimes as Necessity, sometimes as the Power, which is represented as the eternal transcendent realisation and occasional immanent agent of Truth, the Idea. The principal human connections with this figure are through visionary insight and revolutionary will. Shelley's characteristic imaginative habit in this poetry is to swerve sudddenly aside from the natural or human object before the poem's eye, such as a mountain or a girl, to an ideal or intellectual subject, such as revolution or paradise. The connections between object and subject are asserted by the poetry rather than demonstrated. This might be termed the symbolic method; the association of subject with object is a matter of "contiguity" and "constant conjunction", in Humean terms, not inner metaphorical resemblance. The metaphorical method, in which Shelley's detractors find him wanting, is to make the connections exist in the language. Shelley treats words as givens, not as the stuff of thought. Since the unity and meaning of his poetry lies in the transcendent idea to which it refers he feels he does not need to find unity within his language, between his images. Since the central idea is unrepresentable it functions as an absence at the heart of the poem, something which directs all the diverse images as an invisible magnet directs iron filings. Shelley's admirers see here a sophisticated proto-modernist awareness of the limitations of language. Shelley's detractors, not having the benefit of his vision of the Idea, see the diversity as incoherence, the connections as arbitrary, the swerve aside from the natural and human as indifference to the natural and human, and the interest in the limits of language as a distrust of language out of place in a poet. Sometimes this category of poetry becomes topical, polemically revolutionary, as in *The Mask of Anarchy*, parts of the "Euganean Hills", the shorter political poems of 1819–20 and, more obliquely, the "Ode". In these places the poetry's visionary indifference to the human in the name of the ideal can be quite disturbing.

The other principal category includes *Alastor*, the original antithesis to *Queen Mab*'s original thesis; "Julian and Maddalo", *The Cenci, Epipsychidion*, most of *Adonais* and perhaps "The Triumph of Life"; and aspects of "Mont Blanc" and the "Euganean Hills". This is a more dramatic, passion-centred and undidactic poetry, often explicitly critical of the kind of life recommended by its ideal-reformist counterpart, with its search for Necessity and consequent inattention to the human. In this second category poetry appears less instrumental, less subordinated to reform and idea, more a kind of thought in its own right. But there are various shadows falling between the purpose and the performance. The principal shadow is that Shelley cannot distance himself emotionally or dramatically from the leading figures of his renunciatory poems. The Poet in *Alastor*, the Maniac in "Julian and Maddalo", the Tasso figure behind both "Julian and Maddalo" and *The Cenci*, Adonais and the "one frail form" in *Adonais*: in all these cases the poetry passionately extenuates the life it proposes to condemn. The ironies and dramatic qualities Shelley's admirers claim to detect are not sufficient to prevent this; Shelley himself commented on his own inadequacies as a dramatist. More generally these poems offer a view of the world, of the natural and human worlds experienced by the protagonists, as denatured and vain respectively. In order to criticise the search for Necessity Shelley had to show how the world might look without her, and without that ideal light his world looks drab, mankind looks brutal, the human condition which is redeemed in the ideal poetry only by its tenuous connections with the transcendent becomes everywhere disgusting. There is no middle way, no delight in ordinary life, no discovery of courage and vision in the midst of decay and defeat. And finally this category in its focus on the passions merely objectifies them, idealises them, offers them and poetry their vessel or conduit as the latest and best pathways to the Idea. The passions are used symbolically, as representations of some idea, not thought into metaphorically, as constituents of a self.

There is however a third category of or aspect to Shelley's poetry, corresponding to his embryonic third view of poetry. Beginning with the early "Letter to Edward Fergus Graham" (1811) and then "To Constantia" (1817), continuing through the poems for Sophia Stacey (1819–20) and the "Letter to Maria Gisborne" (1820), and culminating in the poems for Jane Williams (1822), Shelley wrote a series of minor occasional poems, mainly for women, in which we can hear the voice of a whole self, see the thinking being done with the passions rather than about them, find metaphorical thought arising from situations that resemble their theme instead of being associated with it symbolically, as a matter of mere physical contiguity. Traces of this kind of poetic thought can also be discerned in many of the poems mentioned above, especially "The Triumph of Life", "Julian and Maddalo", the "Euganean Hills", *Alastor*, *Epipsychidion* and even *The Mask of Anarchy*. An oustanding short example of this kind of thought is "Ozymandias". Unfortunately Shelley showed few signs of regarding this kind of thinking as other than peripheral to his central poetic endeavours. There is just a suggestion that towards the end of his life he may have been forced into attaching more importance to it, but only for want of his usual politico-moral stimuli. Still, this kind of thought showed increasing signs of infiltrating his work. His short career as a poet from 1811 to 1822 can be divided into three cycles roughly corresponding to the cycles of thought about poetry outlined above. *Queen Mab* and its responding antithesis *Alastor* dominate the first cycle. *The Revolt of Islam* and *Prometheus Unbound* in 1817–19 attracted their own criticisms in the same period from "Julian and Maddalo" and *The Cenci*. In 1820–2 the political voice, resurgent in late 1819, seems to fade away in fruitless poems about European liberty, increasingly criticised by the voices of *Epipsychidion*, *Adonais* and "The Triumph of Life", with the poems for Jane promising different things to come and the "Triumph" intimating an increased imaginative power within a more settled mode.

This book is not an unsympathetic and partisan assault on a besieged and misunderstood canonical writer. Its chief purpose is to promote serious reflection on an important poet whose habits of thought may turn out to be more widely significant; and to suggest the continuing value of attending closely to how poetry thinks, of treating it with respect whether or not one happens to like it. This may in the end turn out to be a better way of serving Shelley's poetry than fencing it off behind intimidating referentialist scholarship. The name "Shelley" for most educated younger people now refers only to the author of *Frankenstein.* This is a sign of substantial cultural loss: a loss to which that referentialism has actually contributed, in its self-regarding complacency and in its relativising tendency to avoid evaluative judgements.

Notes

These notes have been kept brief. Wherever possible they simply give page references to the works listed in the Bibliography. See the Bibliography, too, for abbreviations used in these notes. References to *SPP* throughout the book are by page number in parentheses in the text, thus: (p. 234). Poems referred to are in, and all quotations are from, *SPP* unless otherwise indicated. References in parentheses thus (234) are to line numbers within poems under discussion. References to *Letters* are by volume and page, also in parentheses in the text, thus: (ii 234).

1: THE CASE OF SHELLEY

1. Pottle, 604.
2. The pre-eminent names are those of Carl Grabo, Newman Ivey White, Kenneth Neill Cameron, D. H. Reiman, Earl R. Wasserman, G. M. Matthews, and more recently Stuart Curran, Timothy Webb and Kelvin Everest.
3. For example *The Keats-Shelley Review*, the bulletin of the Keats-Shelley Memorial Association, published in Britain as a smaller counterpart to the *Journal*, which is produced by the Keats-Shelley Association of America; and *The Bodleian Shelley Manuscripts*, now approaching twenty volumes.
4. For good accounts of the reasons see Curran, 1985, 598–606, and *PS*, xii–xxxi. *SPP* is the best selection by far; Timothy Webb's Everyman selection (1977), is also very good for the poetry. *PS* is the first volume of a new three-volume complete edition of the poems now in preparation; *PW* is for now still the only complete edition of the poems. The first volume of a new complete edition of the prose edited by E. B. Murray appeared too late, unfortunately, to be used in this book. The edition used here is *Works*, v–vii.
5. Pottle, 608.
6. Blank, 245.
7. Holmes, 1992, 19.
8. Blank, 5.
9. Leavis, 1936, 206, 219, 222.
10. Leavis, 1936, 216.
11. *Ibid.*
12. Everest, 1983, xi.
13. Allott, 7.
14. Donoghue, 12.
15. Arnold, ix 237, xi 317, 327. See n. 38.
16. McFarland, 694.
17. O'Neill, 2.

18. Murdoch, 1970, 59.
19. For Coleridge see Reiman, 1972, 771–2, 775–6.
20. For Hunt see Reiman, 1972, 445, 447.
21. For Lockhart see Reiman, 1972, 104, 110.
22. For Walker see Reiman, 1972, 780–6.
23. See especially his *Essay on the Principles of Human Action: Being An Argument in favour of the Natural Disinterestedness of the Human Mind* (1805), Hazlitt, i 1–49.
24. This over-compressed account of some key features of Hazlitt's thought draws on the *Essay*; on Hazlitt's essays on Bentham, Wordsworth, Coleridge, Byron and Scott in *The Spirit of the Age* (1825) in Hazlitt, xi 5–95; on his *Lectures on the Dramatic Literature of the Age of Elizabeth* (1820), in Hazlitt, vi 175 ff.; and on various of his other writings on poetry, drama and the novel. See also Bromwich, 1983, chapters I and IV, and *passim*; this and Roy Park's are much the best books on Hazlitt's thought. For a deeply penetrating account of the Hazlittean as opposed to the Coleridgean mode of critical thought, an account which goes well beyond the thought of Hazlitt and Coleridge themselves, and one to which I am very much indebted in this chapter, see Bromwich, 1989, chapter 15, "Literature and Theory".
25. Hazlitt, xi 72, 25.
26. Hazlitt, xii 251.
27. *ibid.*
28. Originally entitled "Table Talk" in *The London Magazine* ("Baldwin's"), April 1821. Hazlitt printed the essay under its present title in his *The Plain Speaker: Opinions on Books, Men and Things* (1826): Hazlitt, xii 242–52.
29. Hazlitt, xii 246–7.
30. Hazlitt, xii 245–6.
31. First published in *Table-Talk; or, Original Essays*, 2 vols., 1821–2; Hazlitt, viii 146–56.
32. Hazlitt, viii 146.
33. Hazlitt, viii 148–50.
34. First published in *The Edinburgh Review*, July 1824; Hazlitt, xvi 265–84. The quotations in this paragraph are from 267–9.
35. Hazlitt, viii 265–6.
36. Quotations in this paragraph from Hazlitt, viii 270–80.
37. The essay was first published in *The Nineteenth Century*, January 1888, and in *Essays in Criticism, Second Series* (1888); Arnold, xi 305–27. For quotations from the essay in this paragraph see 320, 324, 327.
38. From the preface to Arnold's *Poetry of Byron* (1881), which later also appeared in *Essays in Criticism, Second Series*; Arnold, ix 218. The famous phrase about the angel first appeared in this essay (ix 237); in the Shelley essay (xi 327) Arnold is quoting himself.
39. Carlyle, 1923, 292, from a letter to Robert Browning of 8 March 1852; and 1972 (original edition 1881), 354.
40. Patmore, 93.

41. Stephen, iii 78, 91–2.
42. Robertson, 235.
43. Kinnear, 325, identified as the author in Houghton, i 744. Kinnear reviewed several recent memoirs of Shelley, concluding that on the whole he had not been well served by his biographers (289).
44. For the quotations, and more on the "ethical imagination", see Babbitt, 161, 202–3, 224, 291, 360–1.
45. All quotations from More, 170–3.
46. Eliot, 1975, 48. From "Hamlet" (1919).
47. Eliot, 1975, 41, 43–4. From "Tradition and the Individual Talent" (1919).
48. Eliot, 1975, 64–5. From "The Metaphysical Poets" (1921).
49. From "The Social Function of Poetry", Eliot, 1957, 17.
50. For all quotations down to the ones referred to in the next note see Eliot, 1933, 89–99.
51. Quotations in this sentence are from Eliot, 1975, 65.
52. See, for example, Bateson, chapters 3 and 11; Blackmur, 51; Brooks, 1948, 58, 230–1, 237–8 and 1949, 1, 166; Ransom, 137–8; Richards, 249–50; Wilson, 20.
53. Hulme, 134; see also 10–11.
54. Empson, 184, 190.
55. Winters, 50–1.
56. Brooks, 1949, 58.
57. All the quotations in this paragraph except for the one referred to in the next note are from Leavis, 1936; see 203, 204, 206, 210, 211, 214, 216, 220, 237.
58. Wellek, 382; Leavis, 1937, 69.
59. From the essay "The Unliteral Imagination; Or, I, Too, Dislike It" (1965): Tate, 1968, 455.
60. The remaining quotations in this paragraph are from the essay "Three Types of Poetry" (1934): Tate, 1970, 92–4. The quotation from Yeats is from his essay "Emotion of Multitude" (1903): Yeats, 215.
61. O'Neill, 1–2.
62. Norman, 143–4.
63. White, 1972, ii 450.
64. White, 1972, ii 111.
65. Browning, 1972, 82, 85–6.
66. See Engelberg, "Introduction", ix–xii.
67. See Webb, 1977, chapter 1, "Angels and Critics".
68. Lewes, 313, 316, 321.
69. Blind, 87.
70. Todhunter, 9.
71. Aveling and Aveling, 5. Eleanor Marx Aveling was the daughter of Karl Marx.
72. Shaw, xxix, 258, 249. The essay in which these remarks appear was first published in *The Albemarle Review*, September 1892.
73. Foot, 13.
74. Cameron, 1951, 37, 240.

75. Grabo, 1936, viii. For a representative selection from the many systems-of-ideas studies referred to in this paragraph see Baker, Barnard, Barrell, Hughes, King-Hele, Kurtz, Rogers, Stovall, Weaver.
76. Pulos, 110–1.
77. Matthews, 1957, 192.
78. Wasserman, ix, 307.
79. "Shelley's symbolic universe will be fully elucidated only after scholars have examined dozens of key words in various contexts in his poetry (and prose) and have then studied the associations of these same words in the philosophical, religious and literary writings that are known to have impressed Shelley": Reiman, 1965, 11.
80. Everest, 1993, 243.
81. Reiman, 1972, 627; White, 1938, 231.
82. Reiman, 1972, 629.
83. Coleridge, 1956–71, vi 849–50; from a letter of December 1830 in which Coleridge was contrasting the reception he would have afforded Shelley in 1811–2 with that which Southey actually did afford him.
84. Swinburne, 1925–7, v 380. The essay was first published in *The Fortnightly Review*, 1 May 1869.
85. Todhunter, 22.
86. Elton, ii 200.
87. Santayana, 180.
88. Yeats, 66.
89. Yeats, 87.
90. Yeats, 294. From the essay "Discoveries" (1906).
91. Lewis, 29–30.
92. Knight, 256, 189, 247.
93. Fogle, 1949, 59, 225; 1952, 27.
94. Butter, 241, 59, 57.
95. Wilson, 18–19, 38–9.
96. Rieger, 193, 215.
97. Wilson, 39; Rieger, 209–10, 274–80.
98. Bloom, 1966, xxxvi, xliv.
99. Bloom, 1959, *passim*.
100. Bloom, 1959, 36.
101. Wordsworth, Christopher, ii 474.
102. Gosse, 200.
103. Saintsbury, iii 102–16.
104. Davie, 133–59.
105. de Man, 40, 65, 69.
106. Tetreault, 1991, 18, 33.
107. Rajan, 86.
108. Tetreault, 1987, 16.
109. Hogle, viii, 10.
110. Cronin, 76:
111. Davie, 157.
112. Keach, 2, 78.
113. Empson, 190–1.

114. Keach, 116, and chapter III, *passim*.
115. Leighton, 1984, vii.
116. Leighton, 1984, 106.
117. O'Neill, 3–5.
118. O'Neill, 7–8.
119. O'Neill, 35–6.
120. O'Neill, 1.
121. Here I must record again my indebtedness to the work of David Bromwich, especially the chapter entitled "Literature and Theory" in Bromwich, 1989. See n. 24 above.
122. Gaita, 39–40, 277, 309–10; and see chapters 3 ("Mortal Men and rational Beings"), 4 ("Remorse and its Lessons"), 12 ("Ethical Other-Worldliness") and 15 ("Moral Understanding"), *passim*.
123. Murdoch, 1970, 22, 34, 59, 71, 77 and *passsim*; 1956, 34, 39, 49, 54–6 and *passim*; 1983, 46 and *passim*.
124. Diamond, 1983, 162–3.
125. Murdoch, 1983, 46.
126. Murdoch, 1983, 49; Diamond, 1988, 261.
127. Diamond, 1988, 270.
128. Diamond, 1988, 263–70.
129. Diamond, 1991, 294–307.
130. See Nussbaum, 1986, 13, 15–16, 45, 69, 300–1, 307, 364, and Parts I and III, *passim*; and also 1990, chapters 1, 2, 4, 5 and 6. For Aristotle and *krisis* see also Hampshire, 52, 61.
131. For key works by Cavell, Taylor, MacIntyre, Booth, Altieri, Siebers, Williams and Baier see Bibliography. For a fuller account of the movement in modern moral philosophy referred to here, and its implications for literary criticism, see Haines, 1993.
132. For an exploration of the term in moral philosophy see Clarke and Simpson, "Introduction", *passim*; for the quotations above see Clarke and Simpson, 3.
133. One such critic was the late S. L. Goldberg, to whose book *Agents and Lives* and to whose conversation the general view of literature and of criticism offered in this book owes a great deal.
134. Warnock, 61–2, 65, 42.

2: SHELLEY'S VIEWS OF POETRY

1. See, for example, Bradley; Cameron, 1974, chapter 5; Flagg; Solve; Schulze; Wasserman, chapter 7. But the tendency is general.
2. Such as Keach, chapter 1; Cronin, at several points; Clark, Part I.
3. Ensor, 263, 283.
4. *Journal*, i 36.
5. *Works*, v 207, 274, vi 39; *PS*, i 381–3. From a note to *Queen Mab* and from the essays *The Necessity of Atheism* (1811), *Declaration of Rights* (1812) and *A Refutation of Deism* (1814).
6. *Works*, vi 6. From the essay *A Vindication of Natural Diet* (1813).
7. *Works*, v 247. From *An Address to the Irish People* (1812).

8. Lawrence, i 130.
9. Godwin, 1985, 762, 764.
10. Wollstonecraft, 35.
11. In particular *A Proposal for Putting Reform to the Vote Throughout the Kingdom* and *An Address to the People on the Death of the Princess Charlotte*, both published in 1817: *Works*, vi 58–82.
12. These remarks are scattered through Peacock's "Memoirs of Shelley" (Peacock, viii 37–141), first published in *Fraser's Magazine for Town and Country* in 1858, 1860 and 1862: Peacock, viii 78, 103, 131.
13. Peacock, viii 78. For Brown see Bibliography. Other romances shaping "the structure of his interior mind" included Ann Radcliffe's *The Italian* (1797), M. G. Lewis's *The Monk* (1796), Schiller's *The Robbers* (1781) and the three novels by Godwin listed in the Bibliography.
14. Peacock, viii 211; this was in a letter of 15 December 1818.
15. Rousseau, 1987, 398.
16. *Works*, vi 88.
17. *PW*, 35.
18. *PW*, 32.
19. *Works*, vi 221.
20. See ii 6–7, 77–81, 83–9; and *Journal*, i 200.
21. From Shelley's poem written at this time, "Lines Written Among the Euganean Hills" (l. 147).
22. Winckelmann, i 355.
23. *Works*, vi 317. The remarks referred to here and in the following notes are from a series of "Notes on Sculptures in Rome and Florence".
24. *Works*, vi 320–1.
25. *Works*, vi 322.
26. *Works*, vi 310–1, 330–2.
27. Winckelmann, i 361, 482.
28. Shelley uses all these terms in his comments on sculpture in the "Notes" and in his letters.
29. Hazlitt, xviii 100.
30. *Works*, vi 323.
31. *Works*, vi 329, 319–20.
32. *Works*, vii 224. From the essay "Discourse on the Manners of the Ancients" (1818).
33. See ii 30 and 152, and *SPP*, pp. 475 ("On Life", 1819) and 506 ("A Defence of Poetry", 1821).
34. From the "Discourse": *Works*, 223–4.
35. *Works*, vii 161; from Shelley's preface to his translation of Plato's *Symposium* (1818).
36. From the "Defence" (484).
37. See ii 29–30, 261, 360; and *Works*, vii 161 and n.
38. See Forsyth, Robert, chapter XVI, "Of the Passion for Reforming the World"; Shelley's phrase is probably taken from this work.
39. Wordsworth, 1974, iii 137–228.
40. See especially *Works*, vii 5–20 (the first chapter of the essay).
41. *Works*, vii 19–20.

42. Drummond, 309.
43. *Works*, vii 91–2, 101.
44. *Journal*, i 186.
45. Keats, ii 322–3.
46. Byron, v 70–2 (I 192–8).
47. See ii 283–4, 309.
48. "But she is now *not* what she was, she is not the singular angelic being whom you adored & I loved": thus Shelley to his close friend Thomas Jefferson Hogg, eleven years before, on the subject of his first wife, Harriet (i 93).
49. Shelley, Mary Wollstonecraft, 1980, i 223.
50. See Peacock, viii 1–25.
51. From an earlier draft of the "Defence", in an unsent letter to the editor of the journal in which Peacock's essay had appeared (*Ollier's Literary Miscellany*): ii 272–4.

3: SHELLEY'S POETRY, 1811–17

1. *PS*, i 166–8, 230–7.
2. Cameron, 1951, 254.
3. But see also King-Hele, chapter 2. The scientific referentialists since Grabo, 1930, have also been interested in the poem.
4. Holmes, 1976, 201.
5. Southey, 23–116; Peacock, vi 167–75.
6. Volney, 6.
7. References to this poem are by canto and line number.
8. See, for example, Cameron, 1951, 240–65; Wasserman, 3–8, 135, 230.
9. See Drummond, 228–78; Evans; Godwin, 1985, 335–60; Hume, 1975, 80–103.
10. See, for example, Kant, 120–75, 257–75.
11. Volney, 87.
12. Hume, 1975, 75.
13. See especially Wasserman, 11–15.
14. See especially "A Summer Evening Churchyard", line 28 and *passim*; "Verses Written on Receiving a Celandine in a Letter from England", line 29 and *passim*; "Mutability"; "Her voice did quiver as we parted", line 5; "Mine eyes were dim with tears unshed"; "Stanzas, April 1814"; "To Harriet"; "O! there are spirits of the air"; and others: *PS*, i 427 ff., and *SPP* 87–9.
15. Godwin, 1805, chapter 4.
16. *Journal*, i 86.
17. For example, Baker, 48–57; Dowden, i 531 (and the nineteenth century *passim*); Holmes, 1976, 305; Hughes, chapter 14; White, 1972, i 418–20.
18. See "Lines, Composed a Few Miles Above Tintern Abbey...", line 22, and "Ode: Intimations of Immortality...", lines 141–2: Wordsworth, 1992, 117, 275.
19. Keach, 81–2.

20. For example Clark, 118–42; Cronin, 84–94; O'Neill, 21–9; Wasserman, 28–46.
21. Fogle, 1952, 27.
22. *PW*, 31–156.
23. For "Stanzas" see *SPP*, 127–8; for the rest, *PW*, 546–7, 559–60, 158–88.
24. *PW*, 536–9.
25. *PW*, 580, 583, 627.
26. Bloom, 30; O'Neill, 45.
27. For the "Hymn" see Coleridge, 1912, i 376–80; for "Tintern Abbey", see Wordsworth, 1992, 116–20.
28. "On Life", *SPP*, 476.

4: SHELLEY'S POETRY, 1818–20

1. Reiman, 1962, 404–5.
2. Davie, 141.
3. See for example Everest, 1983; Newey; Rzepka.
4. Hazlitt, xvi 273.
5. Byron, ii 165–6 (stanzas 123, 124, 126). The canto was principally composed in the second half of 1817 and published in April 1818 (see editor's commentary, ii 314–6).
6. Peacock, iii 1–146.
7. Browning, 76, 79–80, 82.
8. See Peterfreund and Worton, for example.
9. From Mary's note to the poem: *PW*, 337.
10. Hazlitt, xvi 275. "Prosaic" is also Davie's term for the language of "Julian and Maddalo", curiously enough, although Davie means something more complimentary than Hazlitt does by it.
11. At least not in Hazlitt's sense; they are in Davie's.
12. Cronin, 243–4.
13. *PW*, 654–7.
14. *PW*, 667.
15. Bloom, 1959, 178–9, 183.
16. *PW*, 389–409.
17. *PW*, 488–507.
18. *PW*, 616–21.
19. See *PW*, 571–6.
20. "England in 1819", lines 4–7.
21. *Journal*, i 297; Petrarch, 49–68.
22. Leavis, 1936, 204–8.
23. See Swinden, for example.
24. Some good accounts of the poem are those of Bloom, 1959, 65–90; Chernaik, 93 ff.; Cronin, 230–42; Fogle, 1948; Holmes, 1976, 546–7; King-Hele, 219–27; Leighton, 1984, 101–16; Matthews, 1970, 24; Wasserman, 245–51;
25. See Ludlam, and King-Hele 219–27.
26. Leighton, 1984, 106.
27. See Chapter 1, note 97.

28. Bloom, 1959, 73–4. For "Dejection" see Coleridge, 1912, i 362–8.
29. Knight, 247.
30. See Holmes, 1976, 547; Rogers, 19.
31. See Chapter 1, note 85.
32. These are, it should be emphasised, *kinds* of reading, rather than specific readings of this poem by particular critics. Readers should refer again to Chapter 1 for groups of critics who read in these ways.
33. All the quotations from Bloom in this paragraph are from 1959, 75–6.
34. Bloom, 1959, 79.

5: SHELLEY'S POETRY, 1818–20 (CONTINUED)

1. Lewis, 29.
2. Todhunter, 134.
3. Baker, 89. Some of the leading modern accounts of the poem are those of Baker, 89–118; Bloom, 1959, 46–64, 91–147; Cameron, 1974, 475–564; Curran, 1975, 33–118; Knight; Leighton, 1984, 73–100; Lewis; Matthews, 1957; O'Neill, 92–125; and Wasserman, 255–373.
4. See Chapter 1, notes 33, 80, 81.
5. Keach, 44.
6. Keach, 45.
7. Keach, 57–8 and n. 27; Eliot, 1975, 210 (from "Dante", 1929).
8. See Chapter 2, note 38.
9. Lewis, 30.
10. Cameron, 1974, 475.
11. Matthews, 1957, 192. See Chapter 1, note 77.
12. Bloom, 1959, 95, 98.
13. Bloom, 1959, 98.
14. Bloom, 1959, 92.
15. *ibid.*
16. Bloom, 1959, 105.
17. See for example Barnard and Weaver; and also Webb, 1977, chapter 6, "The Christian Mythology".
18. Bloom, 1959, 108, 110.
19. Godwin, 1985, 187–8.
20. Bloom, 1959, 112.
21. O'Neill, 99–100.
22. O'Neill, 96.
23. Bloom, 1959, 115.
24. Keach, 55, and chapter II, *passim.*
25. Bloom, 1959, 128.
26. Holmes, 1976, 507.
27. Grabo, 1930, 151 ff.
28. Knight, 222.
29. Webb, 1977, 257; Bloom, 1959, 141–4.

6: SHELLEY'S POETRY, 1821-22

1. Principally Cameron, 1974, 275-88; Holmes, 1976, 624-40; Wasserman, 417-61; White, 1972, ii 247-70.
2. For example Beatty, 213-21; Bloom, 1959, 205-19; Hogle, 279-86; Leighton, 1991; O'Neill, 157-77; Webb, 1976, 276-309.
3. Webb, 1976, 304.
4. Rousseau, 1987, 386, 398. See Chapter 2, note 15.
5. O'Neill, 158.
6. See especially Cameron, 1948, and 1974, 275-88.
7. Bloom, 1959, 219. For "bodies which think" see "Are Persons Bodies?", Williams, 1973, 64-81.
8. Particularly Clark, 214-23; Cronin, 169-201; Curran, 1983, 165-82; Leighton, 1983, and 1984, 125-49; Wasserman, 462-502.
9. See Coleridge, i 125-31 and Wordsworth, 1983, 123-9.
10. Holmes, 1976, 657.
11. Leighton, 1984, 142.
12. de Man, 67.
13. Bloom, 1959, 220n.
14. The "Triumph" has attracted some fine criticism in recent years. Little specific reference to that criticism is made in this account of the poem, but interested readers should see especially Allott, 239-78, Bloom, 1959, 220-75; Clark, 224-56; Cronin, 202-22; de Man; Holmes, 717-24; Leighton, 1984, 150-75; O'Neill, 178-201; Reiman, 1965.
15. Byron, iv 213-39; composed 1819, published 1821 (see editor's commentary, iv 499-500).
16. Hazlitt, xvi 274.
17. Lucretius, 278 and ff.; Book IV lines 26 and ff.
18. See lines 278-9 on p. 463.
19. From the essay *Proposals for an Association of Philanthropists* (1812): *Works*, v 265.
20. See Bloom, 1959, 232-40. Blake's "Bring me my chariot of fire" is from the prefatory lyric to his poem *Milton*: Blake, 488-9.

Bibliography

ABBREVIATIONS USED IN THE NOTES

Journal   *The Journals of Mary Shelley, 1814–1844*, eds. Paula R. Feldman and Diana Scott-Kilvert, 2 vols., Clarendon Press, Oxford, 1987.

Letters   *The Letters of Percy Bysshe Shelley*, ed. Frederick L. Jones, 2 vols., Clarendon Press, Oxford, 1964.

PS   *The Poems of Shelley*, eds. Geoffrey Matthews and Kelvin Everest, vol. i, Longman, London and New York, 1989.

PW   *Shelley: Poetical Works*, ed. Thomas Hutchinson, 1905, new ed. Geoffrey Matthews, Oxford University Press, London, Oxford, New York, 1970.

SPP   *Shelley's Poetry and Prose*, eds. Donald H. Reiman and Sharon B. Powers, Norton, New York and London, 1977.

Works   *The Complete Works of Percy Bysshe Shelley*, eds. Roger Ingpen and Walter E. Peck, 10 vols., Ernest Benn, London and Charles Scribner's Sons, New York, 1926–30 (the "Julian Edition").

WORKS CITED IN TEXT AND NOTES

Allott, Miriam, ed., *Essays on Shelley*, The University Press, Liverpool, 1982.

——, "Attitudes to Shelley: the vagaries of a critical reputation", in Allott, 1–38.

——, "The Reworking of a Literary Genre: Shelley's 'The Triumph of Life'", in Allott, 239–78.

Altieri, Charles, *Canons and Consequences. Reflections on the Ethical Force of Imaginative Ideals*, Northwestern University Press, Evanston, Illinois, 1990.

Arnold, Matthew, *The Complete Prose Works of Matthew Arnold*, ed. R. H. Super, 11 vols., University of Michigan Press, Ann Arbor, Michigan, 1960–77.

Aveling, Edward and Aveling, Eleanor Marx, *Shelley's Socialism: Two Lectures*, privately printed, London, 1888.

Babbitt, Irving, *Rousseau and Romanticism*, 1919, rpt. University of Texas Press, Austin, 1977.

Baier, Annette, "Secular Faith", *The Canadian Journal of Philosophy*, x:1, March 1980, reprinted in Hauerwas and MacIntyre, 203–21.

——, "Doing Without Moral Theory?", in Clarke and Simpson, 29–48.

Baker, Carlos, *Shelley's Major Poetry: The Fabric of a Vision*, Princeton University Press, Princeton, 1948.

Barnard, Ellsworth, *Shelley's Religion*, University of Minnesota Press, Minneapolis, 1937.

Barrell, Joseph, *Shelley and the Thought of His Time: A Study in the History of Ideas*, Yale University Press, New Haven, 1947.

Blackmur, R. P., *Language as Gesture: Essays in Poetry*, George Allen and Unwin, London, 1954.

Bateson, F. W., *English Poetry, A Critical Introduction*, Longmans, Green and Co., London, New York, Toronto, 1950.

Blake, William, *The Poems of William Blake*, ed. W. H. Stevenson, text by David R. Erdman, Longman, 1971.

Blank, G. Kim, ed., *The New Shelley. Later Twentieth-Century Views*, St. Martin's Press, New York, 1991.

Blind, Mathilde, "Shelley", *The Westminster Review*, xxxviii (NS), 1 July 1870, 75–97.

Bloom, Harold, *Shelley's Mythmaking*, Yale University Press, New Haven, 1959.

——, "The Unpastured Sea: An Introduction to Shelley", preface to *The Selected Poetry and Prose of Shelley*, ed. Harold Bloom, Signet Classics, 1966.

—— *et al.*, *Deconstruction and Criticism*, The Seabury Press, New York, 1979.

Booth, Wayne C., *The Company We Keep: An Ethics of Fiction*, University of California Press, Berkeley, Los Angeles, London, 1988.

Bradley, A. C., "Shelley's View of Poetry", *Oxford Lectures on Poetry*, Macmillan and Co., London, 1909, 149–74.

Brett-Smith, H. F., ed., *Peacock's Four Ages of Poetry, Shelley's Defence of Poetry, Browning's Essay on Shelley*, Basil Blackwell, Oxford, 1921, 2nd edn. 1923.

Brinton, Crane, "The Second Generation of Revolt", chapter IV in *The Political Ideas of the English Romanticists*, Oxford University Press, London, 1926.

Bromwich, David, *Hazlitt: The Mind of a Critic*, Oxford University Press. New York, Oxford, 1983.

——, *A Choice of Inheritance: Self and Community from Edmund Burke to Robert Frost*, Harvard University Press, Cambridge, Mass., 1989.

Brooks, Cleanth, *Modern Poetry and the Tradition*, PL Poetry, London, 1948.

——, *The Well-Wrought Urn: Studies in the Structure of Poetry*, Dennis Dobson, London, 1949.

Brown, Charles Brockden, *Wieland, or the Transformation, an American Tale*, 1798, rpt., 3 vols., Henry Colburn, London, 1811.

——, *Ormond; or, The Secret Witness*, 1799, rpt., 3 vols., Henry Colburn, London, 1800, 1811.

——, *Edgar Huntly, or Memoirs of a Sleep-Walker, A Novel*, 1799, rpt., 3 vols., Lane and Newman, London, 1803.

——, *Arthur Mervyn, Or, Memoirs of the Year 1793*, 1799, 2 vols., Burt Franklin, New York, 1887.

Browning, Robert, *An Essay on Percy Bysshe Shelley*, 1888, rpt. in Brett-Smith (1923), 61–83.

Burnet, James, Lord Monboddo, *Of the Origin and Progress of Language*, 6 vols., A. Kincaid and W. Creech, Edinburgh, T. Cadell, London, 1773–92.

Butter, Peter, *Shelley's Idols of the Cave*, The University Press, Edinburgh, 1954.

Byron, Lord, *The Complete Poetical Works*, ed. Jerome J. McGann, Clarendon Press, Oxford, 7 vols., 1980–93.

Calderón de la Barca, Pedro, *The Rubaiyat of Omar Khayyam and Six Plays of Calderon*, trans. Edward Fitzgerald, J. M. Dent & Sons Ltd., London and Toronto, 1903, 1928.

Cameron, Kenneth Neill, "The Planet-Tempest Passage in *Epipsychidion*", *Publications of the Modern Language Association*, lxiii, 1948, 950–72.

——, *The Young Shelley: Genesis of a Radical*, Gollancz, London, 1951.

—— and Reiman, Donald H., eds., *Shelley and His Circle, 1773–1822*, 8 vols., i–iv ed. Cameron, v–viii ed. Reiman, Harvard University Press, Cambridge, Mass., 1961–86.

——, *Shelley: The Golden Years*, Harvard University Press, Cambridge, Mass., 1974.

Carlyle, Thomas, *Letters of Thomas Carlyle to John Stuart Mill, John Sterling and Robert Browning*, ed. Alexander Carlyle, T. Fisher Unwin Ltd., London, 1923.

——, *Reminiscences*, 2 vols., ed. J. A. Froude, 1881, 2 vols., ed. Charles Eliot Norton, 1887, with introduction by Ian Campbell, J. M. Dent & Sons Ltd., London, 1932, 1972.

Cavell, Stanley, *The Claim of Reason: Wittgenstein, Scepticism, Morality and Tragedy*, Clarendon Press, Oxford and Oxford University Press, New York, 1979.

Chernaik, Judith, *The Lyrics of Shelley*, The Press of Case Western Reserve University, Cleveland and London, 1972.

Clark, Timothy, *Embodying Revolution: The Figure of the Poet in Shelley*, Clarendon Press, Oxford, 1989.

Clarke, Stanley G. and Simpson, Evan, eds., *Anti-Theory in Ethics and Moral Conservatism*, State University of New York Press, Albany, 1989.

——, "Introduction: The Primacy of Moral Practice", in Clarke and Simpson (1989), 1–26.

Coleridge, Samuel Taylor, *The Complete Poetical Works of Samuel Taylor Coleridge*, 2 vols., ed. E. H. Coleridge, Clarendon Press, Oxford, 1912.

——, *Collected Letters of Samuel Taylor Coleridge*, 6 vols., ed. Earl Leslie Griggs, Clarendon Press, Oxford, 1956–71.

——, *Biographia Literaria, or Biographical Sketches of My Literary Life and Opinions* (1817), eds. James Engell and W. Jackson Bate, Princeton University Press, Princeton, 1983.

Condorcet, Antoine-Nicolas, Marquis de, *Esquisse d'un Tableau des Progrès de L'Esprit Humain*, 1795, *Outlines of an Historical View of the Progress of the Human Mind*, trans anon., J. Johnson, London, 1795.

Curran, Stuart, *Shelley's Annus Mirabilis: The Maturing of an Epic Vision*, Huntington Library, San Marino, Calif., 1975.

——, "*Adonais* in Context", in Everest, 1983, 165–82.

——, "Shelley", in *The English Romantic Poets: A Review of Research and Criticism*, 4th edn., ed. Frank Jordan, Modern Language Association, New York, 1985, 593–663.

Cronin, Richard, *Shelley's Poetic Thoughts*, Macmillan, London, 1981.

Dante Alighieri, *The Divine Comedy*, text with translation by Geoffrey L. Bickersteth, Basil Blackwell, Oxford, 1965.

——, *Dante's Lyric Poetry*, 2 vols., eds. K. Foster and P. Boyde, Clarendon Press, Oxford, 1967, vol. i, texts and translations, *canzoni* nos. 59, 61, 69 (the *Convivio* consists of these three *canzoni* and a commentary on them).

——, *La Vita Nuova (Poems of Youth)*, trans. Barbara Reynolds, Penguin Books, 1969.

Darwin, Erasmus, *The Botanic Garden*, 2 vols., J. Johnson, London, 1789, 1791.

——, *The Temple of Nature; Or, the Origin of Society: A Poem, with Philosophical Notes*, J. Johnson, London, 1803.

Davie, Donald, "Shelley's Urbanity", in *Purity of Diction in English Verse*, Routledge and Kegan Paul, London, 1952, 133–59.

Dawson, P. M. S., *The Unacknowledged Legislator: Shelley and Politics*, Clarendon Press, Oxford, 1980.

de Man, Paul, "Shelley Disfigured", in Bloom *et al.*, 1979, 39–73.

Diamond, Cora, "Having a Rough Story about What Moral Philosophy Is", *New Literary History*, xv:1, Autumn 1983, 155–169.

——, "Losing Your Concepts", *Ethics*, xcviii: 2, January 1988, 255–277.

——, *The Realistic Spirit: Wittgenstein, Philosophy and the Mind*, MIT Press, Cambridge, Mass., London, 1991.

Donoghue, Denis, "Keach and Shelley", *London Review of Books*, 19 September 1985, 12–13.

Dowden, Edward, *The Life of Percy Bysshe Shelley*, 2 vols., Kegan Paul, Trench and Co., London, 1886.

Drummond, the Rt. Hon. William, *Academical Questions*, vol. i only, W. Bulmer & Co., London, 1805.

Dunbar, Clement, *A Bibliography of Shelley Studies, 1823–1950*, Garland Publishing Inc., Folkestone, 1976.

Eliot, T. S., *The Use of Poetry and the Use of Criticism. Studies in the Relation of Criticism to Poetry in England*, Faber and Faber Ltd., London, 1933.

——, *On Poetry and Poets*, Faber and Faber Ltd., 1957.

——, *Selected Prose of T. S. Eliot*, ed. Frank Kermode, Faber and Faber Ltd., London, Boston, 1975.

Elton, Oliver, *A Survey of English Literature 1780–1830*, 2 vols., Edwin Arnold, London, 1912.

Empson, William, *Seven Types of Ambiguity*, 1930, Peregrine Books, 1961.

Engelberg, Karsten Klejs, *The Making of the Shelley Myth: An Annotated Bibliography of Criticism of Percy Bysshe Shelley, 1822–1860*, Mansell Publishing Limited, London, 1988.

Ensor, George, *On National Education*, Longman, Hurst, Rees, Orme, and Brown, London, 1811.

Eustace, John Chetwode, *A Tour Through Italy, Exhibiting a View of its Scenery, its Antiquities, and its Monuments*, 2 vols., J. Mawman, London, 1813.

Evans, Frank B., "Shelley, Godwin, Hume, and the Doctrine of Necessity", *Studies in Philology*, xxxvii, 1940, 632–40.

Everest, Kelvin, ed., *Shelley Revalued: Essays from the Gregynog Confer-ence*, Leicester University Press, Leicester, 1983.

——, "Shelley's doubles: an approach to *Julian and Maddalo*", in Everest, 1983, 63–88.

——, ed., *Essays and Studies 1992. Percy Bysshe Shelley: Bicentenary Es-says*, D. S. Brewer, Cambridge, 1992.

——, "'Mechanism of a Kind Yet Unattempted': The Dramatic Action of *Prometheus Unbound*", in *Durham University Journal. Percy Bysshe Shelley Special Issue*, lxxxv no. 2 (NS liv no. 2), July 1993, 237–45.

Flagg, John S., "Shelley and Aristotle: Elements of the *Poetics* in Shelley's Theory of Poetry", *Studies in Romanticism*, ix:1, Winter 1970, 44–67.

Fogarty, Nancy, *Shelley in the Twentieth Century: A Study of the Develop-ment of Shelley Criticism in England and America, 1916–1971*, Salzburg Studies in English Literature, Salzburg, 1976.

Fogle, Richard Harter, *The Imagery of Keats and Shelley: A Comparative Study*, University of North Carolina Press, Chapel Hill, 1949.

——, "Image and Imagelessness: A Limited Reading of *Prometheus Un-bound*, *Keats-Shelley Journal*, i, January 1952, 23–36.

Foot, Paul, *Red Shelley*, Sidgwick and Jackson, London, 1980.

Forman, Harry Buxton, "Preface", in *The Poetical Works of Percy Bysshe Shelley*, ed. Forman, 4 vols., Reeves and Turner, London, 1876–7, xi–xl.

Forsyth, Joseph, *Remarks on Antiquities, Arts and Letters. During an Ex-cursion in Italy in the Years 1802 and 1803*, T. Cadell and W. Davies, London, 1813.

Forsyth, Robert, *The Principles of Moral Science*, vol. i only, Bell & Bradfute, Edinburgh, 1805.

Fortiguerra, Niccolo, *Ricciardetto di Niccolo Carteromaco*, 3 vols., Dalla Societa Tipografica de' Classici Italiani, Milan, 1813.

——. *The First Two Cantos of Richardetto, Freely translated from the Origi-nal Burlesque Poem of Niccolo Fortiguerra, Otherwise Carteromaco*, trans. anon., John Murray, London, 1820.

Gaita, Raimond, *Good and Evil: An Absolute Conception*, Macmillan, Lon-don, 1991.

Godwin, William, *Things As They Are; or, The Adventures of Caleb Will-iams*, 3 vols., B. Crosby, London, 1794.

——, *St. Leon: A Tale of the Sixteenth Century*, 4 vols., G. G. and J. Robinson, London, 1799.

——, *Fleetwood; or, The New Man of Feeling*, 2 vols., I. Riley and Co., New York, 1805.

——, *Mandeville. A Tale of the Seventeenth Century in England*, 3 vols., Longman, Hurst, Rees, Orme and Brown, London, 1817.

——, *Enquiry Concerning Political Justice, and its Influence on Morals and Happiness*, 1793, ed. Isaac Kramnick, Penguin Books, 1985.

Goethe, Johann Wolfgang von, *Faust* (1808), trans. as *Faust: Part I*, Philip Wayne, Penguin Books, 1949.

Goldberg, S. L., *Agents and Lives: Moral Thinking in Literature*, Cambridge University Press, 1993.

Gosse, Edmund, "Shelley in 1892, Centenary Address Delivered at

Horsham", in *Questions at Issue*, Heinemann, London, 1893, 199–218.

Grabo, Carl, *A Newton Among Poets: Shelley's Use of Science in Prometheus Unbound*, University of North Carolina Press, Chapel Hill, 1930.

——, *The Magic Plant: the Growth of Shelley's Thought*, University of North Carolina Press, Chapel Hill, 1936.

Haines, Simon, "Shelley's 'West Wind': Power or Weakness?", *The Critical Review*, 30, 1990, 112–26.

——, "Deepening the Self: the Language of Ethics and the Language of Literature", *The Critical Review*, 33, 1993, 15–28.

Hampshire, Stuart, "Fallacies in Moral Philosophy", *Mind*, lviii, 1949, reprinted in Hauerwas and MacIntyre (1983), 51–67.

Hauerwas, Stanley and MacIntyre, Alasdair, eds., *Revisions: Changing Perspectives in Moral Philosophy*, University of Notre Dame Press, Notre Dame, Indiana, 1983.

Hazlitt, William, *The Complete Works of William Hazlitt*, ed. P. P. Howe, 21 vols., J. M. Dent & Sons Ltd., London and Toronto, 1930–4.

Hoagwood, Terence Allan, *Skepticism and Ideology. Shelley's Political Prose and its Philosophical Context from Bacon to Marx*, University of Iowa Press, Iowa City, 1988.

Hogg, Thomas Jefferson, *The Life of Percy Bysshe Shelley*, 2 vols., Edward Moxon, London, 1858, rpt. in Wolfe (1933), i 1–415, ii 1–158.

Hogle, Jerrold E., *Shelley's Process: Radical Transference and the Development of His Major Works*, Oxford University Press, New York, Oxford, 1988.

Holbach, Baron d', *Système de la Nature, ou Des Lois du Monde Physique et du Monde Moral*, "par M. Mirabaud", 1770, new edn., 2 vols., Etienne Ledoux, Paris, 1821.

Holmes, Richard, *Shelley: The Pursuit*, Weidenfeld and Nicolson, London, 1974, rpt. Quartet Books, London, 1976.

——, "'He Doth Not Sleep'", *The New York Review of Books*, 24 September 1992, 19–24.

Home, Henry, Lord Kames, *Elements of Criticism*, William Creech, Edinburgh, 7th edn., 1788.

——, *Essays on the Principles of Morality and Natural Religion*, William Creech, Edinburgh, 1751.

Houghton, Walter E., *The Wellesley Index to Victorian Periodicals 1824–1900*, 2 vols., University of Toronto Press, Toronto, 1966.

Hughes, A. M. D., *The Nascent Mind of Shelley*, Clarendon Press, Oxford, 1947.

Hulme, T. E., *Speculations: Essays on Humanism and the Philosophy of Art*, ed. Herbert Read, Routledge & Kegan Paul, London, 1924, rpt. 1960.

Hume, David, *A Treatise of Human Nature*, 3 vols., 1739–40, ed. L. A. Selby-Bigge, 1888, 2nd ed. P. H. Nidditch, Clarendon Press, Oxford, 1978.

——, *Essays and Treatises on Several Subjects*, 1753–6, 2 vols. 1777, vol. ii rpt. with some omissions as *Enquiries Concerning Human Understanding and Concerning the Principles of Morals*, ed. L. A. Selby-Bigge, 1893, 3rd ed. P. H. Nidditch, Clarendon Press, Oxford, 1975.

Hunt, Thornton, "Shelley, By One Who Knew Him", *The Atlantic Monthly*, xi, February 1863, 184–204.

Jones, Frederick L., *The Letters of Percy Bysshe Shelley*, 2 vols., Clarendon Press, Oxford, 1964.

Kames, see Home.

Kant, Immanuel, *Immanuel Kant's Critique of Pure Reason* (1781, 1787), trans. Norman Kemp Smith, Macmillan, London, 1929, 2nd impression 1933, rpt. 1970.

Keach, William, *Shelley's Style*, Methuen, New York and London, 1984.

Keats, John, *The Letters of John Keats*, 2 vols., ed. Hyder Edward Rollins, Harvard University Press, Cambridge, Mass., 1958.

King-Hele, Desmond, *Shelley, His Thought and Work*, Macmillan, London, 1960, 2nd edn. 1971.

Kinnear, Alexander S., review in *The Quarterly Review*, cx, October 1861, 289–328.

Knight, G. Wilson, "The Naked Seraph: An Essay on Shelley", *The Starlit Dome: Studies in the Poetry of Vision*, Oxford University Press, London, 1941, 179–257.

Kurtz, Benjamin P., *The Pursuit of Death: A Study of Shelley's Poetry*, Oxford University Press, London, 1933.

Lawrence, Sir James, *The Empire of the Nairs; Or, the Rights of Women. An Utopian Romance, in Twelve Books*, 4 vols., T. Hookham, Jun. and E. T. Hookham, London, 1811.

Leavis, F. R., *Revaluation: Tradition and Development in English Poetry*, Chatto and Windus, London, 1936.

——, "Literary Criticism and Philosophy: A Reply", *Scrutiny*, vi, June 1937, 59–70.

Leighton, Angela, "Deconstruction Criticism and Shelley's *Adonais*", in Everest, 1983, 147–64.

——, *Shelley and the Sublime: An Interpretation of the Major Poems*, Cambridge University Press, 1984.

——, "Versions of a double man", *Times Literary Supplement*, March 30–April 5, 1990, 354.

——, "Love, Writing and Scepticism in *Epipsychidion*", in Blank (1991), 220–41.

Lewes, G. H., "Percy Bysshe Shelley", *The Westminster Review*, xxv, April 1841, 303–44.

Lewis, C. S., "Shelley, Dryden and Mr. Eliot", *Rehabilitations and Other Essays*, Oxford University Press, London, 1939, 3–34.

Lewis, M. G., *The Monk: A Romance* (1796), ed. Howard Anderson, Oxford University Press, London, 1973.

Lucretius, *De Rerum Natura*, trans. W. D. H. Rouse (1924), rev. Martin Ferguson Smith, 1975, 2nd ed. 1982, Harvard University Press, Cambridge, Mass. (Loeb Library).

Ludlam, F. H., "The Meteorology of the *Ode to the West Wind*", in Swinden, 217–26.

McFarland, Thomas, "Recent Studies in the Nineteenth Century", *Studies in English Literature 1500–1900*, xvi, 1976, 693–727.

MacIntyre, Alasdair, *After Virtue: a Study in Moral Theory*, Duckworth, London, 1981, second edn. 1985.

McNiece, Gerald, *Shelley and the Revolutionary Idea*, Harvard University Press, Cambridge, Mass., 1969.

Mason, Francis Clairborne, *A Study of Shelley Criticism: An Examination of the Principal Interpretations of Shelley's Art and Philosophy in England from 1818 to 1860*, privately printed, Mercersburg, Pennsylvania, 1937.

Matthews, G. M., "Shelley's Grasp Upon the Actual", *Essays in Criticism*, iv, July 1954, 328–31.

——, "A Volcano's Voice in Shelley", *Journal of English Literary History*, xxiv, September 1957, 191–228.

——, "Shelley's Lyrics", in D. W. Jefferson, ed., *The Morality of Art: Essays Presented to G. Wilson Knight by his Colleagues and Friends*, Routledge and Kegan Paul, London, 1969, 195–209.

——, "Percy Bysshe Shelley", in *New Cambridge Bibliography of English Literature*, vol. iii (1800–1900), ed. George Watson, Cambridge University Press, 1969, 309–44.

——, *Shelley*, Longmans, London, 1970.

Maurois, André, *Ariel, The Life of Shelley* (1923), trans. Ella D'Arcy, D. Appleton and Co., New York, 1924.

Medwin, Thomas, *Shelley Papers: Memoir of Percy Bysshe Shelley by T. Medwin Esq. and Original Poems and Papers by Percy Bysshe Shelley*, Whitaker, Treacher and Co., London, 1833.

——, *The Life of Percy Bysshe Shelley*, 2 vols., Thomas Cautley Newby, London, 1847.

Monboddo: see Burnet.

More, Paul Elmer, "Shelley", *Shelburne Essays, Seventh Series*, 1910, rpt. in *Selected Shelburne Essays*, Oxford University Press, London, New York, 1935, 168–87.

Murdoch, Iris, "Symposium: Vision and Choice in Morality. II", *Aristotelian Society Supplementary Volume xxx*, July 1956, 32–58.

——, *The Sovereignty of Good*, Routledge & Kegan Paul, London, 1970.

——, "Against Dryness: A Polemical Sketch", *Encounter*, xvi: 1, January 1961, reprinted in Hauerwas and MacIntyre (1983), 43–50.

Newey, Vincent, "The Shelleyan Psycho-Drama: 'Julian and Maddalo'", in Allott, 71–104.

Norman, Sylva, *Flight of the Skylark: The Development of Shelley's Reputation*, University of Oklahoma Press, Norman, Oklahoma, 1954.

Notopoulos, James A., *The Platonism of Shelley: A Study of Platonism and the Poetic Mind*, Duke University Press, Durham, North Carolina, 1949.

Nussbaum, Martha C., *The Fragility of Goodness. Luck and Ethics in Greek Tragedy and Philosophy*, Cambridge University Press, 1986.

——, *Love's Knowledge. Essays on Philosophy and Literature*, Oxford University Press, New York , Oxford, 1990.

O'Neill, Michael, *The Human Mind's Imaginings: Conflict and Achievement in Shelley's Poetry*, Clarendon Press, Oxford, 1989.

Park, Roy, *Hazlitt and the Spirit of the Age: Abstraction and Critical Theory*, Clarendon Press, Oxford, 1971.

Patmore, Coventry, *Principle in Art*, George Bell and Sons, London, 1890.

Peacock, Thomas Love, *The Works of Thomas Love Peacock*, 10 vols., eds. H. F. Brett-Smith and C. E. Jones, Constable & Co., London, 1924–34.

Peck, Walter Edwin, *Shelley, His Life and Work*, 2 vols., Ernest Benn Ltd., London, 1927.

Peterfreund, Stuart, "Seduced by Metonymy: Figuration and Authority in *The Cenci*", in Blank, 184–203.

Petrarch, Francesco, *The Triumphs of Petrarch*, trans. Ernest Hatch Wilkins, The University Press, Chicago, 1962.

——, *Petrarch's Lyric Poems: The Rime Sparse and Other Lyrics*, trans. and ed. Robert M. Durling, Harvard University Press, Cambridge, Mass., 1976.

Plato, *The Collected Dialogues of Plato*, eds. Edith Hamilton and Huntington Cairns, The University Press, Princeton, New Jersey, 1961.

Pottle, Frederick A., "The Case of Shelley", *Publications of the Modern Language Association*, lxvii, 1952, 589–608.

Power, Julia, *Shelley in America in the Nineteenth Century: His Relation to Critical Thought and His Influence*, University of Nebraska Press, Lincoln, Nebraska, 1940.

Pulos, C. E., *The Deep Truth: A Study of Shelley's Scepticism*, University of Nebraska Press, Lincoln, Nebraska, 1954.

Rabaut Saint-Étienne, Jean Paul and Lacretelle Jeune, Jean Charles D. De, *Précis d'histoire de la Révolution française*, Paris, 1792, 1805–6.

Radcliffe, Ann, *The Italian, or The Confessional of the Black Penitents, A Romance* (1797), ed. Frederick Garber, Oxford University Press, London, 1968.

Rajan, Tillotama, "The Web of Human Things: Narrative and Identity in *Alastor*", in Blank, 85–107.

Ransom, John Crowe, *The World's Body*, Charles Scribner's Sons, New York, 1938.

Reiman, Donald H., "Structure, Symbol, and Theme in 'Lines Written Among the Euganean Hills'", *Publications of the Modern Language Association*, lxxvii, September 1962, 404–13.

——, *Shelley's "The Triumph of Life": A Critical Study*, University of Illinois Press, Urbana, 1965.

——, *Percy Bysshe Shelley*, Twayne's English Authors Series, New York, 1969.

——, ed., *The Romantics Reviewed: Contemporary Reviews of British Romantic Writers. Part C: Shelley, Keats and London Radical Writers*, 2 vols., Garland Publishing Inc., New York and London, 1972.

Richards, I. A., *Principles of Literary Criticism*, Routledge and Kegan Paul, London, 1924.

Rieger, James, *The Mutiny Within: The Heresies of Percy Bysshe Shelley*, George Braziller, New York, 1967.

Robertson, J. M., *New Essays Towards a Critical Method*, John Lane, London, 1877.

Rogers, Neville, *Shelley At Work, A Critical Inquiry*, Clarendon Press, Oxford, 1956, 2nd edn. 1967.

Rossetti, William Michael, *Memoir of Percy Bysshe Shelley*, John Slark, London, 1886.

Rousseau, Jean-Jacques, *La Nouvelle Héloïse. Julie, or the New Eloise. Letters of Two Lovers, Inhabitants of a Small Town at the Foot of the Alps*

(1761), trans. and abridged, Judith H. McDowell, Pennsylvania State University Press, 1968.

———, *The Confessions of Jean-Jacques Rousseau* (1781), trans. J. M. Cohen, Penguin Books, 1953, 1987.

———, *Eloisa, or a series of original letters*, trans. William Kenrick (1803), 2 vols., Woodstock Books, Oxford, 1989.

Rzepka, Charles J., "*Julian and Maddalo* as Revisionary Conversation Poem", in Blank, 128–49.

Saintsbury, George, *A History of English Prosody From the Twelfth Century to the Present Day*, 3 vols., Macmillan and Co. Ltd., London, 1910, rpt. 1923.

Santayana, George, *Winds of Doctrine: Studies in Contemporary Opinion*, J. M. Dent and Sons, London, 1913.

Schiller, Friedrich, *Die Raüber* (1781), trans. F. J. Lamport, in *The Robbers, Wallenstein*, Penguin Books, 1979.

Schulze, Earl J., *Shelley's Theory of Poetry: A Reappraisal*, Mouton & Co., The Hague, 1966.

Scrivener, Michael Henry, *Radical Shelley. The Philosophical Anarchism and Utopian Thought of Percy Bysshe Shelley*, The University Press, Princeton, New Jersey, 1982.

Shaw, George Bernard, "Shaming the Devil About Shelley", in *The Works of Bernard Shaw*, 33 vols., Constable and Co., London, 1930–8, xxix, 248–59.

Shelley, Mary Wollstonecraft, *The Letters of Mary Wollstonecraft Shelley*, 2 vols., ed. Betty T. Bennett, Johns Hopkins University Press, Baltimore and London, 1980.

———, *The Journals of Mary Shelley, 1814–1844*, 2 vols., eds. Paula R. Feldman and Diana Scott-Kilvert, Clarendon Press, Oxford, 1987.

Shelley, Percy Bysshe, *Zastrozzi; A Romance*, Wilkie and Robinson, London, 1810.

———, *St Irvyne; or, The Rosicrucian: A Romance*, Stockdale, London, 1811.

———, *Posthumous Poems of Percy Bysshe Shelley*, ed. Mrs. Shelley, John and Henry L. Hunt, London, 1824.

———, *The Poetical Works of Percy Bysshe Shelley*, 4 vols., ed. Mrs. Shelley, Edward Moxon, London, 1839.

———, *Essays, Letters from Abroad, Translations and Fragments, by Percy Bysshe Shelley*, 2 vols., ed. Mrs. Shelley, Edward Moxon, London, 1840.

———, *The Poetical Works of Percy Bysshe Shelley. With Notes and a Memoir*, ed. William Michael Rossetti, 2 vols., E. Moxon, Son & Co., London, 1870.

———, *The Complete Poetical Works of Percy Bysshe Shelley. With Memoir and Notes*, ed. George Edward Woodberry, 4 vols., Houghton Mifflin, Boston, 1892.

———, *The Complete Works of Percy Bysshe Shelley*, 10 vols., eds. Roger Ingpen and Walter E. Peck, Ernest Benn, London and Charles Scribner's Sons, New York, 1926–30 (the "Julian Edition").

———, *Shelley: Poetical Works*, ed. Thomas Hutchinson, 1905, new ed. Geoffrey Matthews, Oxford University Press, London, Oxford, New York, 1970.

——, *Percy Bysshe Shelley: Selected Poems*, ed. Timothy Webb, J. M. Dent & Sons Limited, London, 1977.

——, *Shelley's Poetry and Prose*, eds. Donald H. Reiman and Sharon B. Powers, Norton, New York and London, 1977.

——, *The Poems of Shelley*, eds. Geoffrey Matthews and Kelvin Everest, vol. i, Longman, London and New York, 1989.

——, *The Prose Works of Percy Bysshe Shelley*, ed. E. B. Murray, vol. i, Clarendon Press, Oxford, 1993.

Shine, Hill and Shine, Helen Chadwick, *The Quarterly Review under Gifford. Identification of Contributors 1809–24*, University of North Carolina Press, Chapel Hill, 1949.

Siebers, Tobin, *The Ethics of Criticism*, Cornell University Press, Ithaca and London, 1988.

Smith, Horace, "A Graybeard's Gossip About His Literary Acquaintance", *The New Monthly Magazine and Humourist*, lxxxi, October–November 1847, 227–40, 288–94.

Solve, Melvin T., *Shelley: His Theory of Poetry*, University of Chicago Press, Chicago, 1927.

Southey, Robert, *Poems of Robert Southey*, ed. Maurice H. Fitzgerald, Oxford University Press, London, 1909.

Stephen, Leslie, *Hours in a Library*, 1879, new ed., 3 vols., Smith, Elder & Co., London, 1909.

Stewart, Dugald, *Outlines of Moral Philosophy for the Use of Students in the University of Edinburgh*, 1793, 2nd edn., William Creech, Edinburgh, 1801.

Stovall, Floyd, *Desire and Restraint in Shelley*, Duke University Press, Durham, North Carolina, 1931.

Strout, Alan Lang, *A Bibliography of Articles in Blackwood's Magazine, Volumes I through XVIII, 1817–1825*, Texas Technological College Library, Lubbock, Texas, 1959.

Swinburne, Algernon Charles, *The Complete Works of Algernon Charles Swinburne*, 20 vols., eds. Sir Edmund Gosse and Thomas James Wise, London, 1925–7 ("Bonchurch Edition").

Swinden, Patrick, ed., *Shelley, Shorter Poems and Lyrics: A Casebook*, Macmillan, London, 1976.

——, "The *Ode to the West Wind*", in Swinden, 227–44.

Tate, Allen, *On the Limits of Poetry. Selected Essays: 1928–1948*, Swallow Press, New York, 1948, rpt. 1970.

——, *Essays of Four Decades*, Swallow Press, Chicago, 1968.

Taylor, Charles, *Sources of the Self: The Making of the Modern Identity*, Cambridge University Press, 1989.

Tetreault, Ronald, *The Poetry of Life: Shelley and Literary Form*, University of Toronto Press, Toronto, 1987.

——, "Shelley: Style and Substance", in Blank, 15–33.

Thompson, Francis, *Shelley*, ed. W. Meynell, Burns and Oates, London, 1909.

Tooke, John Horne, *ΕΠΕΑ ΠΤΕΡΟΕΝΤΑ. Or, The Diversions of Purley*, 2 vols., J. Johnson, London, 1798, 1805.

Trelawny, Edward John, *Recollections of the Last Days of Shelley and Byron*, Ticknor and Fields, Boston, 1858, rpt. in Wolfe, ii 159–301.

Todhunter, John, *A Study of Shelley*, C. Kegan Paul and Co., London, 1880.

Volney, Constantin François, *Les Ruines d'Empire*, 1791, *The Ruins of Empire: Or, a Survey of the Revolutions of Empires*, trans. anon., 3rd edn., J. Johnson, London, 1796.

Warnock, Mary, *Imagination*, Faber and Faber, London, 1976.

Wasserman, Earl R., *Shelley: A Critical Reading*, The Johns Hopkins Press, Baltimore, 1971.

Weaver, Bennett, *Toward the Understanding of Shelley*, University of Michigan Press, Ann Arbor, 1932.

Webb, Timothy, *The Violet in the Crucible: Shelley and Translation*, Clarendon Press, Oxford, 1976.

——, *Shelley: A Voice not Understood*, The University Press, Manchester, 1977.

Wellek, René, "Literary Criticism and Philosophy", *Scrutiny*, v, March 1937, 375–83.

White, Newman Ivey, *The Unextinguished Hearth: Shelley and His Contemporary Critics*, Duke University Press, Durham, North Carolina, 1938.

——, *Shelley*, 2 vols., Secker and Warburg, London, 1947, rpt. Octagon Books, New York, 1972.

Wieland, C. M., *The History of Agathon* (1766), 4 vols., trans. John Richardson, C. Heydinger, London, 1773.

Williams, Bernard, *Problems of the Self. Philosophical Papers 1956–1972*, Cambridge University Press, 1973.

——, *Moral Luck. Philosophical Papers 1973–1980*, Cambridge University Press, 1981.

——, *Ethics and the Limits of Philosophy*, Fontana Press/ Collins, London, 1985.

Wilson, Edmund, *Axel's Castle: A Study in the Imaginative Literature of 1870–1930*, Charles Scribner's Sons, New York, 1931.

Wilson, Milton, *Shelley's Later Poetry: A Study of His Prophetic Imagination*, Columbia University Press, New York, 1959.

Winckelmann, Johann Joachim, *The History of Ancient Art* (1764, French trans. 1802), 2 vols., trans. G. Henry Lodge, Sampson Low, Marston, Searle and Rivington, London, 1881.

Winters, Yvor, *In Defence of Reason*, The Swallow Press and William Morrow and Co., New York, 1947.

Wolfe, Humbert, ed., *The Life of Percy Bysshe Shelley*, 2 vols., J. M. Dent and Sons, London, 1933.

Wollstonecraft, Mary, *A Vindication of the Rights of Woman: With Strictures on Moral and Political Subjects*, 1792, published with John Stuart Mill, *The Subjection of Women*, J. M. Dent & Sons Ltd., London, 1929, with intro. by Mary Warnock, 1985.

Woodring, Carl, "Shelley", chapter VI in *Politics in English Romantic Poetry*, Harvard University Press, Cambridge, Mass., 1970, 230–325.

Wordsworth, Christopher, *Memoirs of William Wordsworth, Poet Laureate*, D. C. L., 2 vols., Edward Moxon, London, 1851.

Wordsworth, William, *The Prose Works of William Wordsworth*, 3 vols., eds. W. J. B. Owen and Jane Worthington Smyser, Clarendon Press, Oxford, 1974.

——, *Poems, in Two Volumes, and Other Poems 1800–1807*, ed. Jared Curtis, Cornell University Press, Ithaca and London, 1983 (part of the "Cornell Wordsworth").

——, *Lyrical Ballads, and Other Poems, 1797–1800*, eds. James Butler and Karen Green, Cornell University Press, Ithaca and London, 1992 (part of the "Cornell Wordsworth").

Worton, Michael, "Speech and Silence in *The Cenci*", in Allott, 105–24.

Yeats, W. B., *Essays and Introductions*, Macmillan, New York, 1961.

Index

32400616